Patterns of Highland Development

Patterns of Highland Development

DAVID TURNOCK

Lecturer in Geography, University of Leicester

MACMILLAN

First published 1970 by
MACMILLAN AND CO LTD
Little Essex Street London W C 2
and also at Bombay Calcutta and Madras
Macmillan South Africa (Publishers) Pty Ltd Johannesburg
The Macmillan Company of Australia Pty Ltd Melbourne
The Macmillan Company of Canada Ltd Toronto
Gill and Macmillan Ltd Dublin

Printed in Great Britain at
THE PITMAN PRESS
Bath

Contents

List of Plates

between pages 114 and 115

The publishers wish to thank the following, who have kindly given permission for photographs to be reproduced:
Aerofilms Ltd for Plates 1, 3, 5, 8, 10, 12, 14, 17, 22, 25, 28, 31.
J. K. St Joseph for Plates 2, 4, 7, 9, 11, 15, 16, 18, 19, 20, 29.
The Scotsman Publications Ltd for Plates 6, 13, 21, 23, 24, 26, 27, 32.
The British Aluminium Company Ltd for Plate 30.

List of Figures

List of Tables

Preface

THE Highland problem is no new concern of the British people. The difficulties encountered in enabling this marginal area of the country to receive its fair share of affluence and development have troubled politicians and others for centuries. It is a problem stemming largely from the relative advantages of certain other parts of the country in terms of position and resources, and in the context of the political unit of the United Kingdom one may readily point to the peripheral location of the Highlands and their limited resource base when the Central Valley of Scotland or south-east England is taken as the point of reference. It would nevertheless be highly misleading to argue that the Highlands are naturally an area of poverty, because although a rich mineral endowment would not be expected in a zone of predominantly old primary rocks, this very large area, embracing about one-fifth of the land area of the country, offers many opportunities for agriculture, forestry and fishing. It also possesses abundant supplies of water and excellent facilities for recreation, resources which are by no means insignificant in crowded twentieth-century Britain. Rather the problem arises from the location of these resources on the edge of the country – and also on the edge of Europe – yet in close proximity, in what is a very small island to areas in the south with much richer endowments. This has encouraged underuse in the past, a feature still evident today with the growing emphasis on central places in the national economy for manufacturing and services.

Attention must also be focused on the manner in which the primary sector of the economy in the Highlands (agriculture, fishing, etc.) was managed in the past, for the devastation of the environment which was brought about by the supply of livestock and timber to the south and the starvation of the area of capital investment have served to accentuate the contrast in opportunities and rates of growth, with inevitable and well-known demographic consequences. The problem has been brought on gradually over the years by various economic, social and political processes, and it is important to recognise the importance of these in shaping the economic patterns which exist in the Highlands today. Not only does the historical background place a contemporary study in perspective, but it provides at the same time many lessons which may not be entirely irrelevant today.

The chapter headings are selected to enable the evolution of the Highland economy to be studied systematically, taking each of the main activities in turn. But the sequence is arranged so that a group of chapters on various matters relating to land use are followed by studies of the growth of transport and industry, which have made for growing emphasis on certain nodal points within the Highlands. The final chapters then examine various aspects of this process of selective growth, which brings out a number of developing areas within the general context of population decline over the Highlands as a whole. References and a substantial bibliography are provided in a way which it is hoped will satisfy student needs and at the same time avoid undue confusion for readers with more general interests.

In any regional study there is a danger of becoming inward-looking, with the result that the area involved appears as an isolated entity with unique features and special problems of its own. It is very easy to adopt this attitude of mind in the Highlands, for their history and culture have many distinctive characteristics and their economic problems have sometimes been regarded as being singularly intractable, as indicated by the process of emigration which has proved to be the major long-term response. Yet against this it must be remembered that the pattern of events in the economic, social and political spheres has been conditioned by the proximity of the Central Lowlands, with which the Highlands have found it extremely difficult to work out a satisfactory *modus vivendi*. Highland affairs cannot be divorced from the country of which they are a part, and rather than argue that the Highlands suffer from unique problems which demand special aid, it is perhaps more realistic to see the area as one of several peripheral regions of Britain, or Europe, with characteristics which are distinct in degree rather than kind.

It may seem pedantic to present the demarcation of the Highlands as a problem, but confusion can easily arise in attempting to interpret this popular expression. The Highlands may be taken as the area beyond the Highland Line, which runs across Scotland roughly from Helensburgh to Stonehaven. Yet within this zone there are many districts with a definite 'Lowland' character, especially in Buchan and the Moray Firth coastlands as well as the islands of Orkney. But in addition to the physical contrast between east and west there are the cultural and economic divisions which combine to introduce a contrast between the north-west and south-east districts, the former being the stronghold of Gaelic culture as well as the most inaccessible part of the Highlands approached from the south, whereas the latter have been exposed to the penetration of Lowland influences over a much longer period. It is largely with this last point in mind that the Highlands are defined for the purposes of this book as the seven crofting counties: Argyll, Caithness, Inverness, Orkney, Ross and Cromarty, Shetland and Sutherland.

This unit was first recognised in 1886 as the region where the problem of small-scale agriculture was greatest, and although the gravity of the problem is neither as great nor as extensive as was then the case, it has been a useful division for planning purposes. It is recognised as a sub-region of the Scottish planning region and the area over which the Highlands and Islands Development Board has responsibilities. As will become clear in due course, however, the seven counties do not form an ideally coherent region; the seriousness of the economic problems of the north-west mainland and islands was recognised as early as the 1890s when parishes there were declared 'congested districts', and it is this fringe of the Highlands which today suffers most acutely from a declining and ageing population. Moreover the functional links of the crofting counties with Inverness, the Highland capital, break down in Argyll, where Glasgow's influence is strong, and again in Orkney and Shetland, which are closely linked by air and sea transport with Aberdeen.

In compiling the material presented in this book and in the development of the various arguments put forward I am indebted to many people for their help and inspiration. First of all a great debt is owed to my teachers at Cambridge, Mr A. A. L. Caesar and Mrs H. G. Steers, whose interest and encouragement were invaluable. For a continuing interest in Highland problems the author is grateful to a number of Scottish geographers, including Dr J. B. Caird and Mr H. A. Moisley, but particularly to the late Professor A. C. O'Dell of Aberdeen, whose scholarly work on the Highlands, written with Professor K. Walton, was a source of great stimulation. But recognition must also be made of the kind co-operation and generous help received from many interested individuals and bodies in all parts of Scotland. These involve government and local government organisations and many people living in the Highlands, especially in Lochaber, where the author spent considerable time in 1962 and 1963 collecting material for the Ph.D. thesis which forms the core of the present work. Acknowledgement is made to Mr R. Millman, on whose research Fig. 13 is based, to the editor of *Geografiska Annaler* for permission to reproduce Figs 27, 28 and 29, and to the editor of the *Scottish Geographical Magazine* for permission to reproduce Figs 3 and 9. Great assistance in reading the final draft was rendered by my wife, and I am deeply grateful to her for her patience and constant support.

DAVID TURNOCK

CHAPTER ONE

The Highlands before 1815

IT has been said that the most complete prisoners of the past are those who are least conscious of it. Certainly in the Highlands there are many themes which call for careful study in their historical contexts if a misleading impression is to be avoided. Of the various dates which have been put forward to mark the beginning of the Highland problem 1745 is probably the most popular, since it marks very definitely the opening of a new phase in Highland–Lowland relations. Yet this must not be allowed to obscure the element of continuity running through the whole of Scottish history. The idea of the Highland problem has been taken to reflect the difficulty experienced by the Highlands in reaching a stable relationship with the south, and hence this study must begin rather further back in time than the Jacobite rebellions. Prehistoric settlement, illustrated by Plates 9 and 10, will not be dealt with in detail, however.

THE UNIFICATION OF SCOTLAND

In the days when Scotland was organised into a number of separate kingdoms the Highlands were divided roughly along the main east–west watershed into Dalriada (Scotland) and Pictland. The west was penetrated by Scots from Ireland certainly as far as Applecross, and it is thought that the place-name Glenelg may mean 'Glen of Ireland'. By contrast the area of Pictish settlement, which may be inferred from the distribution of their symbol stones, embraced a territory in the east extending from Sutherland to Stirling. A nominal union was eventually formed between these two Highland units, with Gaelic influence temporarily spreading eastwards to allow the formation of the kingdom of Alba under Kenneth MacAlpin in 843. It comprised only a portion of present-day Scotland, for to the south Strathclyde with its capital at Dumbarton was a largely independent kingdom, and the province of Lothian stretching from the Forth to the Tweed was in Northumbrian hands. Moreover in the north the margins of the Highlands – Orkney and Shetland, Caithness and the Hebrides – were in Norse hands from 780 onwards. The unification of this kingdom of

Alba can hardly have been very effective, but nevertheless here was a case of the greater part of the Highlands constituting a separate political unit; this situation and the close functional links with Ireland by sea gave the region a very different position from the peripheral one it occupies today. Iona, for instance, at the seaward approach to Loch Linnhe and the Great Glen, was an appropriate centre of Columba's church, and Scottish kings were buried there until 1097 (Plate 11). St Moluag, a contemporary of St Columba who came to the Highlands in 562, is associated with Lismore, an island in a similar strategic position. There was a considerable element of commerce on Loch Linnhe and references to diplomatic links with the crusading Catholic empire of Charlemagne.

Norse power could hardly extend inland, resting as it did on control of the northern seas, but their very presence had the effect of unifying some of the groups to the south. Alba thus had an ally in the kingdom of Strathclyde, which could maintain only a shaky independence after the Norse raid on Dumbarton in 870, and went on to acquire Lothian in 1016 from a Northumbria also weakened by Scandinavian invasions. Frontiers were thus established which, except in the north, were little different from those of the present day. From this time the significance of Highland and Lowland in Scotland becomes increasingly prominent, and although the superior economic potential of the latter was unknown and unexploited for a long time thereafter, the centre of gravity of Scotland slowly shifted south, leaving the Highlands in an increasingly marginal position. With poor land communications and the prominence of sea power the coasts assumed a great importance, and in view of the Norse threat the administration of the districts of Moray, Buchan, Mar, Mearns and Angus was placed in the hands of Celtic sea stewards (Mormaers). In the west, the districts of Lennox (Clyde) and Morvern (Great Glen) were similarly governed. But the hold of the central government over these areas was necessarily tenuous and they evolved into practically independent earldoms, providing a constant threat to the authority of the King of Scotland, particularly the outposts of Celtic society in Moray and Argyll.

The lack of a direct line of succession weakened the central government by consistently producing rival claimants, until Malcolm II managed to introduce a direct succession after 1034. A feudal system was also introduced to maintain the unification of Scotland and stress the power of the centre; the policy in the north was to contain the inherent separatism of the Celtic fringe by settling Norman families in the area to replace the Mormaers. The Great Glen was particularly important as a strategic objective, since it offered a direct link between the power centres of Moray and Argyll and was therefore fortified in the reign of William the Lion by a line of castles running from Inverness through Urquhart and Inverlochy to Dunstaffnage (Plate 1). In 1229 the Comyn family moved from Badenoch into Lochaber, becoming wardens of the Great Glen under Alexander II, whose vigorous policy succeeded in pacifying Moray in 1230. With this valuable consolidation the routes to the north over the Mounth lay open, regulated by castles at strategic points on Deeside and Donside such as Braemar and Kildrummy. A measure of ecclesiastical and commercial development followed which saw the founding of various royal burghs and a substantial increase in trade (Plate 12).

But in Argyll society was more staunchly Celtic and patriarchal rather than feudal. Economically too there were distinctions, for the very limited arable land and hazardous nature of cultivation made a settled living almost impossible. Since famine was never far away, the lifting of cattle seemed a natural response and war with a neighbouring clan to gain more land one of the few ways of increasing production. Moreover this independent spirit was partially sustained by Norse occupation, which divided the Celtic areas of the west between Norway and Scotland. King Magnus of Norway was able to extort from King Malcolm III Scottish recognition of Norwegian sovereignty over every island on the west coast of Scotland round which a ship could be steered. But with the decline of sea power and the strengthening of land defences the tide began to turn; in the twelfth century Somerled expelled the Norse from Kintyre, a disputed territory in view of its fertility and the ability of the Norse to circumnavigate it only by dragging a ship over land from East to West Loch Tarbert! He went on to build up a powerful principality in south Argyll under the nominal sovereignty of David I of Scotland, and later moved from this fertile heart of the southern Highlands to annex the islands from Islay to Mull. But it was not until 1266, after a defeat at Largs, that the Norse ceased denying the Hebrides to Scotland and ceded the Kingdom of the Isles for a money payment. Orkney and Shetland remained in Norse hands until 1469, and Scots feudalism was not imposed over the Viking *udal* system of family holdings stretching from the hill crests to the seashore until then.

THE LORDSHIP OF THE ISLES

The King of Scotland, however, was no longer in a position to extend his power personally over this scattered territory, for his relations with the local barons and lords were generally fluid and uncertain after 1286, when Alexander III was killed on the cliffs of Kinghorn, Fife. With him passed the dynasty stemming from Malcolm Canmore which had confirmed the unification of Scotland, for Alexander's heir was his granddaughter, the Maid of Norway, and when she tragically died on her way to Scotland there turned out to be no fewer than thirteen claimants to the crown. This enabled the English king, Edward I, to insist on his doubtful claim to be feudal superior and lord paramount of the Scottish throne and immediately the independence of Scotland was compromised, since separatist elements were now open to subversion from England. Old and feeble kings, child rulers and disputed regencies thus reduced the power of the central authority. Nor can the international context be ignored, for with the rival powers of the Vatican, Spain and France alternately consoling and opposing England, Scotland's strategic situation on England's northern border made her at once an object of favour from the Continent and hostility from England.

This context created new opportunities for Argyll. Somerled had already met his death in 1164 challenging the king's authority on the Clyde, as unsuccessfully as the Norwegians were to a hundred years later, but his successors were able to manœuvre more skilfully during the troubled period of the Wars of Independence with England between 1296 and 1342. For while the Comyns in Lochaber supported the English faction, Argyll was allied with Bruce and could hardly fail to gain territory with the latter's success. Following grants from Bruce and David and with other territories gained by marriage, John of Islay emerged with lands on the western mainland and islands far more extensive than those which once belonged to the Norse Kingdom of the Isles (Fig. 1). They included at their maximum the whole of the Hebrides along with Kintyre, north Argyll, Lochaber and Ross, and were controlled from the castle of Finlaggan on Islay, a more convenient point than the Isle of Man where the Norse had concentrated their power. By 1354 John had assumed the proud title of 'Lord of the Isles' and exercised authority almost independently of the King of Scotland. Here was a veritable sea empire, for the hotly contested acquisition of Ross in 1424 gave complete control of the Minch crossing from the Sound of Sleat to Lewis. Easter Ross was of debatable value, but control of the marginal territory of Lochaber meant that a major land route to the north was blocked; although the alignment of the Great Glen from north-east to south-west and the difficult route further south by Loch Leven and over Rannoch Moor reduced its value as compared with the Mounth routes further east, its strategic value has always been great in terms of controlling

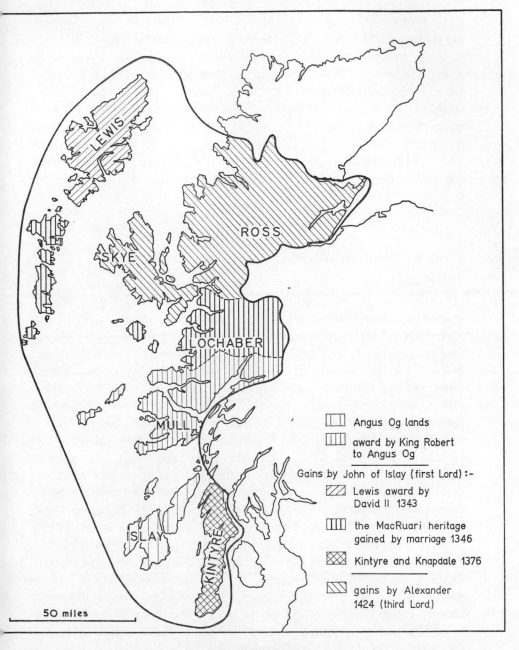

Fig. 1 *The Lordship of the Isles*

the Hebrides, and a stronghold at Inverlochy was for a long time an important government objective. But control of Lochaber created some embarrassment for the Lords of the Isles because their policy of settling MacDonalds in key areas was only partially successful. They settled in Glencoe, Keppoch (Brae Lochaber), Glengarry and further west in Morar and Moidart, Alistair Carrach (Keppoch) becoming Lord of Lochaber, which was controlled from Tor Castle, near Inverlochy. But this hold was insufficient to maintain the allegiance of the remaining native clans, notably Clan Cameron and Clan Chattan, who deserted the Lord of the Isles in 1431 shortly before the first battle of Inverlochy, a critical engagement following a raid by the Lord of the Isles on Inverness.

THE DANTING OF THE ISLES

The fifteenth century, however, marks a determined return to a policy of consolidation from the centre. After 1371 England was not in a position to assert her claim to suzerainty over Scotland with great vigour. The Lord of the Isles was certainly recognised as the main centre of disaffection within Scotland, and he was accordingly encouraged to stake his claim to the earldom of Ross. Though he eventually succeeded in 1424, the first attempt ended disastrously at Harlaw in the Garioch of Aberdeenshire in 1411. More pretentious and unforgivable was the Treaty of Ardtornish–Westminster (1462) between the Lord of the Isles and Edward IV of England, whereby the Lord would be a principal beneficiary in the partition of Scotland. He was forced to yield Kintyre, Knapdale and Ross in 1476, and in 1480, weakened by defeat in the battle of Bloody Bay, was obliged to submit to the vigorous James III. Finally, after an unsuccessful attempt to regain Ross, growing disunity within Clan Donald allowed the Lordship to be abolished in 1493. Attempts by Donald Dubh in the sixteenth century to revive it in a modified form with support from Henry VIII were unsuccessful. Progress in the long process of pacification was thus admittedly slow, but the situation was once again promising. An economic upsurge at the end of the sixteenth century prompted a scheme to regularise the landholding pattern in the Highlands, and chiefs were called upon to submit their titles. This was followed up in 1609 by the Statutes of Iona which compelled the chiefs to accept the King of Scotland and the overlordship of superiors, Argyll and Huntly, who were the chiefs of the Campbells and Gordons respectively.

This imposition of the feudal system on the few outstanding areas of Scotland was logical enough in itself as a necessary step in the process of effective unification. But the policy of using Argyll and Huntly as regional policemen proved to have many shortcomings. Certain clan groups were eliminated, notably the MacIans in Ardnamurchan who declined to become a sept of the Campbells and resigned their lands in 1602; they took up a life of piracy on the high seas after being expelled from Ardnamurchan by 1625. But not all clans could be pacified; in many areas MacDonalds were strong enough to retain their lands and other clans were then left in possession as well, since it was considered expedient to counterbalance MacDonald power in this way. Thus the MacLeans, who were on the worst possible terms with the MacDonalds, were left in possession in Mull and Morvern until later in the seventeenth century, although it was originally contemplated in 1613 that Morvern would be granted to Sir John Campbell of Lawers. Another factor was the successful pressure by Campbells on the lands peripheral to their own territories, which had the effect of cementing alliances between clans who had formerly been living on bad terms with each other: MacLeans, Stewarts of Appin and MacDonalds of Glencoe were all aware of the implications of the superiority lying in Campbell hands and formed a solid front of resistance to further attrition. Nor did Huntly find himself in any better position further north. While it was Campbell policy to absorb feudal gains, the Earls of Huntly could not achieve this since their feudal dependants in the west were far from their main centres of power in Aberdeenshire and Banffshire. He was successful in disrupting Clan Chattan, whose territory was adjacent to his own, and drove a wedge between them and the Camerons, but elsewhere made little progress. The North Isles especially (islands north of Ardnamurchan apart from Skye and Lewis) resisted him, partly on religious grounds with Presbyterian opposition to any increase in power by a Catholic noble. Aware of these weaknesses, Huntly was largely content to reach a *modus vivendi* with neighbouring clans.

Lochaber illustrates the difficulties most strikingly, because although the cattle-raiding activities of Camerons and MacDonalds of Keppoch gave ample justification for more effective control and pacification, the clans were not dislodged (Fig. 2). The Camerons, who had already resisted pressure from MacLeans in 1470 (battle of Corpach) and Frasers in 1544 (battle of Blar nan Leine), remained in possession of their highly strategic piece of territory across the southern end of the Great Glen and indeed placed further pressure on Clan Chattan, from whom they obtained the lands round

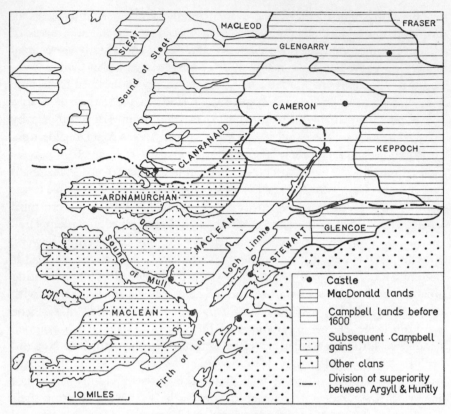

Fig. 2 *Feudalism in Lochaber*

Loch Arkaig by purchase under the terms of the Treaty of Achnacarry in 1665. Nor could the MacDonalds of Keppoch be dislodged from Brae Lochaber, although MacIntosh received title to these lands and, in fact, the last recorded clan battle took place in this area at Mulroy in 1688, which saw Keppoch once again victorious in resisting MacIntosh's legal claim. Perhaps most damaging was the fact that in this highly sensitive region of Lochaber, which required firm and unified control, the superiorities of Argyll and Huntly clashed: even the superiority of Cameron lands was divided and control thereby weakened. Even though the main strategic points were covered with Argyll's control of the castles guarding the Sound of Mull and Firth of Lorn and Huntly's hold on Inverlochy, now rebuilt, there was much scope for clan activity at the local level. Far from destroying the clans it might be argued that 'the danting of the isles' actually made clanship more durable.

Government policy in the islands was even more debatable in its wisdom, for when Lewis was put at the king's disposal after the failure of the MacLeods to produce their title deeds to the land, he granted the island in 1598 to a company of Lowland colonists, the Fife Adventurers. In addition they were granted estates belonging to MacLeod of Dunvegan and Mac-Donald of Sleat in north Skye. The frustration of this planned colonisation, which may be compared with the plantations in Ireland, was therefore a major objective of these powerful clans in Skye and also of Mackenzie of Kintail, who claimed Lewis by marriage. By failing to accommodate the local people as well as the chiefs the expedition failed and Kintail was then able to invade Lewis, crush opposition and successfully force his claim.

THE JACOBITE CAUSE

In view of the lawlessness in the north there was a clear case for firmer central control, but what is to be regretted is the way in which the Highland issue later became clouded and complicated by wider considerations. The history of Scotland as a whole in the seventeenth century was tragic, with a number of complex religious and political issues of international significance. The union of the crowns of Scotland and England in 1603 had great implications for Scotland, for it meant the sharing of a common king in spite of the maintenance of separate parliaments, laws, taxes and churches. It meant, despite King James's protestations of good intent, an absentee king and court living virtually in exile; it gave him new power and, at the same time, freedom from baronial influence. The union increased the flow of English ideas north of the border and added impetus to the renaissance which was affecting Scottish society, but at the same time the autocratic rule of the Stuarts provoked a vigorous reaction in Scotland on constitutional and more especially religious grounds. For the Reformation was compromised by Charles I's rigid policy of episcopacy, opposition to which was formalised in the National Covenant of 1638. Yet this issue split Highland and Lowland, for while the Covenant gained great support in the Lowlands, Catholic and Episcopal elements were more prominent in the Highlands. Certainly Presbyterian influence was strong in Lewis, but clans such as the MacDonalds tended to be mainly Catholic, while the Camerons and Stewarts of Appin were strongly Episcopal and hence were undying supporters of the Stuarts, fully supporting Charles during the subsequent civil war. With Montrose they soundly defeated the Campbells at Inverlochy after carrying fire and sword through their lands around Inveraray and Breadalbane. The Covenanters by contrast, though not anti-royalist, could not bring Charles to overcome his intransigent attitude to the presbytery and therefore handed him over to the English by whom he was subsequently tried and executed.

The Highland–Lowland antipathy was illustrated again after the Restoration, when the Stuarts again persisted in unpopular religious measures. In 1662 the bishops received back their lost power, and so began a second bitter period of covenanting war. By using Highland supporters to quell Lowland opposition in 1678 and force them to accept episcopacy, the government merely earned for Gaeldom further hatred and contempt which provoked a certain indifference to punitive measures against the clans which later governments were to take. For no government could feel happy about separatist elements on the edges of the kingdom, and the Stuarts, when in power, were as sensitive about this as anyone. Thus James II, as Duke of York, showed a harsh lack of sympathy when sent by Charles II to pacify the Highlanders, although he received their support against the forces of Argyll and Monmouth in the 1685 rebellion and again after he was driven from the country on the landing of William and Mary. Religious issues thus tragically divided Scotland precisely at a time when unification was gradually becoming more desirable and more attainable; at the time when a carefully calculated domestic policy was needed to ease the process of unification, government policy served to emphasise the division.

In this connection it is interesting to note in passing that the Commonwealth succeeded in pacifying the Highlands and abolishing the greater hereditary jurisdictions without stripping the Highland clans of their dignity and sense of race. General George Monk was in charge of operations in the Highlands and a fort was erected at Inverlochy, reflecting once again the strategic importance of the Great Glen. Known as the 'Black Garrison', it was protected by water on three sides and by marsh on the other, and timber was cut for ramparts and to secure a clear field of fire. As a result of the efforts of Colonel John Hill, who became governor of the fort in 1656, much progress was made to establish good relations with the clans, and his efforts culminated in Lochiel's voluntary submission at the fort. Had such a genuine policy been able to continue, the subsequent chapters of Highland history might well have been less unhappy, but the death of Cromwell and the end of the Commonwealth brought with it the evacuation of the fort and its subsequent destruction by the Camerons who were left in charge of it. But in this instance there were special circumstances, for the whole of Scotland was treated uniformly by Cromwell as a subjugated province; even the staunch Presbyterians had been reluctant to abandon their king and on his death had immediately proclaimed his son king as Charles II. The subsequent 'usurpation' by Cromwell meant forts not only at Inverness and Inverlochy but at various points throughout Scotland, and the whole country was thus held in peace by Monk's garrisons with little scope for Highland–Lowland prejudice to influence the position.

European affairs also had an important bearing on the fate of the Highlands. The perpetual fear of the government was that separatism in far-flung parts of the kingdom might be exploited by enemies on the Continent who could therefore open up a major war on a second front. It was probably this situation which demanded harsh measures against Ireland, where religious factors made for close links with France and Spain. Similarly Catholic elements in the Highlands posed a danger to Britain's security which seemed to be very acute at the end of the seventeenth century. The rule of James II was generally tolerated in Britain for a time on the grounds that the lack of a male heir would make a Catholic succession improbable, yet the birth of a son in 1688 changed this optimistic forecast and led to widespread speculation that Protestants would become subjected to widespread persecution and loss of rights on the lines of the French model. James fled to France, while William of Orange came to the throne in 1689. Predictably, the clans were raised on James's behalf under John Graham of Claverhouse, Viscount Dundee, at Dalmuccomer near Fort William. The subsequent expedition proved to be largely ineffective, for the clans needed a great leader to maintain and co-ordinate their efforts, and after the death of Dundee at Killiecrankie the resistance petered out in the streets of Dunkeld. The clansmen returned home, raiding Breadalbane yet again en route.

But the sensitivities of the government had been aroused. William, as Stadtholder of the Netherlands, was primarily interested in the security of Holland against Louis XIV of France, and in view of James's presence in France was all too well aware of the possible consequences of French support for the Jacobites in the Highlands. The clans were bound on oath to support James, and it was known that French ships were in the area and that Glengarry had given hospitality to Sir George Barclay, one of James's emissaries, and had surrounded his castle with a ditch and palisades. A military expedition under Buchan was defeated at Cromdale in 1690 but served to highlight the growing threat rather than inspire relief. Moreover Scots in general were dissatisfied at being involved in William's war on the

Continent, especially as they were not necessarily obliged to accept the same king as England. The Stuarts might well be restored to the Scottish throne, and then England would have not only disaffection in the Highlands to contend with but a hostile Catholic country on her northern frontier. William had been defeated off Beachy Head and there was distinct rumour of a French invasion. There were clearly forces calling for a strong hand against the clans. From the military angle Hugh Mackay believed in a tough policy of fire and plunder and had already built a stronger fort at Inverlochy along with the royal burgh and barony of Maryburgh. But there were also William's Scottish advisers to be considered, for the views of Sir John Dalrymple, Master of Stair and Principal Secretary of State for Scotland, could hardly be described as objective where the Highlands were concerned. Stair had abandoned James readily after his flight, and to his new position of trust with William he carried a nagging sense of inferiority to the English, largely through the uncivilised state of the Highlands. Furthermore, the Earl of Argyll, who was leader of the Commission offering the crown of Scotland, enjoyed an influential position and also had an eye to compensation for the destruction wrought in his estates by the Atholl raiders.

A policy of strong repressive measures in the Highlands was therefore likely to gain the full support of Stair and Argyll, and against such pressures the lonely and distant voice of moderation from Colonel Hill, once more governor of the fort, was bound to be ineffective in London and mistrusted in the Highlands, where the Earl of Breadalbane had been given a separate commission to establish peace. It is thus easy to see how the unfortunate event of MacIan of Glencoe being several days late in taking the oath of allegiance to William and Mary should have resulted in the Massacre of Glencoe, for it was later shown to have been a deliberate and unnecessary plot devised by Stair in excess of the king's wishes and carried out by Argyll's men. Fortunately James had belatedly released the clans from their oath of allegiance in time for the majority to take an oath to William before 1 January 1692, otherwise the slaughter, which was very likely premeditated on a large scale by Stair, would have extended throughout Lochaber. Fortunately too the subsequent order to transport those Glencoe men who escaped the massacre was rescinded on Hill's pleading. But the massacre, described by Prebble (1966) as 'the only recorded attempt at genocide in the history of the British peoples', is a sad illustration of the results of the interaction of the forces moulding Highland history. It was a bad omen for the future, for it suggested that force would continue to be the only way to resolve the problem, with a strong prejudice in the Lowlands and a stubborn tenacity to maintain their way of life on the part of the Highland clans.

The political scene remained unstable, however, for some time afterwards. The most satisfactory solution from England's point of view was to remove the possibility of Scotland appointing her own ruler by an Act of Union to bring a common parliament into existence. This was attempted in William's reign but only succeeded in 1707, when a large section of public opinion eventually declared itself in favour of it. Needless to say there was considerable controversy at the time and more so in the following years, when it seemed that Scotland was receiving insufficient government attention. Once again this dissatisfaction found expression in a call to restore the Stuarts, a possibility which seemed by no means unrealistic in view of the fact that Queen Anne had no heir. The war on the Continent was still in progress and French support could be counted on. Unfortunately by the time rebellion had been planned peace was established on the Continent (1713) so that France was no longer interested. Moreover after Anne's death in 1714 and the proclamation of the Hanoverian succession there was sufficient delay and hesitation for the government to take appropriate measures, so that only the Highland component of the rebellion led by the Earl of Mar ever became a coherent force.

On one further occasion the Jacobite cause was to be sustained by force of arms, but never again were internal and external circumstances so favourable. After 1715 further military precautions were taken. No longer did Fort William exist in splendid isolation, for it was supplemented by Ruthven barracks, built near Kingussie in 1718, and also by forts at Fort Augustus and Fort George (Plate 13). Moreover barracks were built at Bernera, Glenelg, in 1722, thus guarding the main ferry point to the Hebrides, while the occupation by regular troops of Duart Castle did the same for the Sound of Mull. The value of these forts was then increased by the military roads built under the direction of the Commander-in-Chief in Scotland, General Wade, linking the Great Glen forts together and also with Crieff and Dunkeld between 1725 and 1737. Among his achievements was the construction of High Bridge over the Spean, completed in 1736, and the series of hairpin bends which took the road over Corrieyairack Pass, at a height of 2,507 ft. It is noteworthy that Wade selected this route for a road to the south, a reflection of the difficulty of travelling from the end of the Great Glen, one which has always reduced its value as a through route.

ECONOMIC CHANGE

But it was not only these developments that inhibited independent military action on the part of the Highlanders (though ironically much use was made of the military roads by Prince Charles Edward during the '45), for economic factors were equally potent in destroying the fabric of resistance. It is often assumed that many of the economic developments in the Highlands came after Culloden, when the butchery of Cumberland's troops had reduced the area to a state of bankruptcy, but in fact many of the changes were much in evidence before. The droving trade in black cattle was a thriving one, and other enterprises, such as the lead mining at New York and Strontian and the Invergarry iron furnace, began in 1723 and 1736 respectively. In view of these growing contacts with the south, 'long before the last Jacobite rebellion there was a marked inclination on the part of the Highland chiefs to ape the customs and manners of the south' (Nicolsen, 1930, p. 266), and more gracious living was increasingly sought. More comfortable houses began to replace draughty castles, for in 1633 the Laird of Grant was repairing Urquhart Castle and in the same year a house for modern comfort was built at Duart Castle in Mull. There are even reports of the extravagant living in Edinburgh by the eighteenth chief of Dunvegan in the late seventeenth century, bringing the clan to the brink of ruin; mortgages and debts were thus a feature of the seventeenth as well as the eighteenth and nineteenth centuries.

But the changes were going deeper still. The whole system of landholding was coming under review. It was a system traditionally geared to the patriarchal character of the clan and its important function as a military unit. It ensured that the whole population had a stake in the land through a process of letting and subletting from the chief to his tacksmen and on to the small tenants, who might themselves have dependants, cottars or servants, on their small patch of arable land, and a stake in the grazing. This system maintained the social fabric of the clan, giving each member a definite though fixed position in relation to the chief, and could readily be applied in a military situation. But agriculturally it was inefficient, for the proliferation of tiny holdings, usually without leases, in the infield (the small section of the farm which could be used as arable) rotated perhaps annually on a run-rig basis, and grazing in common did not encourage land improvement or permit capital accumulation. The system did not permit a pattern of rational farming units even though the clan was forced to depend on very limited land resources for livelihood. But the breakdown of the cohesion of the clans in the seventeenth and eighteenth centuries, with the decline of their military function, led gradually to the introduction of improvements by way of consolidation and the granting of leases. Thus on the Campbell estates in 1678 incoming Lowland and Campbell gentlemen held half the land of Kintyre. The tacksman system was later abolished in Kintyre and leases given to the former joint tenants, a process which was later carried through in 1737 by Duncan Forbes of Culloden for the Campbell chief in Mull, Morvern and Tiree. In many cases the amenity value of properties was enhanced by the planting of policies of oak, fir or birch (Plate 14).

It is possible therefore to take the view that in 1745 many of the Highlanders were peaceful and law-abiding. The clan system was certainly breaking down in the more accessible parts of the Highlands, and even in remoter areas the forfeiture of estates after 1715 and the long absence of some chiefs inevitably weakened the link. Moreover, the Church of Scotland, re-established as Presbyterian in 1690, had taken up the evangelisation of the Highlands, with consequent attrition of the Jacobite cause. At the same time, however, the effect of these developments was to accentuate the difference in character between the north and south of the Highlands which was noted earlier. For it was essentially the southern and eastern fringes where Lowland influences spread relatively early, while the less accessible lands north and west of the Great Glen retained far more of the old form of organisation. Thus it is not surprising that many of the Young Pretender's supporters were out under duress and that by 1745 the Jacobite party could with reasonable confidence call only on less than half the fighting strength of the Highland clans. But it is equally significant that the bulk, though not all, of his support came from beyond the Great Glen, where society was still capable of being moved, albeit with deep misgivings in some quarters, by a passionate and romantic attachment to the *de jure* royal house. Culloden serves therefore not as a beginning but only as a crude marker of the emergence of the Highland problem, which was brought on by the penetration of Lowland influences and, equally important, their introduction at an uneven rate in different parts of the Highlands.

The long-term results of Culloden can be exaggerated. The punitive expeditions indulged in by Cumberland's troops and the forfeiture of certain estates until 1784 were certainly disrupting influences, but these can to some extent be offset by much good work which the forfeited estates commission carried out in the meantime in agricultural improvement and industrial growth. Again, the temporary measures taken against Highland society by way of abolishing heritable jurisdictions and proscribing Highland dress did not affect the relationship between the chief and his people, for where the patriarchal system had existed before, it largely continued in force, and there were cases of rents still being paid to the chief even in his absence after 1746. What was now different, however, was the status of the clan as a military force, for this function was now utterly lost and gradually taken over by various Highland regiments which were recruited for government service, for Parliament was not slow to realise the value of Highlanders in battle if their energies were funnelled along more acceptable channels. Often these regiments were raised by tacksmen, for under conditions of peace their role was now reduced to a modest agricultural involvement. Thus in 1777 John Macdonnell raised the 76th Regiment (the MacDonald Highlanders) and in 1793 Alan Cameron of Erracht formed the 79th Regiment.

There was some further weakening then in the cohesiveness of the clan system, and to that extent agrarian reform became even more practicable. It might even seem as if Culloden, by indirectly accelerating the decline of traditional society, encouraged the possibility of greater uniformity throughout the Highlands in economic development. Not only had the main centres of resistance been crushed, but accessibility was improved by another wave of road building. In 1749 schemes began to link Fort William with Stirling by way of Glencoe and Rannoch Moor and Coupar Angus with Fort George, followed in 1760 by the Contin–Poolewe project and in 1770 by the road to Bernera, the first roads to penetrate beyond the Great Glen. But though it might seem as if progress could now be made on a broader front, the reverse proved to be the case.

EVOLUTION OR REVOLUTION?

It is an unfortunate feature of Highland geography that the richest and most easily traversable areas tend to be on the eastern and southern fringes, that is, precisely those areas which are most accessible from the Central Lowlands. The poorer lands of the north and west, with a higher proportion of ill-drained peaty ground, much bare rock outcropping and a bleaker climate, thus have the added disadvantage of being much less accessible (Plate 5). The Hebrides represent an even greater problem in terms of resources and accessibility, with the extreme case being reached in the case of a small Hebridean island such as Mingulay or St Kilda, where communications with the main islands pose considerable difficulties quite apart from links with the mainland of Scotland (Plate 7). Developments have tended to have the unfortunate effect of increasing these contrasts rather than minimising them, for while access to the north-west Highlands and islands has certainly improved over the years, the rate of improvement further south has been greater. This can readily be seen by examining the road network in the Highlands. With each succeeding phase of building they pushed further into the north-west mainland, but even after the Telford phase there were few good roads on the islands, while roads on the margins of the Highlands were more comprehensive and of better quality. Thus in the eighteenth century agricultural reform could continue gradually on the Lowland fringes of the Highlands through a substantial measure of voluntary emigration (with small tenants going seasonally and later permanently to the industrial Lowlands) and richer land resources to ease the process of consolidation.

Reform was also encouraged by increasing demands for livestock in the south. The agricultural revolution in central Scotland in the eighteenth century led to a great expansion in cereal production (the acreage of wheat in Midlothian rising from 1,000 in 1750 to 7,000 in 1800), whereas the Highlands seemed marked out as an area of cattle and sheep raising. Arable farming in the Highlands suffered many hazards, and unless there was a demand for self-sufficiency a greater concentration on the grazings seemed most appropriate, with arable devoted to turnips and artificial grasses to sustain the livestock through the winter. This was encouraged by the Union of Parliaments in 1707, for while this ended certain commercial contacts which Scotland once had with the Continent, it did open up the English market and offer increased possibilities for the sale of livestock.

But once again it was the more accessible richer grazings on the Highland margins which could profit most, for further north and west the quality of the grazings and the supply of good arable were such that cattle could not be fattened for market. Sheep were more appropriate here and larger holdings necessary. Yet the north and west had seen little emigration at that time other than the disappearance of tacksmen, many of whom felt themselves superfluous under conditions of peace and emigrated, especially when relations with the chief became embittered through rent increases or religious issues. Since they had carried on a variety of small though useful entrepreneurial functions in society, the effect of their departure was to rob the north-west of a valuable source of leadership and initiative, while the population as a whole continued to increase. Under these physical and demographic conditions land consolidation could not be achieved without greater overcrowding, for a considerable number of families would have to be resettled in order to create one commercial grazing farm. The full extent of the dilemma can be appreciated by the need on the part of the chief to raise rents in sympathy with the financial demands of a higher standard of living which increased intercourse with the south encouraged. The tenantry must pay more, yet increasing pressure of population on limited land resources reduced their ability to do so and the patriarchal relationship precluded any drastic action for some time.

Rents did rise substantially in the late eighteenth century, however. At Dunvegan in Skye, for instance, the rental was £1,589 in 1724 and had risen to £7,266 by 1811. Three factors in particular are important in sustaining these increases. First, the greatly increased demand for cattle was naturally accompanied by an increase in price. About the time of the Union in 1707 the average price of cows in Scotland appears to have been a little over £1 sterling, whereas by 1763 prices at the Falkirk Tryst were of the order of £2 per head. By 1794 the average price had risen to £4, and it then climbed steeply during the Napoleonic wars to reach as much as £6 per head. The second factor was the introduction of the potato in about 1740, which enabled a greater number of people to subsist off a given area of land than formerly. To this extent the increasing population could be accommodated – albeit at a very low level of living – and a limited amount of land consolidation could be attempted. Thirdly came the kelp industry; this was an alkaline seaweed extract and was in great demand as a source of soda, especially when supplies of Spanish barilla were cut off during the Napoleonic wars. Over 2,000 tons were produced annually in the late eighteenth century in the Western Isles and on the mainland of Morvern, Ardnamurchan and Arisaig. Prices rose from £8 per ton in 1775 to £10 in 1800 and reached a peak of some £22 per ton by 1810; the profits to the landowner were such that people could be kept on the land far beyond its agricultural potential.

But the situation was highly unstable. Much of the financial benefit from cattle and kelp passed directly or indirectly to the landowner, the lot of the small tenant hardly improving at all and in some cases probably deteriorating, circumstances which made it more necessary yet more difficult to move. Change could not come gradually in these remoter, poorer and overpopulated districts: instead it came more suddenly and dramatically, following, significantly, the fall in cattle and kelp prices after the Napoleonic wars. This period serves well to define the end of an era, when confident planning gave way to nervous attempts to hold together the agrarian structure. In the following chapters, which deal with attempts to come to terms with the nineteenth century, a basic theme will be the contrast between the evolutionary processes at work on the Highland margins and the more revolutionary measures which were implemented in the north-west Highlands and islands.

It would seem in conclusion that the exploitation of the Highlands and the depression of their economy were the result of forces emanating as much from the Central Belt of Scotland as from England. Inevitably, with the Union of 1707 London became the centre of power, carrying responsibility for Highland affairs, and the greater economic contacts certainly affected these northern areas. Yet Highland–Lowland relations before the Union do not suggest that the continuation of Scottish independence would have significantly modified the pattern of events there. But it was regrettable that the effective political and economic unification of Scotland should have been accomplished by force, with the inflammation of the inherent cultural separatism of the area by a number of major religious issues. More conciliatory policies might have created a better atmosphere for subsequent development. But the widely contrasting conditions in different parts of the Highlands, and the tendency for these to be exaggerated rather than lessened with time, show that improvement is most difficult where it is most necessary. An absolute gain yet relative decline is a typical feature of the development performance of many countries today, in that rates of growth in certain countries do not measure up to those in others, so that the gulf widens rather than contracts. But this is also true in the case of a country and its sub-regions and furthermore at local level. Viewed in this light, a study of the Highlands and their constituent areas becomes at once more explicable and more illuminating.

CHAPTER TWO

The Improving Movement

THE farming pattern in the Highlands until the changes of the late eighteenth century had an important subsistence element, with cattle as the main export product. There was a premium on arable land and even the least promising tracts were taken in for cereals (oats and barley) and potatoes, introduced from the mid-eighteenth century. Generally, however, much of the land was rough grazing, but in view of the limited ranging ability of cattle only the lower slopes were incorporated into individual joint farms, along with the infield and outfield. The higher grazings were used seasonally and allocated to the joint farms as quite separate grazings, known as shielings. The layout on the Lochiel estate in 1772 (Fig. 3) may be regarded as typical for the western districts, and contrasts with the east-coast layout, where the lowland arable component is much more prominent.

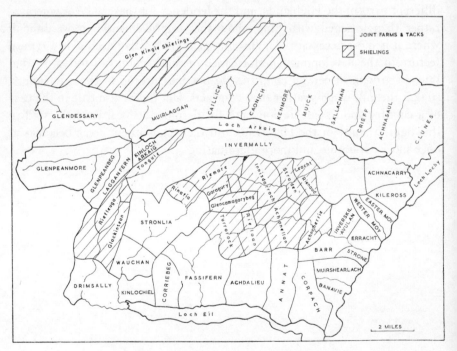

Fig. 3 *Organisation of the Lochiel estate, 1772*

THE YEAR OF THE SHEEP

The improving movement, however, was a growing force for stable conditions and removed one of the constraints which had prevented the Highlands taking full advantage of the commercial possibilities offered by the Union of 1707. Backed by such bodies as the Highland Society of Scotland founded in 1784, and agricultural surveys of the northern counties, new enterprises were advertised and the old system placed under increasing scrutiny. Although Lowland areas could be geared to the production of feeding stuffs with a fat cattle economy in mind, the appraisal of the Highland grazings in a wider national context for the most part suggested commercial sheep rearing as a principal farming activity. Almost all the rough grazings could be used by hardy breeds, and the problem of limited amounts of good arable could be overcome by the limited demands of sheep for feeding stuffs as compared with cattle. Sheep moved into the Highlands in increasing numbers after 1745 and the frontier was pushed progressively further north, to Perthshire by 1760, the Great Glen by 1780 and Sutherland by 1795.

The implications for the existing farming population were serious, and the year 1792 was for long remembered in the northern Highlands as 'the Year of the Sheep', when the men of Ross made a determined but unsuccessful attempt to expel the Cheviot sheep from the north. These intruders, whose growing numbers hailed the dawn of a new economy in the Highlands, had been regarded with deep misgivings ever since 1762 when Sir John Lockhart-Ross retired from public life to develop his estates at Balnagowan on the Dornoch Firth. The improvements he initiated were many, but most significant was the attraction of Lowland sheep farmers north of the Great Glen for the first time. The momentum gained by the import of these black-faced Linton sheep was followed up by the Cheviot, a breed which found a champion in Sir John Sinclair of Ulbster, Caithness. His diligent experiments with this breed at Langwell farm constituted a veritable model for improvers to follow.

Here indeed was a challenge to the established pattern of farming. As J. MacCulloch, a great exponent of commercial sheep farming, remarked (1824, p. 111), 'in these mountainous and boggy tracts black cattle cannot consume all the pasture. Sheep can; and consequently there is a saving on this head alone by the exchange.' This was true, though it should be remembered that the cattle did not monopolise the rough grazings but co-existed with the deer which constituted an important component of the traditional land-use pattern. But change could hardly be resisted provided it was introduced gradually and with due account taken of all the interests affected. Sir John Sinclair, in fact, advocated that commercial sheep farming should not necessitate the eviction of small tenants; rather they should be encouraged to amalgamate their holdings and capital resources and manage small flocks of sheep in common.

But sheep farming tended to be introduced in a more exclusive manner, for, as MacCulloch points out (1824, p. 111), 'sheep cannot be cultivated to a profit unless in large flocks and by a well regulated system. Small farmers cannot thence manage them: and thus arises the necessity of large sheep farms.' Such units would merge the rough grazings of several joint farms into large grazing tracts for sheep, whose ranging ability would be such as to allow shielings to be incorporated without the differentiation which was necessary under the cattle economy. More ominous still were the implications of demands for winter shelter and feeding stuffs, requirements which 'render it compulsory to take from petty agriculture the smaller interspersed tracts which are adapted to this purpose' (MacCulloch, 1824, p. 111). At a time when improvement of any sort was a measure of enlightenment, it was perhaps to be expected that the assured high rentals of southern graziers should have been preferred to the problematical returns gained under the old system. Once this choice was made, disturbance and disruption of the existing agricultural system, practised for centuries by the tenantry, was inevitable. Now 'it became inevitable on the proprietors to eject the small tenants, for the general benefit as well as for their own'. To the small farmers, however, secure in their system of 'petty agriculture' and the society which they had customarily associated with it, the benefits arising from the 'great sheep' economy were less tangible. The men of Ross therefore decided to take matters into their own hands and drive all the Cheviots from the county. Their failure was predictable, for the landowners received the instant backing of the law in the form of military support from Fort George. But it was a symbolic gesture, pointing to the shortcomings of exlusive land-use policies in general and those concerned with the 'great sheep' in particular.

The great commotion in Ross in 1792 was a local affair spontaneously conceived, but the sheep farming there was merely part of a growing movement which was to affect the whole of the Highlands. Now that the pacification of the Highlands was effective, the flocks could move up from the southern margins of Argyll and Perthshire to the northern counties. The sheep frontier pushed north relentlessly, but while the new sheep economy was generally welcomed by landowners in preference to the old type of subsistence farming, there are many important regional and local differences. It would be wrong to assume that all Highland landlords suddenly abandoned their tenantry in one massive co-ordinated policy shift. In certain cases the introduction of the new economy posed few problems: on the southern and eastern margins of the Highlands there was an early voluntary movement of people to the south which eased pressure on land and made reorganisation more feasible. Recruitment of men for military service on some estates made for the same end, especially during the Napoleonic phase. Finally there are also a number of cases of major emigration movements before the end of the eighteenth century. Thus the Clanranald chief, an ardent Presbyterian in a clan of predominantly Catholic and Jacobite convictions, found himself faced, in 1771, with the emigration of one of the cadet families, John MacDonald of Glenaladale. The latter purchased land in Prince Edward Island in Canada and took with him the majority of his subtenants from Moidart and Arisaig in 1772. Hence there are few references to clearances in this part of Lochaber.

IMPROVEMENT IN LOCHABER

On many estates therefore change was introduced gradually in the decades after 1745, and Lochaber provides some interesting examples. These concern policies on various estates in the area, lands which in many cases were similar to the clan lands as recognised before 1745. In an age when so much depended upon the energies and resources of the landowners and principal tenants, as opposed to those of local and national government, it is perhaps not surprising that the estate pattern of the time is an essential context for study. For this reason Fig. 4 shows the mid-nineteenth-century estate layout as well as the land use. However, the variations between estates do not hide a general contrast in the timing of improvement and the extent of resettlement between the east, where change came sooner and more gradually, and the west. This contrast moreover is part of a wider distinction between the north and west as opposed to the southern and eastern fringes of the Highlands, which acquired a 'Lowland' aspect at a relatively early date (Moisley, 1962b, p. 84).

In the Braes of Lochaber MacIntosh made changes in the late eighteenth century, moving his small tenantry down to the lower reaches of Glen Roy, where they were resettled in the townships of Bohuntine and Inverroy, and also in smaller groups around the hill of Galmore. Holdings were lotted to each tenant to be held in perpetuity in place of the former run-rig

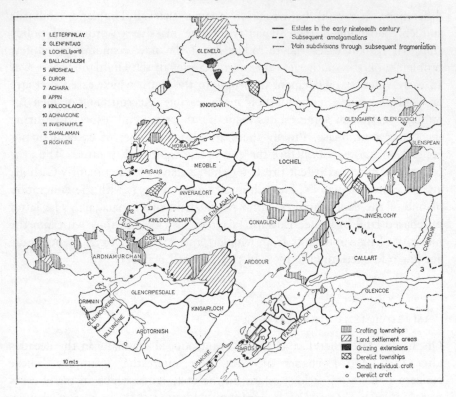

1 LETTERFINLAY
2 GLENFINTAIG
3 LOCHIEL (part)
4 BALLACHULISH
5 ARDSHEAL
6 DUROR
7 ACHARA
8 APPIN
9 KINLOCHLAICH
10 ACHNACONE
11 INVERNAHYLE
12 SAMALAMAN
13 ROSHVEN

— Estates in the early nineteenth century
-- Subsequent amalgamations
⌐···· Main subdivisions through subsequent fragmentation

Crofting townships
Land settlement areas
Grazing extensions
Derelict townships
• Small individual croft
o Derelict croft

10 mls

Fig. 4 *Croft land in Lochaber and north Argyll*

pattern, where holdings rotated at short intervals. This in turn prompted a new settlement pattern, with the morphology of the township taking on a strong linear appearance, the houses in a discontinuous row, each on its own strip of land, in place of the former nucleated clachan. Generous grazings were allocated, to be used in common by all the crofter tenants, and each was given a fixed quota or souming to ensure that overgrazing was avoided. The common grazing or pasture was often only large enough to support a cattle stock, the landlord holding the view that the land base was a means of producing basic foodstuffs, but that this support should be supplemented by some other employment in the area. The Glen Roy grazings were very large, however, and allowed a sheep stock as well as cattle. Hence relatively prosperous communities evolved and at the same time the introduction and development of commercial sheep grazing in the upper glens was not prejudiced.

Similar measures were adopted in other parts of the Great Glen area. On the Glengarry estate there was considerable dwindling of the population through the emigration of tacksmen and small tenants forced out by rent increases and non-renewal of leases. Moreover recruitment for the armed forces was vigorously pursued; in 1777 John Macdonnell raised the 76th Regiment (the MacDonald Highlanders), an operation followed up in 1794 when the Glengarry Fencibles were raised by Alistair Ranaldson, the first chief. It was as early as 1782 that Thomas Gillespie came to Glengarry to lease a large sheep grazing in Glen Quoich, as the lofty upper reaches of Glengarry are known. It was unlikely that this displaced large numbers of people, since Glen Quoich was a shieling area and Roy's map of 1755 shows no permanent settlement whatever around Loch Quoich. But it was a typical beginning, the sheep grazier moving first into the upper reaches of the glens and then putting pressure on the lower reaches, which were appreciated for their shelter and arable land. There were further clearances in Glengarry therefore in 1785 and 1787 which maintained the flow of emigrants sailing from Fort William. Yet again in 1802, after the Glengarry Fencibles were disbanded, some small tenants were disturbed, and though there are further reports of emigration at this time it is significant that a substantial area of grazing at Balmaglaster and Mandally was set aside for resettlement and that the changes came during the construction of the Caledonian Canal, a venture which it was thought might provide some local employment.

Developments on the adjacent Lochiel estate came slightly later. This great landholding, which embraced the land between Loch Quoich, Loch Arkaig and Loch Eil and also the land on the eastern side of Loch Linnhe south as far as Loch Leven, was forfeited after 1745 in view of the Camerons' prominence in the rebellion. Indeed it was Lochiel's decision which tipped the scales in favour of embarking on this disastrous expedition. It was not until 1784 that the estate was returned to the family, and most probably sheep had made only a scant impact by that time. The manpower requirements of British imperialism, however, made their customary demands: in 1793 Alan Cameron of Erracht raised the 79th Regiment, and later in 1799 Lochiel himself applied the usual forms of pressure on his tenantry to secure recruits for the Lochaber Fencibles. Side by side the sheep economy was developed; beginning in the glens of Glen Pean and Glen Dessary it spread along Locharkaigside, pushing out the small farmers to new sites on the damp moss of Blar Mor at Corpach and the stony raised beaches of Achintore, Corran, Onich and North Ballachulish. The main movement took place in 1803, contemporaneous with the beginning of the Caledonian Canal, and many of the tenants, certainly those who found themselves lotted holdings at Banavie, must have found additional employment in this great public work.

In all these cases, and in the cases of adjacent estates around the Great Glen such as Ardgour and Glencoe, the process of change was gradual; new forms of livelihood were found and there was sufficient land of reasonable quality to allow groups of smallholdings to exist alongside the sheep farms. Naturally these townships, all of which are still prominent in the crofting landscape today, were sited on land which would least prejudice the development of an efficient sheep-farming economy and, in the case of the coastal townships particularly, on poor land where reclamation can only be understood in the context of very low living standards with meagre subsistence the only objective. Coastal resettlement was normally the rule in the Highlands, since this combined opportunity for fishing with minimum interference with the rest of the estate, but on landlocked estates this was obviously not possible. In these cases, of which there are several in Lochaber, the equivalent site lay at the point where a tributary valley opened up into the Great Glen. The crofts in Glengarry, Glenfintaig, Glen Roy and Glen Spean all fit into this pattern.

THE DILEMMA IN THE WEST

Further west, however, change did not come so soon. The grazings of the west coast itself and the islands were often rockier and less desirable, as well as being less well known and relatively inaccessible. For the road network of the Highlands scarcely embraced areas beyond the Great Glen until Telford began his work early in the nineteenth century. Lacking the necessary stimulus the old ways persisted, and although the population was certainly increasing rapidly in many western districts, the potato crop and the kelp industry prolonged the life of the old social and economic order. But the situation was highly unstable; with the failure of the kelp industry after 1815 the problem of overpopulation became acute, since this semi-industrial population was now thrown back on the meagre resources of the land, which could no longer sustain the increased numbers. At the same time the road-building programme initiated by the state had now penetrated to Moidart, Arisaig, Loch Hourn and even to Skye. The first quarter of the nineteenth century witnessed a forward surge in the opening-up of the country which was far greater than all earlier achievements. Thus the ideas of the agricultural revolution could no longer be resisted and were now belatedly introduced in sudden and often revolutionary fashion, in contrast to the gradual consolidation which had been effected on the southern and eastern margins during the previous decades.

Generalisations are, however, again rather misleading in view of the significant variations between estates. There is a great danger in assuming that revolutionary improvement in the Highlands followed the same pattern everywhere. Too often the tactics of Patrick Sellar and James Loch in the Sutherland clearances between 1809 and 1821 have been translated into a general Highland model and applied indiscriminately throughout. The burnings in Strathnaver in 1814 which led to the trial, and acquittal, of Patrick Sellar in 1816 should rather be treated as a special case of injustice and oppression – one of few exceptions to the more general rule of moderation (Plate 15). Perhaps the very term 'clearance', even when linked with 'resettlement', is now so loaded that it would be more appropriate to think rather of 'reorganisation' or 'consolidation' of Highland agriculture.

Certainly events in Ardnamurchan indicate a fairly balanced approach. Here was a large estate comprising the whole of the long but narrow peninsula parish of Ardnamurchan and Sunart. After the expulsion of the MacIans the land had passed to Sir Duncan Campbell of Lochnell. He sold the estate to Murray of Stanhope who began the lead mining at Strontian. The population grew during the eighteenth century and reached a peak of 3,311 in 1831. An early estate map drawn up in 1807 by William Bald shows that the clachan form of settlement persisted in most cases, with the land still unlotted into fixed holdings; only at Ardnastang at the mouth of the Strontian valley had the land been consolidated into lotted holdings. Moreover the sheep economy was then conspicuous by its relative absence on much of the estate. In the more mountainous area of Sunart a number of sheep walks are evident, but very few existed in the western parts of the peninsula (Storrie, 1961*b*).

Growing pressure in the nineteenth century called for more thorough reform. Arrears in rent were steadily accumulating, the situation reaching a climax in 1838 when the factor of the estate recommended that the rent roll be purged of all tenants whose payments had fallen behind. The result of this was the removal of all tenants from the small group of townships around Ben Hiant, a mountain which is naturally well drained and supports good grazing. The tenants of Camusnagal, Corrievullin, Bourblaige, Skinad and Tornamoany were therefore transferred to other townships in the West End which were now reorganised on the basis of lotted holdings. It is interesting to note, however, that in a number of cases the clachan form of settlement survived the abolition of run-rig, with which pattern it is normally associated; Achnaha and Ockle are good examples of the persistence of this grouping of cottages. Again, after the destitution and havoc wrought by the potato famine another wave of reorganisation was launched. In the early 1850s tenants were removed from Swordle, a section of the estate on the north coast of Ardnamurchan, which was then organised as three joint farms, namely Swordlemore, Swordlechorrach and Swordlehuel. But again it is significant that emigration was not imposed as a necessary part of the process: instead new townships were laid out around Sanna Bay (named Sanna and Portuairk) where smallholdings were allocated to each tenant as potato land in the hope that fishing would sustain the families for the rest (Fig. 5). Furthermore the moss lands between Acharacle and Kentra were reclaimed around their periphery and holdings lotted in the new townships of Shielfoot, Newton and Kentra to resettle tenants removed from the Laga and Glenborrodale areas to the west (Plate 16).

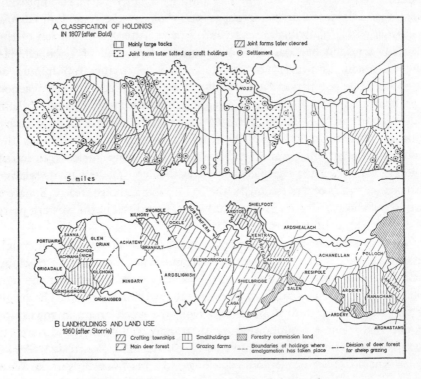

Fig. 5 *The improving movement in Ardnamurchan*

Something of a contrast is provided by the estate of Knoydart, perhaps the most inaccessible part of the *garbh chriochan* ('rough bounds'), as the western districts of Lochaber are known. Telford's roads reached only to Kinlochourn, the far northeastern corner of the estate, and it was a long and difficult journey by track from there to Barrisdale and thence to Inverie, which has always been the centre of the estate. The population of Knoydart numbered 1,000 in 1790, according to the Old Statistical Account, but by the time the census was taken in 1841 numbers had fallen to roughly 900. Being then part of the Glengarry estates, Knoydart had been affected by the dwindling process already described in Glengarry proper: around 1817 for instance there are reports of evictions from Kinlochnevis and other townships on the eastern part of the estate. By 1841 therefore the bulk of the small tenants were crammed into the western coastlands in a group of townships stretching from Niagard at the mouth of Glen Guseran, through Samadalan, Airor and Dunn as far as Ridarroch on the Bay of Sandaig. Other more scattered groups lived at Kylesknoydart in the south and at Skiary on Loch Hourn. In these areas the commercial sheep economy was not inhibited and could expand freely through the major glens of Knoydart, Glen Guseran, Glen Dulochan and Glen Meadail, not to mention Glen Barrisdale and Glen Cosaidh to the north-east. The lonely shepherds' dwellings up these glens contrasted with the dense populations of the townships and illustrated the dichotomy between the two economies (see Fig. 8, insets).

What has provided so much food for thought, however, was not so much this gradual process of reorganisation in Knoydart, which produced such an unbalanced population map in 1841, but rather the measures taken after the potato famine by the widow of the 16th chief of Glengarry. Arrangements were made with the Highland Emigration Society to transport the small tenants who had survived this period of destitution to Australia. The events of 1853, when the population was forced to board the emigration vessel anchored in the Sound of Sleat, are well documented and summarised by Prebble (1963); those who resisted saw their homes burned, and the few who evaded the holds of the *Sillery* passed a winter under extreme conditions within the grounds of the chapel of Sandaig, which was one of the few reliable refuges.

This more extreme action was the result of a number of circumstances. First there was the local situation, with a relatively prosperous sheep-farming industry competing for land with a numerous but poverty-stricken tenantry of small subsistence farmers. The arable and low ground of the crofters was coveted by the large farms of Scottas and Inverguseran; hence the clearance took the form of a pincer movement from both sides, leaving only the township of Airor undisturbed in the centre, straddling the march. Airor was also the ferry point for the estate at the time, and no doubt this was another factor in the decision to leave undisturbed this small community of families, many of whom had come over from Skye around 1835. The only other section of the estate where small farmers remained was at Skiary, where some small potato patches were enclosed on a stony beach which in view of its isolated and peripheral position could not be readily integrated with the rest of the estate. At the same time, as with Airor, Skiary lay at the door of the estate in terms of land transport, for it was the first settlement belonging to Knoydart on the track which continued on to Inverie from the end of the Glengarry road at Kinlochourn.

Much of the Glengarry estates had already been disposed of in the 1830s after the death of the 15th chief, Alistair Ranaldson Macdonnell. Mr Edward Ellice acquired first Glen Quoich (1838), and in 1860 Glengarry (first sold by the Macdonnells in 1842) also passed into his hands. He developed the estate for the most part as a series of sheep farms, with well-built houses and steadings at Kinlochourn, Glen Quoich, Greenfield, Tomdoun, Ardochy, Invergarry, Aberchalder and South Laggan. A buyer was now found for Knoydart – Mr James Baird, an ironmaster – and since he was unwilling to accept the burden of a large, underemployed and near-destitute population, it was considered by Mrs Macdonnell, the 16th chief's widow, that the removal of the tenantry to the New World was the obvious solution. Indeed Aeneas, the 16th chief, had himself emigrated to New South Wales in 1840.

But there is a further national consideration. Emigration, which had originally been generally regarded as escapism in the late eighteenth century, when British army regiments were hungry for recruits, now seemed an acceptable solution to overpopulation problems at a time of peace. Many argued that such an opportunity would be a happy release from a life of toil and low returns. Thus MacCulloch (1824, p. 134) argued that emigration 'should be carried into effect by any means, even by force should that be necessary, and before the period of real excess and want arrives. That which is called oppression is here in fact humanity. The longer a chance is protracted the more severe in every way it will be because greater numbers will be added to greater poverty.' Some stopped to question the ethics of arranging a programme of emigration without consulting those involved, but the majority balanced long-term gains favourably against short-term social cost. Even Stewart in 1822, while highlighting the deplorable conditions on the emigration vessels and the iniquities of compulsory emigration, declared it was 'irreconcilable with every principle of sound policy and humanity to attempt to check emigration' (1822, p. 188), which he considered was the best antidote for a crowded population. The government was content to limit its role to the general supervision of emigration and the administration of a largely ineffective poor-relief programme.

Thus the Knoydart tenants were victims of many oppressors, and they were not alone in their troubles. Throughout the west coast and islands the population had outgrown the capacity of the land: whereas further east and further back in time the requirements of commercial farmers and small tenants had been largely reconciled within the confines of each estate with limited upheaval, the delay in the penetration of the necessary stimuli to the far north and west only enlarged the problem. Sudden waves of clearance and resettlement on rocky coasts were the result. All west-coast estates therefore show radical changes in their agricultural structure by the middle of the nineteenth century. As Fig. 4 shows, Arisaig, Glenelg and Morvern estates employed somewhat different resettlement policies, in the same way as differences of emphasis emerge from a study of Ardnamurchan and Knoydart, but the commercial farming element accounted for an overwhelming proportion of the land in every case. This same pattern was repeated throughout the north-west mainland and again in the Outer Hebrides, where pressure on the limited land resources was so great as to force resettlement of small tenants on the most inhospitable sites along the rocky Minch coast, where arable land had often to be artificially created by building what have been most misleadingly referred to as 'lazy beds'. Several detailed field surveys exist which portray the course of events in specific Hebridean areas, notably Park (Caird *et al.*, 1958) and Uig (Moisley *et al.*, 1961) in Lewis.

Landowners were as much affected as their tenants. Indeed many delayed resolving the dilemma which was becoming annually more formidable until they themselves became the first victims. Discussing the fortunes of the kelp industry and the declining profits from this activity, Gray writes (1951, p. 208) that 'when they disappeared they left the kelp estates in the same precarious state as at the beginning of the boom. From then on the disastrous fall in money income and the recurring problem of maintaining on a faltering rental a tenantry which had outrun the yield of the land slowly submerged many of the greater properties.' In Lochaber it is a striking feature that almost without exception estates which remained intact throughout this time are all in the Great Glen area, where change was spread over a long period, while sale and subdivision of landholdings are more typical of the more revolutionary trends further west. Thus the Clanranald and Glengarry estates were partitioned and even the Ardnamurchan estate was divided after Sir James Miles Riddell became bankrupt in 1848. It was frequently only at times such as this that evictions took place. Certainly the chequered history of Glenelg ties in with the sale of the estate first in 1798 and again in 1811, 1824 and 1837 (Plate 2). It was James Baillie of Dochfour, who then acquired the estate, who contributed some £2,000 to enable 500 of his tenants to emigrate to Canada in 1849.

A SYSTEM OF SMALL FARMS?

It was perhaps only natural that these upheavals on the whole provoked such an indignant response. The unilateral abandonment by many landlords of their obligation to society was construed as a gross breach of faith and roundly condemned. The honourable trait of the chief's generous attachment to his people, which had survived the rebellion of 1745, had now, it seemed, become dispensable. Yet it is perhaps unreasonable to attach all blame to the landowners: many of them were perhaps hardly fitted to manage an estate efficiently or regulate their finances realistically; they were as much victims of circumstances as were the tenants exposed to their decisions. It was particularly unfortunate that the pacification of the Highlands should have come at a time when the resources of central Scotland for agriculture and industry were being diligently exploited, for it meant that the proximity of a veritable growth pole to the south in an age of individualism and *laissez-faire* would force the Highlands into an almost colonial relationship. Aid to the Highlands came largely in the form of state road building, and though this was a necessary preliminary to development it was, without backing, an incentive to migrate south, at least from the most accessible areas. The Highlands remained an underdeveloped region, the inevitable corollary of the growth area in the Central Valley, and despite their inner feelings and wide powers over their own estates the landlords could not escape from this inhibiting context.

The sheep economy could not be denied a prominent place in Highland agriculture. But why could this new source of wealth not be introduced so as to unleash the energies of the small tenants rather than restrict them to very small, rocky and ill-drained coastal sites? This was a theme developed by an anonymous critic of MacCulloch's warm approval of improvement practices:

Had the Northern Proprietors commenced their course of improvement by granting leases to their tenantry, by dissolving the joint farms, by encouraging the introduction of improved implements of husbandry and the green crop system, by pointing out to their tenantry the advantage of rearing stock on those parts of their estates which were either not susceptible of cultivation, or at least could not be cultivated to advantage; in short, had they given to their old, loyal, attached, and faithful tenantry but one-fourth of the encouragement which they have spontaneously given to shepherds from the Moffat Hills, and other interlopers . . . they would have been accounted the protectors and the benefactors, not the calumniators and oppressors, of their people; and would have promoted their own best interests (Anon., 1826, pp. 26–74).

As if in reply to this anonymous outburst of 1826 a scheme of improvement was drawn up for the North Morar estate in 1834. North Morar constitutes the southernmost third of Glenelg parish and is clearly demarcated by Loch Nevis to the north and Loch Morar to the south. Extremely elongated in shape (some sixteen miles long but only two-thirds of a mile wide in the centre), it is also very rough and steeply graded. Yet it has remained in the hands of the Frasers of Lovat continuously since it was sold by the Macdonnells of Glengarry to Simon Fraser, 16th of Lovat, in 1768, and presents an interesting study, since here is a case of a west-coast estate in the hands of a prominent east-coast landowner. Early estate policy therefore tended to be influenced by the intensive measures applied in the more fertile east, with greater emphasis on small agricultural units, rather than the more usual west-coast practice of creating large sheep farms with consequent discouragement and disturbance of small tenants.

Thomas Fraser of Strichen, 18th of Lovat, inherited the Lovat estates in 1815, and in North Morar we are told that he 'found his crofter tenantry in a very reduced and helpless condition and the cultivation of their holdings carried on in a very rude and superficial manner'. Overpopulation was not serious at the time, and on coming of age in 1827 Lord Lovat was able to plan the reorganisation of the estate with the minimum of disturbance by abolishing the old pattern of run-rig joint farms and shielings and establishing small grazing farms and crofting townships, let in some cases on a system of nineteen-year improvement leases at nominal rents. In the words of his factor, John Peter (Scotland, 1895, p. 295), 'he had it surveyed and laid out and put into squares of different sizes according to the means of the people and particularly in regard to crofter tenants so that they might each have their own ground laid out for them'. This striking departure from the normal pattern of west-coast improvement is shown on an estate map drawn from a survey in 1834 (Fig. 6).

Most of the farms consisted of separate independent units of varying size, while others had something of a township structure, with allowance for two holdings and a common grazing at Wester Stoul and Ardnamurach, and three holdings, with apportionment of grazings, at Brinnicorry. In the townships the arable is shown lotted into permanent holdings, roughly four acres each in size at Bracara but rather smaller at Mallaig and Kylesmorar, where fishing was expected to be more prominent. Lotting would encourage a linear settlement pattern in place of the nucleated clachan, though rough terrain inhibited a regular layout at Mallaig especially. Taking the estate as a whole, therefore, farm sizes fell into a continuum rather than a pattern of stratification. By avoiding too strict a distinction between crofter and farmer it was thought possible for the industrious small tenant with capital to graduate to a larger holding, without the same social barriers as the old order had imposed.

From census enumeration material, however, it seems that the scheme was not implemented immediately. The 1841 census shows nucleations of small tenants at Stoul, Ardnamurach and Kinlochmorar, where farms were proposed in the plan, while at Mallaig, where sixteen holdings were envisaged, there were only four families in residence then. Moreover, in the words of the enumerator, sheep farming 'had been but to a limited extent introduced to North Morar'. However, changes became evident as the century progressed, but it is significant that they did not always follow the lines suggested by the 1834 plan. The small sheep grazings 'did not pay very well', for 'the sheep stock is never so good as it is in the regular type farms with proper people regularly trained' (Scotland, 1895, p. 297). It is doubtful from census evidence whether many of them ever attracted a tenant of their own, for the grazings were too small for the capitalist sheep farmer, who needed a large area to achieve efficient shepherding and to justify the investment of his capital and technical ability. At the same time they were too large for the small man to stock adequately with modest capital resources exhausted by the fall in cattle prices and the potato famine of the late 1840s. The conflict between the needs of the large farmer and the capabilities of the small tenant proved to be too great for compromise to bridge, even with the utmost goodwill and benevolence, and hence a rental for the estate in 1879 shows a more definite pattern of stratification. The two large farms, Kinlochmorar and Beoraidmore, accounted for 54 per cent of the total

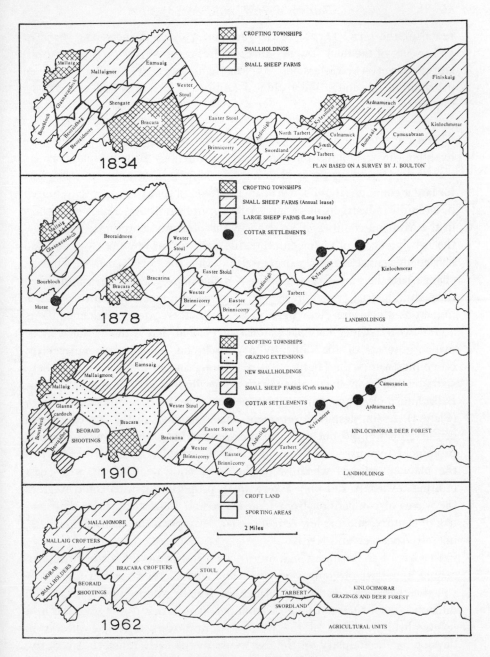

Fig. 6 *The improving movement in North Morar*

rental of the estate (£720), while the eleven other farmers paid £500 or 37 per cent of the total. Twenty-three crofter tenants paid £108 (9 per cent) and the twenty-two cottars only £5, less than 1 per cent. The highly uneven distribution of capital and technical ability could hardly fail to make its impact on the landscape.

The Highland clearances may have a history of their own, yet they are by no means a unique phenomenon. Throughout Britain small farmers were being forced off the land during the agrarian revolution to make way for larger commercial units, whose greater food output was urgently required by a rapidly industrialising society. After the upheavals of the early enclosures in the Midland counties of England in the fifteenth century, demanded by the growing needs of the medieval textile industry for raw wool, opinion had hardened against further reorganisation. But the social costs of agrarian change later became accepted as part of the unavoidable expense incurred through industrial growth in the eighteenth and nineteenth centuries, when numerous Enclosure Acts were passed. To this extent Highland affairs accord with a wider national pattern of change, but a distinction can be made in terms of the difficulty of developing satisfactory replacement economies within the Highland area. Mining and iron smelting were both sporadic and short-lived, albeit with some notable exceptions such as the Ballachulish slate quarrying, which persisted well into the present century (Plate 3). Again, despite government encouragement in the late eighteenth century, textiles did not thrive in the west, although linen was sufficiently prominent in north-east Scotland for it to provide the economic base of the planned villages which were the local equivalent of the west-coast crofting township. But only a very small proportion of this could weather the waves of competition from Lancashire and Leicestershire in the nine-teenth century, and the few remaining concerns are all in the larger centres, notably Aberdeen and Keith.

In view of the manifest inability of kelp to sustain an adequate return, fishing appeared the only alternative and was therefore seized upon as a valuable base for resettlement schemes. Small groups of tiny crofts on difficult coastal sites can only be understood in terms of the great faith in fishing held by many of the west-coast improvers after the success in developing the industry on the east coast in the early nineteenth century, for these tiny holdings were never envisaged as sufficient to support a family in themselves. But for reasons discussed in the following chapter this industry never lived up to its expectations, and hence the tenantry were often forced back to a meagre land base whose frontiers, far from advancing, were being constantly encroached upon by a farming economy enjoying its golden age. The 1860s and 1870s provided numerous examples of eviction and injustice endured by a highly insecure tenantry, and the inevitable corollary of emigration generated customary controversy. It was, as Stewart remarked in 1822 (p. 189), a subject 'too melancholy to contemplate without the deepest commiseration', yet the gradual awakening of the nation's social conscience, with its demands for greater security and regulation, begged the question then, as it still does today, 'Security to do what?'

CHAPTER THREE

Fishing as a Replacement Economy

THE limitations of the Highland environment for agriculture inevitably encouraged the local population to look to the resources of the sea as a source of livelihood. Attention was all the more merited in view of the many sheltered creeks and harbours along certain sections of the indented coastline and also in view of the wealth of the seas on all sides of the Highlands for fish. Thus in the Loch Roag area of Lewis the fine system of natural havens close to the fishing grounds offered obvious possibilities, and a remarkable local fishery for ling developed and persisted into the present century. But the natural endowment is very varied, and other parts of the Hebrides, such as the machair townships facing the Atlantic, have never enjoyed a great stake in the fishing on account of the limitations of their site and situation in relation to the grounds.

It is also necessary, however, to discriminate between the various types of fish, for the possibilities and patterns of activity vary very considerably. Briefly, a fourfold classification into white fish, herring, shellfish and salmon may be suggested. Shellfish are only available locally in commercial quantities, and white fishing, though often reliable, is restricted in scope on the west coast, though more prolific off the east coast and Shetland. Herring are abundant off both coasts, but on the west coast the seasonal migrations, though regular in a broad sense, did not assure attachment to a particular sea loch every year and supplies have therefore fluctuated very greatly in the past. Salmon, like shellfish, are valuable in some areas but limited in potential overall, and are moreover only a source of strictly seasonal summer fishing. Clearly, therefore, fishing had an important subsistence value, but commercial potential lay more specifically with white fish, especially on the east coast, and with herring, though in this case development had to await the discovery of a satisfactory cure. On the west coast, moreover, the migration habits of the herring suggested that a viable industry would demand among other things a full-time specialist interest and an ability to fish at a considerable range beyond the home loch.

Another point which may be made at this early stage is that the areal pattern of fishing, unlike agriculture, cannot be closely regulated. There is no layout of fixed holdings and boundaries to restrict activity to a particular location. Rather it is a free-for-all 'robber' economy with local fisheries open to exploitation from further afield. The unfortunate situation soon arose whereby west-coast fisheries, though invaluable resources for the local population, were developed largely by commercial forces over which they had little or no control and with which they could not compete effectively.

EARLY DEVELOPMENTS

There was a steadily growing interest in fishing through the seventeenth century, with a preoccupation with white fishing. Scope on the east coast especially was considerable, and doubtless in sympathy with the improving movement in agriculture most coastal parishes contained at least one fishing settlement by the early eighteenth century. Circumstances were such that a clear separation in function between agriculture and fishing could be effected. The specialist fishing function of such settlements as Findochty (1716), Macduff and Gardenstown (1720) indicates the cleavage between the fishing and farming communities which grew up then. In Shetland too white fishing became important and was known as *haaf* fishing, but the resources and social fabric of the community were such that here the two functions could not be entirely divided and the traditional duality continued. It was the same on the west coast; where fishing was particularly important in the islands there was a certain amount of curing of white fish for export, and since curing involved only gutting and air-drying remoteness was no great handicap. But the population remained resolutely farmers first and fishermen second.

The consequences of this failure to specialise were various. A division of interest was bound to reduce the single-mindedness with which a man could pursue one activity, irrespective of his initiative and capital resources. Applied to the agricultural conditions on the west coast in the eighteenth century this meant that profits from fishing would tend to be absorbed by agriculture, which frequently left the small tenant in debt to an exacting landlord. Even where the landlord encouraged fishing, the unreliable outlets in the west meant that he could obtain the bulk of the profits by offering the only market, albeit a guaranteed one. Fishing thus had a function akin to that of kelp, in that it boosted the landlords' income and enabled a dense population to be maintained on the land at a very low standard of living. The profits falling to the landlord were no doubt considerable, but were normally necessarily channelled into paying off old debts or supporting a more sophisticated household. Fishing was thus effectively starved of development capital, in sharp contrast to practice on the east coast. Here greater interest and more prolific fishing grounds produced rapid progress and profits were devoted to new equipment, so that the fishermen were in the forefront of the developing fishing technology. They were moreover better placed physically with regard to distant markets and developed sounder contacts with outside sources of capital.

Thus there were two extreme positions, arising basically from relative advantages of position and resources. But there was the social factor too, inasmuch as the west-coast fisherman displayed a marked reluctance to depend entirely on the sea for a living, which cannot be entirely explained in terms of uncertain supplies and outlets. As late as 1900 the Congested Districts Board reported (p. 12) that

> The west coast crofters are not historically a seafaring people. While in many cases both good boatmen and daring sailors they cannot be persuaded to trust entirely to the sea for a living . . . and the means of resorting to the sea for fish when necessary. Their environment inevitably fosters a life made up of spurts of work and spells of idleness and the effect of this attitude is to produce a disinclination to change to a life when there can be little or no idleness.

These reasons put forward for failure to develop the fishing may be considered somewhat uncharitable, and local opinion would be more inclined to stress the limited opportunities for commercial development. But there were certainly some exceptions, and perhaps the most notable, though admittedly away from the west coast, was the *haaf* fishing in Shetland which has already been referred to. This was deep-sea fishing for cod, ling and tusk, cured by gutting, salting and air-drying on stony beaches. Tenants were obliged by landlords to participate in the fishing, with a truck system of payment completing their economic subjection. Yet the industry flourished into the nineteenth century and was later succeeded by other forms of white fishing as far away as the Faeroes, Rockall and Iceland. Although steam trawlers eventually ousted the Shetlanders from this deep-sea fishing and restricted their activity more to the local haddock fishing in winter, the local people clearly displayed a willingness to travel far to the fish. The thriving crofter–fisher communities on the Shetland islands of Whalsay and Burra today are a fitting survival of this long-standing tradition.

HERRING FISHING

The development of herring fishing provides an even more striking illustration of the difficulty of maintaining even rates of progress throughout the Highlands. Although herring abounded off both east and west coasts, local interest was slow to realise the vast potential. The Dutch, however, had first discovered the correct cure for herring and were the first to venture into the open-sea herring fisheries on a large scale. They were certainly active off the east coast of Scotland in the sixteenth and seventeenth centuries and, with no effective competition, were able to retain this position until the Napoleonic wars destroyed their fleets. In view of the established position of the Dutch it was therefore the west-coast herring fishery which seemed to offer the best prospects for a domestic industry in the eighteenth century, and it was here that the British Fisheries Society, founded in 1749, made great efforts. They dispatched a herring bus to Stornoway and laid out Ullapool in 1788. Tobermory (Mull) was another site to be developed, and growth was encouraged at such places as Stein (Skye) and Shieldaig (Loch Torridon). This was not all, for bounties were offered by the government as a further incentive: a bounty of 30s per ton was payable on boats built and operated in Great Britain (with a 20-ton minimum), and this was followed in 1787 by a barrel bounty which extended aid to small fishermen too. Certain local proprietors made strenuous efforts to develop the fishing: in Lewis, Lord Seaforth introduced Dutch fishermen and around 1786 Captain MacLeod, proprietor of Harris, introduced east-coast fishermen to Rodel.

But these external stimuli were inadequate as far as the local population were concerned. Their outlook and circumstances did not permit rapid development, and the problem of market outlets remained acute. At Ullapool in particular the long haul south was certainly a hindrance to progress in spite of the road improvements in the early decades of the nineteenth century. Again, the cure was not entirely satisfactory and frustrated by the veritable famine for salt which the Salt Laws imposed. It was a famine alleviated only by the erratic operations of certain southern entrepreneurs, some of whom established curing houses on the west coast. But their contacts with any one locality were necessarily unreliable, in view of the precarious attachment of the herrings to individual lochs. Years of plenty such as 1773 in Loch Torridon and 1782 in Loch Hourn were separated by long periods of poor returns which could not possibly justify many permanent local shore installations.

This failure to make maximum use of local herring fisheries was perhaps most manifest in the Outer Hebrides. Indeed, as Caird and Moisley have commented (1961, p. 96),

> the lack of local enterprise and initiative in the development of commercial fishing in the outer Hebrides is quite astonishing. From time immemorial the sea has provided part of the subsistence livelihood of the people; it represented, as it still represents, a potential natural resource but the people seemed either unable or unwilling to develop it on a substantial scale.

This is all the more remarkable in view of the very limited agricultural resources, which would have made income from fishing of particular value in these islands, and since the landlords had made vigorous attempts to stimulate interest. Yet it was mainland companies from the south which had been prosecuting fishing in the Hebrides from as early as the sixteenth century, and this trend was never reversed. The failure in the islands to develop fishing widely beyond the subsistence level can probably only be understood by a combination of economic and social factors, one of which must be the continual draining of the islands of sources of leadership and innovation, especially after 1745. Here the problems of remoteness and poor land resources, coupled with a population still growing in terms of total numbers, reached their extreme. Yet the comparison with Shetland, a group of islands equally peripheral, but where local factories were more systematically developed, produces an anomaly which is still not fully understood.

The general outcome of eighteenth-century efforts was that herring fisheries in the west were first developed mainly by boats from the Clyde and Loch Fyne areas, where the curing was concentrated. With superior equipment, resources and marketing facilities major forays were made throughout the west, following the shoals to whichever lochs their seasonal movements happened to favour. These campaigns obliterated the modest local efforts made by a firmly land-based population of small tenants. The presence of outside fishermen in large numbers had the further effect of depressing the crofter fishermen by driving them from the best grounds and damaging or destroying their gear. Despite various efforts, therefore, the first notable success in establishing herring fishing in the Highlands came not on the west coast but at Wick, where there were 200 boats by 1795 and where a new harbour was built at Pulteney town in 1808. The British Fisheries disposed of their assets at Stein in 1827, in Mull in 1838 and at Ullapool in 1847.

THE IMPROVING MOVEMENTS

Events took a new turn, however, after the Napoleonic wars with the search for replacement economies now that agrarian reform in the west was becoming unavoidable. In view of the controversy then over the desirability of emigration, a controversy which is still potent today, it is hardly surprising that responsible proprietors reluctant to implement policies of complete clearance should have looked to fishing as a way out of their dilemma. The solution was to remove tenants to convenient coastal sites as bases for fishing with lotted holdings which would provide potatoes and grazing for a cow. The amount of land occupied by these essentially part-time holdings would be minimal and would certainly not prejudice the formation of large sheep-grazing farms in the interior.

A good example of this comes from Loch Hourn, one of the sea lochs closely associated with nineteenth-century herring fishing. Glenelg, the estate on the northern shore, was sold by the MacLeods of Dunvegan in 1811 and from about 1825 there were sporadic clearances in the area affecting Glenmore, Glen Beag and Glen Arnisdale (Plate 2). With the spread of sheep farming from the upper parts of the glens the small tenants became increasingly restricted to small pockets of land by the seashore at Glenelg and Arnisdale. In Glenmore the townships of Beolary, Scallasaig, Achuirn, Edinvaich, Moyle, Leanachan, Swordlan and Bailanailm were cleared and the people moved to Eilanbuie, Fawlin, Cosaig and Kirkton, while in Glen Arnisdale the settlement was now confined to the coastal townships on either side of the burn at Corran and Camusbane. The crofts were only about one acre in size and clearly intended merely as a means of supplementing an income to be derived mainly from the sea. To Baillie of Dochfour, who owned Glenelg through much of the nineteenth century, this no doubt appeared a balanced solution and certainly offered some advantages compared with the large-scale emigration which seemed the only alternative.

But there were many weaknesses. Although the removal of the Salt Laws made this commodity more readily available and cheaper in price, the cost of producing a barrel of cure locally allowed only a very small profit margin even if outlets functioned satisfactorily and waste was avoided. Again developments in equipment meant that whereas a boat could be obtained for £15 in the eighteenth century, it now cost £100 and was quite beyond the resources of a small crofter, constantly embarrassed by the ailing subsistence agriculture. Even with only small crofts the dualism of agriculture and fishing remained, as indeed it had to, for without adequate harbours, training and equipment there could be no question of effective competition with the Clyde and east coast, where the herring fishing had developed even more rapidly. With the end of Dutch competition the herring industry began to move south from Wick around 1813, aided by Sir John Sinclair, who had introduced Dutch curers into Caithness from whom the local population derived the necessary skills. The ports on the Moray Firth, formerly concerned exclusively with white fishing, were able to take fuller advantage of the favourable bounties offered under the 1807 Act. These amounted to £3 per ton on all fishing vessels of 50 to 100 tons and 2s per barrel on fish cured on the shore (plus an additional 2s 8d for each barrel exported). By 1830, when the bounties were discontinued, all the major ports around the Moray Firth were involved in herring fishing. Total production of cured herring in Scotland rose from 90,000 barrels in 1811 to 1 million in 1873, and continued to increase with the opening of vast markets in Germany and Russia through late-nineteenth-century railway developments there. But boats, nets and catches remained small in the west, and while they maintained their former level through the nineteenth century there was no element of expansion commensurate with the activity on the east coast, where there were over 1,000 boats fishing out of Wick for the 'Great Summer Fishing' by 1862. Indeed, from as early as 1816 the catch on the east coast exceeded that of the west.

In the west, however, agriculture and fishing continued to stultify each other, with any profits from the latter immediately absorbed by rent arrears and other outstanding debts rather than invested in better equipment. Periods of plenty were never quite sufficient for this vicious circle to be broken, and local organisation was insufficient to maintain the west-coast industry in its own right. Significantly the factor of the Knoydart estate, speaking before the Deer Forest Commission in 1892, considered that the small tenant would make a better fisherman if he had no croft at all. 'If they were exclusively fishermen they would make capital fishermen but they are a blend between the crofter and the fisherman and the result is that they do not work either of these occupations to advantage' (Scotland, 1895, p. 1053). Only with radical agrarian reform could herring fishing establish itself, as it did at Helmsdale in 1813 as a result of the vigorous and controversial policy of clearance and resettlement on the Sutherland estates.

Very often the landlord was as financially embarrassed as the small tenant. In the case of Glenelg, Mr Baillie incurred considerable expense at the time of the potato famine by paying the passages of his tenants who opted to emigrate to Canada. It can be appreciated that this must have absorbed much of the income derived from a commercial sheep-farming economy entering its golden age and discouraged heavy investment in uncertain fishing ventures. This situation on the land then further prejudiced the position of the crofter-fisherman, who was now deprived of his few remaining grazings. The grazings at Culindune and Galder were taken in 1852, though it is believed that these encroachments were largely the work of the factor, who apparently concealed from the tenants their landlord's willingness to allow them to remain on their crofts rent-free during the potato famine should they have preferred this to voluntary emigration. If this is true it highlights the consequences of absentee landlordism, from which Glenelg undoubtedly suffered through its detachment from other Dochfour estate lands. But broadly speaking the case of Glenelg shows how attempts to exploit the possibilities of the nineteenth century merely served to exaggerate the relative advantages of the east coast and Clyde and left the west-coast industry in a position of greater inferiority than had been the case in the previous century.

In 1883 Mr James Baillie succeeded to the Dochfour properties and some amelioration in conditions followed his greater personal interest in Glenelg. Grazings were allocated to supplement the small crofts at Galder (340 acres), Kirkton (80 acres) and Camusbane (200 acres), while those at Bernera were enlarged from 600 to 860 acres. In 1890 Mr Robert Birkbeck, who purchased the Arnisdale section of the estate, made similar provision at Corran and rebuilt the two rows of insanitary hovels on the edge of the loch. These moves were no doubt eased by declining returns from commercial farming and encouraged by the awakening of a social conscience in the nation as a whole over the condition of the crofters in the Highlands. But such developments could have no effect on fishing, which remained starved of any direct stimulus. In 1901 the Congested Districts Board mentioned the people of Arnisdale as being mainly fishermen, but the situation was precarious and many people were now moving seasonally to the employment offered by the deer forests inland around Loch Quoich.

TECHNOLOGICAL CHANGES

Technologically the fishing industry continued its rapid progress, notably with the introduction of steam trawling at the beginning of the twentieth century. Such vessels required better harbours, which in turn made for greater nodality and specialisation (Plate 29). The new boats cost some £3,000 each and served to exaggerate the widening technological gulf between the east-coast fleet and the small domestic industry of the west coast. Not only did this increasing disparity in catching power affect the local fishermen, but the sweeping of banks by trawlers ruined certain inshore white fisheries and destroyed much of the gear of the small local boats previously prosecuting them. Fraser Darling mentions the case of the Loch Roag fishery in Lewis, which did not survive the First World War, as a case in point. Some protection was afforded to trawlers in 1889 in the Minch, along with the Moray Firth, but this was only of limited value since only recently has this restriction been applied to foreign trawlers also. With the introduction of new fishery limits in 1964, base lines from Cape Wrath to the Butt of Lewis and from Barra Head to the Mull of Kintyre were made fully effective. There are still occasional complaints, however, of illegal fishing by trawlers off Skye, which undermines the economy of the local crofter-fishermen and damages their gear.

Local fishermen on the west coast now acted increasingly as crew members on the east-coast boats which were monopolising the industry. Already in the 1880s, although 500 large boats were fishing from Stornoway, less than 100 were locally owned, and the bulk of the smoking installations too were in the hands of outsiders, many of them English. Meanwhile some 2,500 men from Lewis and Harris were going to the east coast, almost all as hired hands. At the same time the industry was being concentrated on the fewer ports which could offer the necessary facilities. The construction of the West Highland Railway's Mallaig extension from its former terminus at Fort William in 1901 had as one of its objects the invigoration of the ailing fishing industry in the Sound of Sleat, through the provision of a good harbour and a rail outlet to the south (Plate 28). This development transformed the small crofting settlement laid out by Lord Lovat at the time of the potato famine into a thriving port and curing centre. But predictably the subsequent decades saw the concentration of all activity in the region at Mallaig, and with these several pressures the complete disappearance of fishing based on the smaller creeks such as Glenelg (Table 1).

At this stage the case of the island of Barra, as dealt with by Storrie (1962*d*) is an interesting one, for here the proprietrix, Lady Emily Gordon Cathcart, was attempting to develop the fisheries and planned several land settlement schemes for fishermen from 1883 onwards. In view of the acute congestion on the island a number of crofters had petitioned Lady Cathcart for more land, suggesting that Vatersay, an island south of Barra

Table 1. CONSOLIDATION OF THE FISHING INDUSTRY
IN LOCHABER, 1901–61

Area	Number of fishing boats operating in		
	1901	*1925*	*1961*
Loch Hourn	30	1	–
Mallaig and Loch Nevis	46	13	25
Arisaig	15	1	3
Moidart	14	8	–
Loch Sunart	25	5	1
Loch Eil	42	19	–
Appin	10	2	–
Lismore	10	3	–
Total	192	52	29

Source: *Scottish Sea Fisheries Statistical Tables*

and then part of a large farm, should be settled by crofters. However, aware of the dangers of combining agriculture with fishing and aware also of the fact that Barra could not be wholly agricultural, she rejected the proposal and concentrated on developing Castlebay as a non-agricultural fishing village and source of livelihood for landless families (Plate 19). Already a hotel, several shops and a school had been built, along with piers, curing stations and telegraph communications with mainland markets. But in order to overcome difficulties in the supply of milk and potatoes, smallholdings were proposed on the hilly peninsulas of Bentangavel and Garrygall surrounding Castlebay with the aim of providing each family with sufficient land on which to grow potatoes and winter fodder for a cow. In no way were the holdings intended to be large enough to detract from the main interest in fishing, and this was further emphasised by the proposed siting of houses in Castlebay itself, close to the port, and not on the croft holdings. This scheme was similar in many ways to the earlier attempts at Arnisdale, but coming as it did in the late nineteenth century it showed a greater appreciation of the forces making for centralisation and the need for adequate investment in capital works and other facilities.

But like the Glenelg case this scheme failed too, and the reasons were basically similar. There was first an unwillingness to concentrate whole-heartedly on fishing, evidenced by the fact that the tenants continued to reside in their old townships rather than move to Castlebay, thus maintaining their old attachment with the land. Moreover not all the shares were taken up anyway, and the subsequent raising of the souming (i.e. the stock allowed to each tenant) to increase the agricultural utilisation of the land served also to detract further from a full-time interest in fishing. Like the Arnisdale and Glenelg holdings they could not by their very nature prove successful agricultural holdings, so that today they are generally underused, with a predominantly aged or absentee tenantry, thus representing an extreme case of the crofting problem which is discussed separately later. But there was also the factor of the rapid rate of change in the fishing industry generally, which made Lady Cathcart's progressive idea anachronistic almost before its inception. Great fluctuations in the catch of herring were the rule after the boom of 1889, and only sporadic part-time employment could be obtained on the larger east-coast drift-net boats until 1914. Further problems were to arise after the war, with the loss of markets for cured herring in eastern Europe depressing the industry further. But the consequent concentration on fresh herring for the home market placed obvious advantages in the hands of mainland ports with rail facilities such as Oban, Mallaig and Kyle of Lochalsh, so that the effects of the war proved to be particularly disastrous for island ports such as Stornoway and Castlebay, which could no longer attract landings on any scale.

Fishing in the nineteenth century thus provides a clear example of the economic subjugation of the west to the superior forces from without. It indicates a failure to keep pace with technological change and the long starvation of the area of capital investment, deriving partly from local mismanagement but largely from an unfortunate combination of relative advantages exaggerated by a *laissez-faire* economic policy. The separation of fishing and agriculture has largely been achieved, but only as a result of the decay of the local industry. The main legacy of the traditional dual economy lies mainly in certain islands such as Whalsay and Burra in Shetland and the Hebridean islands of Scalpay and Eriskay, and in dwindling numbers of small inshore fishermen working the lobster and crab fishing. This branch of the industry has always remained a small-scale enterprise and has thus enabled the crofter with modest resources to maintain a grip. It has been helped by recent improvements in lobster storage at the ports which have gone a long way to avoid the mortality and dehydration of lobsters in transit.

For the rest the industry has largely fallen into the hands of east-coast and Clyde fishermen, and it was migrants from such areas who settled in the ports which developed around the railheads along the west coast at the turn of the century. Mallaig is an interesting case of such growth, for this original crofting–fishing community is now a specialist fishing port and steamer terminal with only limited connections with the agricultural hinterland. Mallaig attracted landings by east-coast boats from 1903, and soon afterwards boats from the islands were landing their catches there in preference to the island ports, where curing was the only means of disposal. It was some time before east-coast fishermen overcame their reluctance to stake their whole future in the town, and permanent settlement did not develop in a big way until after the war. But in the 1920s numerous families from Rosehearty and Fraserburgh in north-east Scotland, as well as from Burnmouth and Eyemouth in Berwickshire, settled in Mallaig, and the port developed its own fleet of ring-net boats. With a more pronounced swing to home market production the curing stations which had earlier grown up in the Point area gave way to kippering kilns, of which there were fifteen by 1930. The rapid growth of this period, much of it in a rather unco-ordinated manner, has largely obliterated the croft holdings which survived as a legacy of the earlier planned township.

MODERN PROBLEMS

While many east-coast fishermen responded to the contraction of markets for cured herring by turning back to white fishing, using the Danish seine net, herring remained the principal interest in the west. There is only limited scope on white fishing in the winter between Dunvegan and Barra Head for hake and skate using great lines, while ground nets can be used in the Sound of Rona for hake, ling, saithe and whiting, which are landed mainly at Kyle, where a new fishery pier was opened in 1953. Great progress has been made since 1960 with prawns during the May–August season, a fishing largely followed by the seine-net boats which can then switch back to white fishing later in the year. Herring fishing is, however, far more important, though landings are now restricted to six ports: Tarbert (Loch Fyne), Oban, Mallaig, Ullapool, Gairloch and Stornoway. It is significant that an island port is still able to maintain a stake in the industry, but also that Kyle is omitted from the list. This railhead port, however, has always been poorly placed in relation to the North Minch fishery, and with the road improvements in the direction of Inverness, Ullapool and Gairloch have been able to realise the potential which the British Fisheries Society tried unsuccessfully to exploit in the eighteenth century.

The Minch herring fishery is distinctive in that it lasts throughout the year. There are, however, two main seasons of activity, the summer season from June to September and the autumn and winter season from November to February, thus leaving a lull in the March–April period when local boats tie up for annual overhaul and east-coast boats return home along the Caledonian Canal. Considerable differences occur in the composition of the fish on the grounds at these times, and there is no close similarity between the two seasons; the autumn and winter fishing is usually more productive in quantity, but the quality of the catch is better in summer. East-coast boats are mainly of the drift-net type, but the method of capture used by local boats and those from the Clyde ports is the ring net, which requires two boats to operate in fairly sheltered waters. A new development is the introduction of the purse-seine net for herring fishing; this may prove to be more economical and efficient than the methods in use at the moment. Much greater distances are travelled now than was the case in the days of the uncertain loch fishing, and boats from the mainland ports in the South Minch fish off Barra and Uist in winter and nearer Skye and the Small Isles in summer.

The herring industry has experienced a number of difficulties, however, especially over finding adequate markets. The decline in cured herring has accelerated since the First World War with the loss of the German and Russian markets. 226,878 barrels were cured in the western Highlands and islands in 1913, but only 87,406 barrels in 1935 and 4,127 in 1961. As the industry was thrown back on the home market more vigorous government interest was needed, and state participation entered a new phase when the Herring Industry Act was passed in 1935. This established the Herring Industry Board to regulate the industry and provide financial assistance in the form of grants and loans for the building and conversion of fishing boats, and the industry is now subsidised by way of payments to each boat and guaranteed minimum prices.

Reduction in demand has made contraction of the herring industry inevitable. Unfortunately catches are subject to fluctuation at port, regional and national level from year to year, and hence it is difficult to keep closely in step with demand. Indeed, it is estimated that a surplus of one-third is necessary to ensure a steady supply to meet the demand for fresh herring, which command a higher price than herring sold for curing, canning or klondyking, etc. So to find a use for the inevitable surplus the Herring

Fishing as a Replacement Economy

Industry Board set up a chain of oil and meal factories after 1948, and 45 per cent of the total catch in the U.K. was disposed of in this way in 1953. But this proportion fell to 21 per cent in 1959 as declining catches (in East Anglia especially) threatened the scheme (Table 2). The viability of the

Table 2. DISPOSAL OF THE U.K. HERRING CATCH,
1960–6
('000 cran)

	1960	*1962*	*1964*	*1966*
Home consumption				
Fresh/kippered/quick-freeze	251	313	313	291
Canned	10	7	7	6
Cured	3	4	3	3
Export				
Canned	27	35	28	35
Quick-freeze	16	3	6	3
Cured	27	14	12	14
Redded	22	14	16	16
Kippered	22	20	21	14
Klondyked	29	31	2	44
Marinated	14	17	18	24
Miscellaneous				
Pet food	144	46	72	68
Meal and oil	88	7	59	133
Total	653	511	557	651

Source: *Herring Industry Board*

oil and meal factories was compromised, yet their closure would merely accelerate the downward spiral and depress the whole industry further. So efforts were made to expand the fleet, and output rose from 110,000 tons of herring in 1958 to 137,000 tons in 1959, but now the prices of herring going for meal and oil has slumped because of the depression in the fish-meal industry through competition from Peru. To prevent herring fetching nominal prices, as low as 2s 6d per cran, the government agreed in 1960 to underwrite, for the time being, losses sustained by the Herring Industry Board in paying a guaranteed price of between £1 and £2 per cran for herring disposed of for oil and meal. The subsidies have proved to be a valuable safeguard and the Herring Industry Board strongly resisted the Fleck Committee's recommendation (H.M.S.O., 1961) that they should be

3

stopped. Their withdrawal could well have the effect of attracting existing herring fishermen to white fishing or shore employment and affect ports heavily dependent on herring landings, as are most of the Highland fishing ports. Existing fishermen have gained through this element of protection, but the anticipated growth has not altogether occurred and there is a shortage on the home market in summer when herring are in greatest demand. On these grounds there is room for a 25 per cent increase in the catch, and it may be that improved catching methods, using the mid-water trawl or purse net, may achieve this.

The general situation on the west coast has tended to be favourable, however, since supplies have been maintained during the period of national shortage. Moreover national demand is greatest during the summer fishing in the Minch, and hence disposal patterns at this time show proportions of herring used for meal and oil which are far below the national average (Fig. 7). West Highland ports are therefore not over-anxious to see the introduction of new catching methods which would greatly increase the supply and possibly depress prices. In 1965, for instance, a trawler's herring catch was not accepted at Oban after threats by ring-net boats to boycott the port. But the processing side of the industry on the west coast does not give the same ground for satisfaction, since the growth of large firms has tended to result in the closure of installations at Mallaig (where processing is most important) as part of rationalisation programmes. Only two kippering kilns are now in operation, and the growing emphasis on the east coast is the inevitable result. The situation over herring used for oil and meal has been under review, since the supply often exceeds the capacity of the Fraser-burgh factory and the long haul to this factory tends to depress prices available on the west coast. Schemes for fish-meal factories at Mallaig and Ardrishaig have therefore been supported by local fishermen but not by other residents, who feel that such installations would have an adverse effect on the important local tourist trade. The success of this opposition is a sign of the diversification of industry achieved by certain west-coast ports.

Fish farming would seem to be a promising line for the future in the West Highlands, for while farming the open sea is out of the question, development of the small inlets which abound along the coast may well prove feasible once initial difficulties have been overcome. Activity is being pursued on an experimental basis at Ardtoe, in Ardnamurchan, by the White Fish Authority, and nearby at Lochailort by Marine Harvests Ltd, a subsidiary of Unilever. These stations are located partly with local employment problems in mind and will be able to draw on several small rural

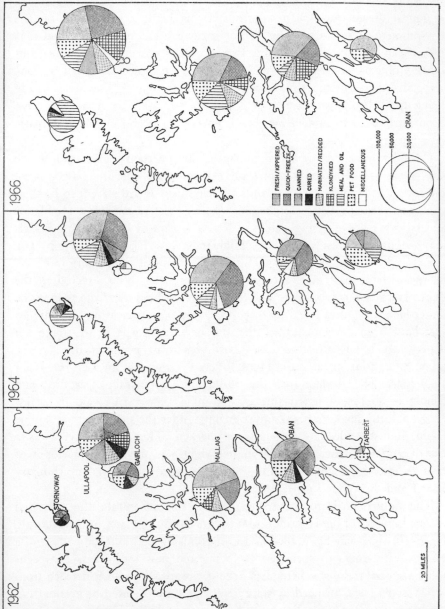

Fig. 7 Use made of herring landed at west Highland ports

communities, including Acharacle–Salen and Arisaig–Glenfinnan–Glenuig respectively. The projects have the backing of the marine research laboratory at Dunstaffnage near Oban, where study is being concentrated on the environment of sea lochs. The Ardtoe scheme has demonstrated that it is possible to hatch and rear marine fish in captivity to marketable size, but other problems have to be solved before commercial operation can be contemplated. Some methods borrowed from fish farming are, however, already being applied to lobster fishing at Kinlochbervie, since artificial pens have been introduced to protect lobsters from predators and enable systematic cropping to be followed.

Considerable energy is being devoted to help certain island areas where fish stocks are considerable yet local fishermen are showing only modest interest. The Highlands and Islands Development Board state it to be their concern to 'ensure that an increasing share of the resources of Highlands and Islands inshore fishing waters is derived by locally based fishing vessels manned by men resident in the Highlands and Islands' (1967, p. 19). Convinced that the resources of Highland waters can stand more intensive fishing without imperilling future stocks, interest has been directed to the Outer Hebrides in particular. The Fleck Report stated that fishermen in the Outer Hebrides 'have failed to keep pace with the newer fishing techniques that have been developed since the war or to take part in the seine net fishery which has attracted east coast vessels to neighbouring waters' (H.M.S.O., 1961, para. 179). The Crofters Commission, in their report for 1957 (para. 45), consider that 'the traditional combination of crofting and fishing is no longer practicable except on a very small scale in a few geographically favoured areas and then only under the shelter of a full time fishing industry adequate to sustain a market'. They found there was a lack of capital, experience and confidence which was preventing development from proceeding under the grants and loans offered by the Herring Industry Board and the White Fish Authority.

The failure of Lord Leverhulme's bid to concentrate the scattered fishing industry of the Hebrides, first in Stornoway and later in Leverburgh, Harris, in 1924 may be recalled as an unpromising sign, but indications of a greater willingness to specialise have merited new incentives. In recent years a special training scheme has been in progress to train fishermen from the Western Isles, financed by state loans and supplemented by grants from the Macaulay (Rhodesia) Trust and the Highland Fund. By the end of 1962 forty-nine men had been trained and nine boats delivered to men who had completed their training. The momentum has kept up and in Eriskay new boats will justify the call for the new jetty, while in Portree (Skye) the local fleet of prawn-fishing boats will be increased from three to five with the aid of loans from the White Fish Authority and the Highland Fund. More important still is the Highland and Islands Development Board's fishery development scheme, under which twenty-five boats are to be built. Practically all the applications for the boats have come from the Outer Hebrides, Lewis and Scalpay especially. This injection of capital should therefore go a long way to maintain interest in traditional fishing areas and prevent complete concentration of boats and landings on the main ports on the mainland. The introduction of local organisation in the islands to market lobsters is also proving a very welcome development.

It may well be that a larger local fleet will have a positive effect on the local processing industry in Stornoway, which is badly placed for supplying the home market. Stornoway still cures and kippers herring, but a high percentage of landings there are processed for oil and meal (Fig. 7). Prospects in Shetland would seem to be rather more promising as regards processing, since not only is there a substantial local fleet but large numbers of boats are attracted from the east coast for the summer fishing, once the first stage of the southward movement following the shoals as far as East Anglia. Problems arise, however, through low prices in Lerwick, which force landings to Aberdeen in many cases in spite of the considerable distance involved. Moreover the irregular patterns of supply over the year make it difficult to justify the provision of a large capacity and the maintenance of separate facilities for herring and white fish. Special attention should be directed to the freight charges for processed fish consigned south from Shetland, while the fact that Shetland lies close to routes frequented by distant-water trawlers offers interesting possibilities.

CHAPTER FOUR

The Deer-Forest Era and the Policy of Land Settlement

THE late nineteenth century saw a number of important changes in Highland affairs. The landscape continued to react violently to changing economic and social conditions, with a great resurgence in the popularity of sport on the Highland moors in the period up to 1914 especially. But whereas the government had been largely passive during the early decades of the century, it now began to initiate a programme of protective legislation in an attempt to ensure by legal statute a state of stability long denied by normal economic processes. The protection was first afforded in the 1880s in belated response to the growth of commercial farming over the previous century, but by the time the first programme of amelioration had begun operation, the changing land-use pattern demanded further government attention, thus revealing, as the tip of an iceberg, the beginnings of the long search for a planned solution to Highland problems.

CHANGING ATTITUDES TO DEER STALKING

It is important to see land-use changes as swings – albeit sudden and substantial – in the balance of power between contending land-users rather than as the introduction of entirely new dimensions. Thus deer stalking in the Highlands was a long-established interest, and many forests were in fact created during the medieval period for royal pleasure and were probably contemporaneous with the extension of effective central government control over much of the Highland area of Scotland. Deer were certainly numerous and constituted an important export item from the northern ports as well as being prominent on the tables of the aristocracy. Interest shifted more from the crown to individual landowners in the seventeenth century, and began to wane as the traditional combination of deer and black cattle, grazed on the summer shielings, was superseded by the 'great sheep' economy.

This does not, however, signify a break in continuity. As O'Dell and Walton (1962, p. 332) point out, the year 1800 saw not only the last Atholl hunt in full traditional style but also the beginning of a new era with the letting of shootings on the Abergeldie estate. On the whole the deer frontier was certainly pushed back during the early nineteenth century, but this swing was neither comprehensive nor permanent. Indeed reaction to the commercial sheep economy can be noted as early as 1786, long before the introduction of sheep to the west coast and islands, when the sheep stock was removed from the north side of Glen Tilt. Throughout the nineteenth century there was a small but steady flow of affluent southerners to the hunting grounds in the north. But it must be added that there were few comforts for the early sportsmen who pioneered the new 'season', and it was not until after 1850 that landowners came to appreciate the commercial potential of their properties for sport.

The prosperity of sheep farming was one important factor in the timing. Having consolidated its hold throughout the Highlands during the first half of the nineteenth century, it went on to enjoy a 'golden age' which lasted until about 1866. Prices of both mutton and wool maintained high levels until this time but then began to weaken, certainly in the case of wool, the price of which slumped from 27s for 24 lb. in 1866 to 22s in 1867 and 15s in 1868. Although there were fluctuations after that, prices rarely if ever reached their former levels now that competition from the New World was beginning to be felt. Prices for mutton and lamb showed rather greater stability, no doubt on account of the technical difficulties of exporting meat as opposed to wool. Effective refrigeration was a critical factor here. Nevertheless it was the beginning of the slide, and with the prospect of depressed rents in mind landowners were not slow to appreciate the higher offers of sporting tenants.

In this growing competition the sheep valuation system was a valuable ally of the sportsmen. It was conventional for the stock of an outgoing tenant to be taken over by the estate or the new tenant not at market price but rather at a substantially higher figure, in view of the fact that the sheep had the advantage of being well acclimatised to their particular hill. In the context of a buoyant industry the system worked tolerably well, but with difficult conditions its abuses became more obvious. There was, for instance, nothing to stop an unscrupulous tenant bringing in unacclimatised sheep shortly before surrendering his lease and thus making a large profit after valuation, for the difference between valuation and open-market prices might be as high as 20s per sheep. This in turn made it more difficult to find new farming tenants, and landlords were then obliged to accept a lower price from a new farmer or else prefer the sporting tenant, thus incurring a heavy loss on the sheep stock in return for a higher rent.

Difficulties were accentuated by the requirements of the sportsman.

A small deer forest was most unsatisfactory, since the animals could not be confined in such a space without fencing, which was totally uneconomical, and hence could easily be driven off on to adjacent properties. At best a small unit could only provide a mere two or three days' sport – and that level of usage could hardly justify the construction of tracks in the hills or lodges to provide accommodation for tenants. A large area of roughland, punctuated by corries and gullies, was necessary for a good forest, and it was precisely on large tracts of land that the valuation system was most open to abuse. A further problem arose over the mutual exclusiveness of sheep and deer; on some of the early deer forests a reduced sheep stock might often be retained, but as the afforestation movement gathered momentum there was increasing competition between landowners and the removal of the sheep altogether was one means of attracting more custom. Ultimately, therefore, sportsmen ceased to be interested in forests with even a small sheep stock, since it could easily result in the deer being disturbed at the critical stage in the stalk.

DEER FORESTS IN LOCHABER

Accompanied by a rising tide of publicity and also by royal patronage, the pace of afforestation quickened. With the popularity of the 'season' assured, landowners now went ahead with the provision of what were often very lavish facilities. The need for an adjacent sheep farmer to pay for part of the cost of a march fence (clearly necessary at the frontiers of the deer-forest land) also tended to work against agriculture and encourage the process of afforestation to extend from the high grazings further and further down the glens. It is perhaps appropriate to take a sample area and follow changes in some detail. Fig. 8, therefore, shows the pattern of change in the knot of wild, mountainous country bounded by the Great Glen in the east and the Sound of Sleat in the west and extending north–south from Glengarry to Loch Eil. At the beginning of the deer-forest era it was divided into four large estates, Glenelg and Knoydart in the west, Glengarry and Lochiel to the east.

The greater part of the land was organised into sheep grazings and crofting townships. There were excessive contrasts in the sizes of land units, especially when it is remembered that a number of grazings were often let in plurality as a group to one tenant. This was common practice, particularly in the late nineteenth century when it became more difficult

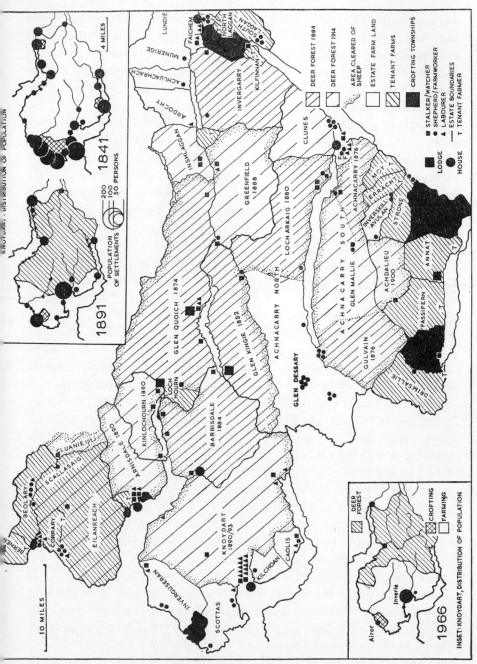

Fig. 8 *The deer-forest era in Lochaber*

KNOYDART: DISTRIBUTION OF POPULATION

1841

1891

POPULATION OF SETTLEMENTS

200
100
50 PERSONS

4 MILES

10 MILES

DEER FOREST 1884

DEER FOREST 1914

AREA CLEARED OF SHEEP

ESTATE FARM LAND

TENANT FARMS

CROFTING TOWNSHIPS

STALKER/WATCHER

SHEPHERD/FARMWORKER

LABOURER

ESTATE BOUNDARIES

T TENANT FARMER

LODGE

HOUSE

INSET: KNOYDART, DISTRIBUTION OF POPULATION

1966

DEER FOREST

CROFTING

FARMING

Airor

Inverie

to find tenants. Thus the domains of John Cameron on Locharkaigside were very extensive in the 1830s, when this prominent local character was colloquially known as 'the Lochaber Drover'. Later in the century much of Ratagan and Glenelg was let, first to James Mitchell and later to William Bean. But with the exception of Glenelg, which was a detached portion of the Dochfour estates and thus constitutes one of the many cases in the Highlands of absentee landlordism, substantial areas were set aside on each estate as the home farm. Certainly on the Lochiel estate much if not all of the southern shores of Loch Arkaig were managed from the home farm at Achnacarry, while in the case of Glengarry the grazings stretching over the hill to Kilfinnan had a similar function. In Knoydart the absence of sheep farmers on the southern part of the estate from Kilchoan round to Kyles-knoydart and Carnoch (Kinlochnevis) suggests that this area was managed by the owner himself.

It is probable, therefore, that these areas were treated as deer forests, at least in part, from the early nineteenth century. Information from the evidence submitted to the Napier Commission by George Malcolm, factor at Invergarry, is a very useful source at this stage (Scotland, 1884, pp. 2840–67). One of the few regular deer forests in the county of Inverness-shire was on the Lochiel estate, probably on the Gulvain section of Achnacarry South (Robertson, 1813, p. 265). But Invergarry was certainly used for stalking by the Macdonnells even if it was not officially constituted as such until after it passed into the hands of Mr Ellice in 1860. Afforestation for letting begins in the 1870s with a successful sheep farmer in Glen Quoich giving up his lease in favour of a sporting tenant around 1874, and in the following decade the adjacent areas were converted: Glen Kingie and Loch Arkaig on the Lochiel estate and Barrisdale on the Knoydart estate. Later the frontier advanced further outwards in all directions to embrace most of Knoydart, Arnisdale, Greenfield, Clunes and Achdalieu by 1900. Moreover, the sheep stocks were removed from the central core, with the notable exception of Glen Dessary on the Lochiel estate which was retained throughout as a sheep-grazing unit of outstanding quality.

The farming element thus disappeared altogether from much of the region or else was drastically cut back. Around Loch Quoich, for instance, a new landscape of shooting lodges appeared, and sporting lets frequently ran in plurality in the same way as the sheep grazings which they superseded. Thus Lord Burton's territory covered 50,000 acres and embraced not only Glen Quoich but also the adjacent let of Glen Kingie from Lochiel. The farming interest was cut back either side at Greenfield in the east and

Kinlochourn in the west, where the spacious buildings and steadings built to serve a large grazing area stretching eastwards to Glen Quoich still stand illogically in the centre of a small tenant farm of some 400 acres. Again in Knoydart the sizes of the main farms of Inverguseran, Scottas, Kilchoan and Caolis were all much reduced. The pattern of employment in the area at the time, in so far as it can be deduced from Valuation Rolls and other scattered sources, endorses this situation, with a group of shepherds in Glen Dessary the only main diversifying element in a country of stalkers and watchers.

Perhaps the legacy of the deer-forest period is most striking at Kinlochourn, not on the southern side of the burn, which is now part of the Glen Quoich estate, but rather on the northern bank, where the steep rocky slopes have never supported a prosperous agriculture. The very position of this piece of land on the southeastern edge of Glenelg, which was itself for long merely a mainland appendage of the island empire of the MacLeods of Dunvegan, implied neglect. With the sale of Glenelg at various times in the early nineteenth century and the coming of the sheep economy it was then integrated with the farm of Arnisdale, several miles further along Loch Hourn. In 1890, however, Robert Birkbeck purchased the Arnisdale section of the estate and proceeded to build up Kinlochourn as a deer forest. A lodge was built and extensive policies with a number of exotic species were planted over the lower slopes. Much labour and capital was then deployed on the construction of paths which gave access well up to the higher slopes. The labour force employed on these various forms of outdoor and indoor work ran well into double figures and thus supported a very substantial total population, which was accommodated in a group of cottages built along the loch side adjacent to the lodge and also, as the map shows, on detached and now deserted sites further along towards Arnisdale such as Torrachoit and Caolas.

Indeed, population figures for this period as brought out in the 1891 census show Loch Hourn's most easterly projection as a focus of a local population explosion. It was similar to the case of the island of Rhum, where the population increased from 53 in 1891 to 116 in 1901; employment as gardeners, coachmen, gamekeepers and servants was considerable following the import of red deer into the island and the construction of a castle and policies at the head of Loch Scresort. On Loch Hourn, however, not only did the new stalking economy support the estate population on the northern side but there was an element of growth on the south side too. For although the lodges for Glen Quoich and Knoydart were sited at Loch

Quoich and Inverie respectively, there was a scatter of houses for watchers on the periphery such as Runival, while the old farmhouse at Barrisdale was converted into a lodge. In view of its humbler and earlier origins it stands out architecturally in contrast to the Victorian architecture of the more contemporary buildings. Since it penetrated into the heart of the deer-forest area, Loch Hourn was visited by the yachts of the more affluent tenants, again with implications for local employment, as the crofter-fishermen at Skiary found to their advantage.

The reactions of the native population to these developments was consequently mixed. On the one hand they viewed with apprehension the steamrolling expansion of the frontier towards their smallholdings, yet on the other the employment which the deer forests offered was often relatively lucrative. As a witness before the Napier Commission put it (Scotland, 1884, p. 2848), 'the ghillies are drawn from the crofter class themselves and the crofters would really be the last people to wish for the abolition of forests as far as they personally are concerned because they derive great pecuniary benefit from them'. During the season especially there was a substantial migration from the crofting townships on the west-coast fringes in Arisaig, Morar and Glenelg inland to the deer forests, and it was income from such sources that enabled the crofting economy to maintain a precarious acceptability in the eyes of the small tenants.

But the price of the stalking boom was an element of depression and uncertainty in crofting agriculture. There were no cases of eviction of crofters to make way for deer, for as the Napier Commission reported (Scotland, 1884, pp. 84–5), 'the existing deer forests . . . have been, as far as made known to us, formed out of large farms by simply removing the sheep and allowing deer, of which there were generally a greater or lesser number already there, to fill up the ground so vacated. Depopulation, therefore, cannot be directly attributed to deer forests unless it can be shown that they employ fewer people than sheep farms.' Nevertheless the pace of afforestation in some areas was so brisk that feelings of insecurity can well be understood, especially in Knoydart, where the estate which the Macdonnells had sold to the ironmaster Mr James Baird in 1857 had now passed into the hands of a Mr E. S. Bowlby. The new owner accelerated the process of afforestation to include not only Barrisdale (1884–5) but also Upper Scottas (1890–1) and Kilchoan–Inverguseran (1893). Not only was there a territorial imbalance in favour of sporting interests, but the gross overstocking of deer increased the possibility of crops being mauled by the depredations of these animals, forced to low ground in times of severe winter weather. A carrying capacity of one deer to 40–60 acres has been suggested as satisfactory to avoid excessive degeneration of grazings, yet at the peak of the era in 1912 some forests were carrying one deer to 15–20 acres. The best that could be expected by farmers and crofters under the circumstances was a certain amount of fencing around the arable.

GOVERNMENT SUPPORT FOR CROFTING

It was significant during this period of rapid change and uncertainty that state intervention to regulate the pattern of land use in the Highlands assumed new and large proportions. For long the main interest of governments had been pacification, especially at times when disaffection and separatism in the Highlands indicated embarrassing implications for British foreign policy. Consolidation after 1745 was partly negative (forfeiture of estates and privileges and prohibitions on certain aspects of local dress and culture) and partly positive, with schemes to develop the economic potential of the Highlands. However, the most tangible aspect of this was the construction of roads and canals, with Telford following up the efforts of the military road-builders of the previous century to consolidate this network and extend it from the Great Glen to the west coast and islands. But unsupported by appropriate levels of capital investment in primary and secondary industry these improved communications merely speeded the process of emigration, already encouraged by reorganisation in agriculture and the inadequacy of social benefits to cope with the growing poverty problem of the later nineteenth century.

The situation was indeed difficult. The potato famine exhausted any modest capital resources which the crofters might have accumulated, and they found their holdings being more rigorously enclosed by the booming sheep economy at precisely the time when the replacement economies were proving unreliable. What could be done about this growing dilemma, which emigration alone seemed unable to solve? MacCulloch (1824, p. 119) argued that

> no other circumstances than a crowded population and a low value of labour, can preserve the cultivation of such lands; and whenever those cease, or when capital and labour shall seek for more legitimate and profitable employment in the breaking up of larger tracts, the occupation of the crofts as such must be abandoned. The labours of crofting, therefore, are merely the parts of a temporary system, not a permanent one, and so, far

from being the first stage of general improvement they are but the last improvements of an ancient system which may be repaired but cannot be rendered perfect.

Crofting, according to this analysis, was doomed to disappear even without any further pressure from landowners.

The crofters, Kellas says (1962, p. 281), 'were congenitally passive and politically inexperienced with the result that no great movement of unrest was born through starvation and eviction'. It is frequently pointed out how meekly the more oppressive and radical forms of clearance were tolerated by the small tenants, who collectively represented a substantial physical force. But as conditions deteriorated through the century, agitation grew and found expression in a number of acts of violence and lawlessness the like of which had not been seen since the Ross-shire sheep riot of 1782. Publicity was forthcoming from a number of newspapers which took up the crofter cause, notably *The Highlander*, which was launched from Inverness as a platform to attack the landowners. Moreover there was the Irish precedent; the serious problem of land hunger in Ireland provoked demonstrations by a militant organisation known as the Irish Land League and led to the Acts of 1870 and 1881, which began the long process of transferring ownership of land from the estates to the tenants. By the 1920s, therefore, the landlord–tenant relationship had disappeared in Ireland.

Here then was a precedent which the crofters followed up in 1882 with the formation of the Highland Land League, advocating a system of peasant proprietorship. For the next ten years it was to be a major force in Highland politics and was represented by four Members of Parliament after the elections of 1885. Meanwhile, however, in response to a number of disturbances in Skye at Braes (1882) and Glendale (1883), a Royal Commission was set up under Lord Napier to inquire into the condition of the crofters and cottars in the Highlands. They carried out their task speedily, hearing evidence at places throughout the area, beginning significantly at Braes (Skye) on 26 May 1883 and ending on 26 December in the same year at Tarbert (Loch Fyne).

The report of the Napier Commission was presented in 1884. It viewed the economic circumstances, and by recording and reproducing all the evidence submitted by witnesses as an appendix running into three volumes enables a striking insight to be gained into local conditions in different parts of the Highlands. The report with its evidence thus stands as a major source of material for any historical study of the Highland economy. The crux of the question was, of course, the acute land shortage and the crofters' strong attachment to land in spite of resettlement and attempts at introducing new industries:

> When the people of the Northern Highlands were removed from their native glens to the shore, in the hope that they would at once become fishermen, without either boats or harbours, or the knowledge how to make use of such, they were provided with crofts of sufficient size to support a family with difficulty in a favourable season. The people naturally looked upon themselves still as crofters rather than fishermen; and they took to the sea only when it was absolutely necessary to supplement the outcome of their stock and crops (Scotland, 1884, p. 58).

The enlargement of townships thus seemed an obvious recommendation, but the Commission were well aware of the difficulties this posed:

> In most cases our proposal translated into practice would simply mean a moderate restoration of the hill pasture which the grandfathers of the existing hamlet enjoyed sixty years ago. It must be admitted, however, that in some parts of the country the plan would not work or would work with insufficient rapidity. There may be, especially in Skye, the Long Island and on the coasts of Sutherland, overpeopled tracts contiguous to which lands might not be found in sufficient extent adapted for the useful enlargement of the township, whether on account of the nature of the soil or the size of the farms, or the duration of existing leases (p. 26).

Indeed, working from the tendency of landowners to lay out crofting townships on sites where, on account of accessibility or quality of land, there would be the minimum interference with commercial sheep farming, it might be predictable that such areas would not be the most suitable basis for a major policy of enlargement.

Thought therefore moved to more radical reforms of the landholding structure, notably resettlement. If there was insufficient land to make adequate enlargements everywhere, then large farms might be divided into groups of smallholdings and population pressure in the more overcrowded townships thereby relieved. But was this the optimum solution? If it was assumed that the population of the Highlands should be maintained and that every family should be supported by agriculture, then it was logical. But the weaknesses were underlined in a minority report by one of the members of the Napier Commission, Mr K. S. Mackenzie. His point was that 'if the clearances are the melancholy result of economic theories, it is to be feared that at the present day the revulsion of feeling these have inspired is leading persons of most excellent intention into the opposite extreme and causing them to urge a division of the land in relation to the numbers upon it rather than in relation to the numbers it is calculated to support in prosperity'. He went on to point out that the crofters 'whom it is proposed to turn into farmers have no sufficiency of capital to make profitable use of a holding large enough to give the occupier a certain livelihood', and mentioned a further obstacle to the creation of such holdings in that 'a subdivision of the large pastoral farms would involve the erection of a number of small homesteads at an expense which neither proprietors nor tenants are very able to undertake' (p. 117). The land-use pattern might leave much to be desired, but clearly an agricultural solution to this problem of high levels of underemployment in the crofting townships could be of very limited benefit. If long-term stability was the objective, then agriculture could be only one aspect of a co-ordinated development plan.

Faced with these thorny implications, the government preferred to avoid the issue and instead fell back on a negative policy of protection. In 1885 a Bill was introduced giving individual security of tenure for holdings under £30 and the right to fair rent, but with no provision for enlarging holdings or for a system of peasant proprietors such as was being evolved in Ireland. This was similar to a Bill introduced the following year by the new Liberal Government which was passed by Parliament as the Crofters' Holdings (Scotland) Act of 1886. For the short term it was satisfactory, in that a number of injustices such as arbitary eviction and rack-renting were stopped, and by 1890 most crofting parishes were visited by the newly constituted Crofters Commission and fair rents fixed. Yet in the long term it held out little hope, since the much debated question of land settlement was shelved. Accordingly, the Crofters' Party forced a division on the Third Reading of the Bill, and the opinion expressed by Mr J. Ramsey, the Member for Falkirk Burghs, that the Bill 'must prove illusory as far as the distressed districts of Scotland are concerned' (*House of Commons Papers*, vol. 302, p. 1324), was typical of feeling in the Highlands. Granting security of tenure to tenants of the smallest crofts could well be construed as security to live in poverty; it was certainly contrary to the recommendations of the Napier Commission, which argued that this 'would tend to fix them [the crofters] in a condition from which they ought to be resolutely though gently withdrawn' (Scotland, 1884, p. 39).

In short, the effect of the legislation was to fossilise the crofting landscape as it happened to appear in 1886. Change is now frustrated by the high degree of security which crofters enjoy as well as by the essentially communal nature of the system, which allows a conservative minority to obstruct a progressive majority. Such a policy 'preserves an anachronistic labour-intensive system of agricultural production . . . while it compels the population to emigrate for want of alternate employment opportunities' (Simpson, 1962, p. 1). Another point is that the Act affects not only the individual and the township but has proved to be a potent influence in planning. For it was the 1886 Act which introduced the 'crofting counties' region into the administrative and legal scene. The seven counties (Orkney, Shetland, Sutherland, Ross and Cromarty, Caithness, Inverness and Argyll) were grouped thus because they embraced the effective crofting area of 1886. There were undoubtedly areas outside to the east and south where groups of smallholdings had been a prominent element in the landscape, but the process of evolution to commercial farming had had earlier origins and was complete by 1886. Similarly there were a number of parishes within the crofting counties (notably in eastern Inverness-shire and south Argyll) where crofting had disappeared and which could not therefore be declared 'crofting parishes' for the purpose of applying the provisions of the Act. Later legislation has ignored these anomalies, however, and deals with the seven counties as a whole. But the crofting landscape has contracted further since 1886, and it may therefore be questioned to what extent a region delimited with agricultural conditions in the late nineteenth century in mind is suitable as a context for remedial legislation in the present century.

LAND SETTLEMENT

The legislative activity of the 1880s was a reaction to the excesses of the sheep economy. Yet action was delayed for so long that protection was not afforded until this commercial farming system was itself being eclipsed by the processes of afforestation already discussed. The impact of this new order on the crofting population had many desirable elements even if it was a mixed blessing on the whole, and one of these was a reduction, if not a complete elimination, of the stranglehold which sheep grazing held over crofting agriculture. Farm rents tumbled down from their dizzy heights of the golden days to levels more reconcilable with the means of the crofters. The result was that enlargement of existing holdings and resettlement on new smallholdings, so long held as the main objectives of crofter agitation, could go forward on a private basis. A striking example of this comes from Arnisdale, purchased from Baillie of Dochfour by

Mr Robert Birkbeck in 1890. The development of the sporting potential at the Kinlochourn end has already been mentioned, but equally noteworthy was the reorganisation at Arnisdale, where the common grazing was enlarged at the expense of Arnisdale farm, which was taken over by the manager of the former pluralist tenant, Mr Milligan.

The crofters' houses were improved as well, for their condition was deplorable. Before rebuilding there were two rows of insanitary hovels with no segregation of living quarters from the cow byres. The lower of the two rows was particularly badly sited, being exposed at once to the spring tides and the refuse from the upper row of houses and byres: 'the sea at high spring tides often flooded the lower row, hardly a house was watertight, the roofs and walls being equally rotten and in damp weather the floors were literally mud' (Scotland, 1895, p. 434). The whole village of Corran was rebuilt, the lower row being completely demolished and replaced by a row of new slated houses a short distance away, while the best houses in the upper row were rebuilt. A separate row of byres was built, draining into the burn so that the dwellinghouses were not affected, and the surplus stones from the old structures were used for a sea wall.

Similar improvements had been made elsewhere in Glenelg after Mr James Baillie succeeded to the Dochfour properties in 1883. Grazings were provided at Galder (340 acres), Kirkton (80 acres) and Camusbane (200 acres). In Knoydart Mr Bowlby, who purchased the estate about 1890, improved the houses at Airor and added Samadalan grazings to the existing croft land, a move which was contemporaneous with the afforestation of much of the interior portions of Scottas, Inverguseran and Kilchoan farms. In addition there was some attempt by private enterprise at resettlement, notably in North Morar where Lord Lovat's balanced estate policies merit further comment.

Here, as in Knoydart and Glenelg, afforestation at Kinlochmorar and Beoraid in the 1880s was balanced by encouragement of the crofter element. Thus when Beoraidmore farm came out of lease in 1881 the area not let as shootings was split into small individual croft holdings with separate grazings apportioned to each, in contrast to the earlier pattern of lotted holdings and common grazings. This resulted in a more dispersed and irregular settlement pattern compared with the linear layout of the orthodox township of the early nineteenth century. The same procedure was followed in 1905 and 1907, when the remaining farms on the estate, Bourbloch, Glasnacardoch and Tarbert, were divided into smallholdings, with portions (Fig. 6) set aside for the extension of the common grazings at Mallaig and Bracara.

This encouragement of the crofting system is reflected in the lack of any record of complaint in the evidence submitted to the Royal Commissions (Scotland, 1884, 1895) by witnesses from North Morar, in contrast to the position on other estates in the area.

In all these cases, however, the crofting element had been reduced so much by previous measures that successful private resettlement schemes could be usefully initiated. Further north and west, however, as the Napier Commission had predicted, the far more problematical balance of population and land resources made small local adjustments less appropriate. Certainly the amount of croft land increased, but overpopulation continued. For whereas the population of many mainland parishes began to show a net loss after 1831 or 1841, in the Hebrides increases were frequently recorded until as late as 1911. It was this particular island problem, as well as awareness of the dangers of unbridled afforestation, that prompted the appointment of another Royal Commission to schedule land in the Highlands and islands which they considered might be suitable for either township common grazing extensions, new townships, or for small farms.

This distinction between small crofts and larger smallholdings reflects the two types of attitude to land held by crofters. In their report this Deer Forest Commission (Scotland, 1895, p. 20) explains that

> while the evidence taken not only discloses a demand for self-supporting holdings and a readiness and willingness to take them up, it is not to be left out of view that the kind of holding to which, for the most part, crofters are accustomed is one affording a home but making it necessary for the crofter to supplement what he derives from his holding by labour or fishing or by carrying on a trade or business. In various districts those who came forward to give evidence rather showed that they had not reached the idea of a self-sustaining holding and craved our attention to the great demand for the smaller size of holdings and the extension of their present holdings, both as arable and pasture.

Action on the report was taken in respect of those areas which were declared congested districts under the Congested Districts (Scotland) Act of 1897. The criteria used were industrial resources and valuation; a parish was declared a 'congested district' if its industrial resources were insufficient to provide for the needs of the population and if the valuation (excluding shootings and holdings rated at more than £30) did not exceed £1 per head. The areas so designated were mainly the islands and certain parishes on the north-west mainland which on the whole stood out against the more satisfactory conditions in the eastern and southern districts. In their area the Congested Districts Board had a mandate to develop agriculture, create and enlarge smallholdings, aid migration, and develop fishing and communications. It was, in fact, a regional development authority, though it is perhaps fair to say that its responsibilities were probably greater than the capital it was given to carry them out.

However, considerable progress was made on the basis of the lands scheduled by the Deer Forest Commission for resettlement. Between 1897 and 1912 (when the functions of the Congested Districts Board were transferred to the Board of Agriculture, along with those of the Crofters Commission) 640 new holdings and 1,138 enlargements were created. This on top of the efforts of the Crofters Commission at effecting 2,051 enlargements thus constitutes a major effort which resulted in the almost complete elimination of farming in many districts of the islands. Thus in the Long Island there was now a move back to the more fertile land along the Atlantic coast, and in Skye, for instance, the Kilmuir district at the northern part of Trotternish stands as a prominent example.

The smallholding policy was carried on further, however, and strengthened by later legislation, namely the Small Landholders (Scotland) Act of 1911 and the Land Settlement (Scotland) Act of 1919. The latter was clearly geared to the needs of returning servicemen after 1918, for the Secretary of State for Scotland at the time argued in the Commons that 'the men from the land in Scotland have proved to be a tower of strength in the hour of national peril and their ranks, which have been thinned by the scythe of death must be replenished by men who, if need be, will vindicate the claim of heroism which they have so fully established' (*House of Commons Papers*, vol. 119, p. 1807). In the years following the Act a number of farms were acquired and divided into smallholdings throughout Scotland. In the crofting counties, however, where the new holdings qualified for croft status along with the original lotted holdings created in the early nineteenth century, no fewer than 44,000 acres of arable and 507,000 acres of grazing went to form 1,999 new smallholdings and enlarge 1,922 others between 1912 and 1933. It was a record far superior to that even of the Congested Districts Board, who only dealt with 3,000 acres of arable and 130,000 acres of hill in their resettlement schemes.

Even so it may be argued that the economic objective of creating viable holdings was compromised too much by the socially desirable aim of settling as many families as was reasonably possible, given the economic depression and high rates of unemployment. Admittedly by the 1930s the rate began to slow down, and in more recent times the process of resettlement has been discouraged by the levels of support for commercial hill farming and the economic pattern in general, making for increasingly large holdings, not to mention the high costs of acquiring and developing land for resettlement. Smallholdings, it is felt, should provide work for two men, thus enabling the son of the family gradually to take over. To improve and stock land on this scale would require £5,000–£20,000 per holding, in addition to £20,000 for building a farmhouse and steadings with necessary services.

THE LEGACY OF THE DEER-FOREST ERA

The legacy of the various expressions of the deer-forest era is certainly considerable. First, the deer forests themselves eliminated the former pattern of tenant farms from much of the Highlands and restricted it to the better farms around the fringes of the mountains, where it is still a prominent feature of the agricultural structure. While practically all the forests were restocked with sheep during the First World War, often on what proved to be a permanent basis, control was retained in the hands of the landowners, giving today's pattern of large estate farms with acreages up to 100,000 being organised as one agricultural unit (Fig. 9). This has frequently led to criticism on the grounds that it must result in a low level of intensification and a certain amount of underuse. Would not a pattern of smaller owner-occupied farms be more appropriate to the conditions and give greater employment and production? This thinking inspired the swing to smallholdings at a time of general depression in hill farming, but their efficiency and social desirability as a way of life has been compromised in modern times, since, as with all small or marginal farms, intensification does not always give an adequate return. Yet compromised though they may be, the protective legislation enacted in 1886 has given these small farms, as well as the earlier crofts, a measure of durability and rigidity, which makes for a complex yet challenging land-use problem today.

But, secondly, the deer forests still make an important contribution to the Highland economy, and some 2,233,000 acres are still designated as deer forests, compared with 3,327,000 in 1892 (Scotland, 1895), not to mention an additional area of shootings where deer may occasionally be found. Although levels have fallen considerably over the last sixty years, the rateable values of deer forests make a significant contribution to the income of local authorities, and the employment of stalkers and shepherd–stalkers offers some support to the local population. Unfortunately there are many misconceptions which linger on from the days when the deer-forest era

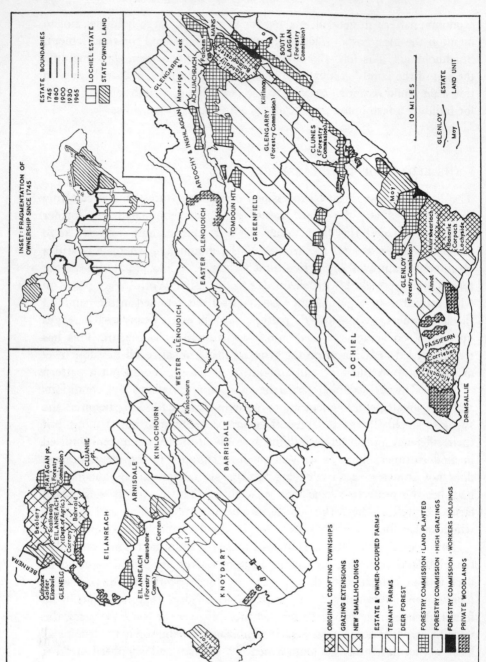

ESTATE BOUNDARIES

1745
1860
1900
1930
1965

LOCHIEL ESTATE
STATE-OWNED LAND

INSET: FRAGMENTATION OF
OWNERSHIP SINCE 1745

10 MILES

GLENLOY ESTATE
Moy   LAND UNIT

GLENGARRY

Munerigie &
Leek
ACHLUACHRACH
Faichem
MANS
Laddie Mill
SOUTH
LAGGAN
(Forestry
Commission)

AROCHY & INSHLAGGAN
Killinnan
GLENGARRY
(Forestry Commission)
CLUNES
(Forestry
Commission)
Moy

TOMDOUN HTL.

EASTER GLENQUOICH
GREENFIELD

LOCHIEL

GLENLOY
(Forestry
Commission)
Annat
Muirsheartlach
Banavie
Corpach
Lochyside

WESTER GLENQUOICH

Kinlochourn

FASSIFERN
Corriebeg
Kinlochiel
DRIMSALLIE

KINLOCHOURN

KNOYDART

BARRISDALE

Kinlochourn

ARNISDALE

CLUANIE
pt.

Corran

Li

Corran
Camusbane
EILANREACH
(Forestry
Comm.)

EILANREACH

BERNERA
Cullindune
Calder
Ellanbuie
GLENELG
RATAGAN pt.
(Forestry
Commission)
Brolary
Scallasaig
EILANREACH
(Dept. of Agric.)
Corrary
Balvraid
Balvraid

ORIGINAL CROFTING TOWNSHIPS

GRAZING EXTENSIONS

NEW SMALLHOLDINGS

ESTATE & OWNER-OCCUPIED FARMS

TENANT FARMS

DEER FOREST

FORESTRY COMMISSION : LAND PLANTED

FORESTRY COMMISSION : HIGH GRAZINGS

FORESTRY COMMISSION : WORKERS HOLDINGS

PRIVATE WOODLANDS

Fig. 2. The present land-use pattern in Lochaber

reached its heights. The use of a large proportion of Highland land for the pleasure of a few has always been a controversial point, but it should be noted that today it is only in a few cases that deer forests are still let to wealthy tenants: much of the stalking is now done by estate staff, not so much as a form of recreation but rather for purely economic reasons, for there is a steady demand for venison, especially from the Continent. There is no longer the same justification for working up what Darling and Boyd (1964, p. 89) have described as 'a personal animus against a very beautiful animal because its hunting has been confined to a certain class in society'. Many of the Victorian shooting lodges have ceased to fulfil their original functions and have frequently been converted into hotels or centres for other forms of recreation.

It must be stressed too that unlike forestry, which excludes areas laid aside for planting from other land uses, deer forests are normally used for stock grazing as well as stalking. The extent of stocking has varied considerably, of course, over the years. In 1940 some 279,000 acres were stocked with 50,426 sheep and 1,593 cattle, but under conditions of war the figures had arisen by 1945 to 148,179 sheep and 4,230 cattle. Since then the density has fallen, but continued support for hill farming maintains present levels above those of the inter-war period. In 1957, therefore, 775,187 acres of deer forest were used additionally for grazing and supported 94,191 sheep and 1,866 cattle. The main question, it seems, is what is the optimum level, because clearly numbers of deer must have a bearing on the level of sheep and cattle stocking. In many cases deer must represent the optimum form of land use, for neither cattle nor sheep have the mobility of deer and cannot take advantage of short spells of fine weather to graze the top pastures.

On many deer forests where much of the land is high and exposed further replacement of deer by sheep may not result in any increase in income. But on the other hand the numbers of deer must be controlled because of the competition which arises in winter for the sheltered, low-lying ground. Overstocking may well lead to marauding and thus create special difficulties, since the animals tend to do most damage at times when they are protected by law. However, considerable progress has been made since 1959, when the Deer (Scotland) Act was passed and the Red Deer Commission set up in Inverness charged with the task of 'furthering the conservation and control of red deer'. For a long time these apparently contradictory objectives had not been reconciled by law, for neither the Deer and Ground Game (Scotland) Bill of 1939 nor the Poaching of Deer (Scotland) Bill of 1954 succeeded in becoming law.

CHAPTER FIVE

The Role of Forestry in the Highlands

WOODLAND is an integral part of the Highland environment and in the days of the great 'Caledonian Forest' probably covered the lower slopes of the hills in a fairly continuous manner. Indeed, faced with such a barrier the original colonists who came to settle in the Highlands may well have established settlements at high altitudes to avoid the need to clear large areas of land lower down. But while forest flourished in the boreal and sub-boreal climates which followed the Ice Age, gradual deterioration set in with colder and damper conditions in the sub-Atlantic period. Woodland, therefore, contracted and was replaced by bogs and wet moorland plants on the less freely drained soils. Indeed sphagnum moss grew so luxuriantly that it felled the forest as effectively as axe or fire.

Human activity cannot be blamed for all the deforestation in the Highlands, but it is nevertheless a key factor and over the short term at least man must be burdened with what Watson (1939, p. 160) describes as 'the chief responsibility for the fate of the living landscape'. Pine forests such as those of Rannoch and Lochaber were deliberately fired to destroy the lurking places of wolves, but such losses were small in relation to those sustained when Highland woodland became valued by the wider Scottish and later British economies. The charcoal phase in iron smelting and demands for shipbuilding, especially at times of war when Britain was flung back on to her dwindling domestic resources, all took their toll. Less obvious but nevertheless significant were the depredations of the commercial sheep economy, when farmers 'cashed in on the accumulated fertility of thousands of years' (Darling, 1945, p. 135). Metamorphosed gneisses and schists are no good foundation for an indefinite period of extractive pastoralism in a countryside of heavy rainfall. Sheep in particular accounted for considerable areas of birch wood, and the hydrological implications of this were that since water could no longer be retained at the surface to the same extent as is possible with a forest cover, downhill wash increased and the peat-forming process accelerated.

This was just one facet of a general process of degeneration. The grassland itself was adversely affected, for whereas cattle graze with a coarse, tearing action, sheep nibble selectively, concentrating on the better grazing such as young heather, thus leaving the poorer grasses to spread and gradually become dominant. Moreover, while sheep are not necessarily any worse than deer or rabbits in this respect, the continuous grazing of land without fertiliser or rotation is damaging. Bracken, no longer kept in check by the bruising action of cattle hooves, spreads out, while the more nutritional grasses are replaced by mat grass. Bracken has therefore become a menace, especially where soil fertility allows the utmost luxuriance of growth. It is further encouraged by burning, a procedure made necessary by the selective sheep grazing in order to remove what the sheep do not require. Besides being a partial admission of failure, burning impoverishes the variety of flora and tends to bring the plant association down to a few dominants, one of which is bracken. Burning is often therefore most common where the sheep–cattle ratio is high, and it has changed the soil from a friable mould with some mineral particles to a tough, dense, rubbery peat, which serves as an insulating layer and prevents access to any basic material nearer the rock.

THE BEGINNINGS OF COMMERCIAL FORESTRY

Thus throughout the nineteenth century the Highlands were not only starved of capital investment at a time when the resources of the Lowlands were enjoying unprecedented expansion, but the pattern of land use was tantamount of land-mining. The Highlands tended to become devastated environment with very little evidence of thought for conservation. But any generalisation produces exceptions. With the move to more settled conditions in the late eighteenth century many landowners successfully improved the amenity value of their properties by laying out attractive policies adjacent to their houses. The activities on the Atholl estates were probably the most impressive; here larch was first planted as early as 1737. It later became appreciated as a forest tree and was planted in large numbers by the fourth Duke of Atholl, the 'planting Duke', who developed large areas of the estate for commercial forestry, with shipbuilding in mind as a possible outlet. Atholl became a great centre of innovation, with enlightened ideas being diffused around to the estates of other prominent improvers. Exotic species were introduced in the late nineteenth century, notably Japanese larch in 1883 which replaced the domestic species now stricken with disease. Douglas fir and Sitka spruce were others to be introduced, this time from America.

There was a positive element to be considered, therefore, and it persisted through the century with the planting of woodlands to improve the amenity of the now fashionable deer forests. But activity was piecemeal and sporadic and scarcely sufficient to keep pace with the heavy fellings. Moreover, since forestry is of necessity a long-term investment, the need for a favourable taxation system is obvious. Any planting is bound to constitute to some extent a declaration of faith, since costs may not be recovered to the full if the price of timber falls in the meantime, not to mention the thorny problems of working out what should constitute an adequate return on capital with continually fluctuating interest rates. But if in addition death duties are assessed so as to penalise a progressive landowner by making the immature woodland liable to duty, although estate income would have been reduced at that stage with expenses in planting, this may well constitute a deterrent. An unfavourable taxation system and imports of cheap foreign timber destroyed the economic foundation of the industry, while the First World War made serious inroads into the dwindling reserves.

Government interest was not entirely lacking, however. The Select Committee of 1885–7 was the first body to consider forestry from a national point of view, but little was done in terms of planting in the next twenty years, although the Board of Agriculture had a mandate from the government to undertake afforestation and the Congested Districts Board had funds at its disposal. Inverliever forest, however, was started in 1908 by the Office of Woods. In 1911 the Departmental Committee on Forestry in Scotland (Scotland, 1912) recommended a forest area of at least 400,000 acres but no property was acquired. This record may well be criticised as a manifest lack of progress, but it is pertinent to ask what objective was supposed to lie behind a programme of woodland afforestation. If it was to be advocated as a simple commercial proposition, then costs might well prove to compare unfavourably with the price of imported timber, which was soaking home demand. If it was to be encouraged merely to allow a better ecological balance in the hills and as a means of making better use of land resources, especially the poorer land which is of limited value for agriculture, then Parliament was unlikely to consent to a scheme which it might justifiably condemn as philanthropic. In the end a state forestry scheme only got under way when the Acland Report (H.M.S.O., 1918) advocated a vigorous forest policy for strategic reasons so that, should the need arise, Britain would have a domestic reserve. The Forestry Act was passed in 1919 establishing the Forestry Commission with wide powers to acquire land and plant it with trees. A forest area of 250,000 acres was planned for Britain over a period of twenty years, and 150,000 acres of this total national figure was to be planted by the state body. To this end many properties were acquired in the Highlands, where land was fairly cheap in view of the difficult conditions in farming. Either whole estates were purchased or alternatively large sections were acquired from some of the biggest landowners.

Ploughing, draining and fencing are essential preliminary activities before planting itself can take place. Fences 6 ft high are normally necessary in the Highlands to keep out deer, which would uproot the seedlings and do much damage in the early stages of growth. This work may well be complicated by access problems, and conventional crawler tractors are widely used. Experiments have been conducted with the 'snow-trac', a light track vehicle, and helicopters have been used in Glen Duror, Argyll, to carry materials and spread phosphate fertiliser. Draining and ploughing are normally done mechanically; a trench is excavated by the plough and the earth piled up on the sides in the form of a 'lazy bed'. An 18 in. plough is used on the peaty land and a shallower one on rougher ground, while on the steepest slopes work must be done by hand. Planting can then go ahead using seedlings grown on Forestry Commission nurseries, which are to be found on a number of their properties, notably in the Black Isle. The nurseries are important employers of female labour in contrast to forests proper, which are predominantly employers of men. The most prominent species in the Highlands is Sitka spruce, the emphasis on such quick-maturing softwoods being well suited to the wet climate of the west coast especially. On the drier east pine is still popular, although the native Scots variety has been replaced by exotic species, notably Corsican pine on the Culbin Sands of Morayshire. Some European and Japanese larch is also to be found; it is planted partly for its amenity value, in order to break up the regimented stands of Sitka, and partly on account of its fire-resisting properties.

Routine work in the forest includes cleaning (brashing) and a certain amount of beating-up in areas where the initial planting proves unsuccessful. Moreover fences, drains and roads must be maintained. Road construction is not necessary in the early stages but becomes essential later on when the trees reach the thinning stage and a certain proportion has to be drawn out. Itinerant road squads are therefore employed by the Commission to carry out these tasks in the various forests, and occasionally to improve access to forests as a whole where existing public roads are not strong enough for heavy timber lorries. This is the case in Glen Hurich in north Argyll, where a new road has recently been completed along Lochshielside from

Glenfinnan to Polloch to provide a more satisfactory alternative to the difficult route over Bellsgrove to Strontian on Loch Sunart. Some clear felling of trees may be necessary to make way for roads, but until maturity is reached thinnings account for the bulk of the timber felled. Such trees are marked and measured and then either sold in sections to contractors for felling, dragging out and processing or dealt with by the Commission themselves. Sawmilling may well be carried out locally on a small scale, with sawn logs and fencing stobs as important end-products. The scope will obviously increase as woodlands approach maturity, and there are high hopes that the present development of timber-using industries such as the Fort William pulp mill will mark the beginning of a new trend and thus give the Highland economy an important new dimension.

Commentary on the success of the forestry programme in the Highlands is, however, necessarily complicated. Not only are there various criteria which could be used as the basis of any assessment, but there is the underlying problem of fitting a national policy into the very distinctive conditions of the Highlands. Frustrations were introduced by the substantial cuts in forestry grants made first by the Geddes Committee (H.M.S.O., 1922) and later by the May Committee (H.M.S.O., 1931). The Geddes Committee in particular rejected the strategic and social arguments for forestry and argued (para. 8) that 'to create employment on an uneconomic basis cannot be justified'. This raised the point about the objective of a national forest policy. If it is examined purely as an economic exercise then it becomes necessary to plan long-term investment on the basis of present assumptions. Though there are well-established methods for calculating the likely return over a period, these cannot forecast changes in the price of wood or levels of future demand. It would seem, therefore, that once the initial decision has been taken, the industry should be spared the disruption of having its essentially long-term programme upset by short-term variations in the supply of capital.

Inter-war policy tended to follow a 'stop–go' pattern, with the availability of money showing considerable fluctuations. But this did not inhibit progress in the Highlands so much, since the relatively depressed state of agriculture made land acquisition an easier process than would have been the case if the farming lobby had been in better heart. Accordingly a considerable number of estates were acquired and intensively developed by the Commission. This pattern of acquisition made it possible to combine forestry with the smallholdings policy which was carried forward with renewed vigour after 1918. A portion of the arable on the estates acquired was therefore divided into separate units, especially after 1924, when the Commission was instructed to pursue a definite land settlement policy. Smallholders were allowed to take up to twenty-four days' unpaid leave annually, in addition to their holidays, without penalty, in order to tend their land, and at the same time were guaranteed 150 days' work per annum in the forest. In practice, however, the smallholders tended to work as regularly in the forest as employees without holdings. The smallholding policy has a number of advantages in providing a stable labour force and maintaining a link between forestry and agriculture. In addition it ensures that a number of people are on hand to deal with any emergency which may arise, such as fire. But though these forestry workers' holdings do not carry croft status, they nevertheless make for a similar land-use pattern, with a proliferation of small units, and in spite of the guarantee that the tenantry will be of working age it must be questioned whether this policy still reflects the best use of land today.

PLANTING IN THE HIGHLANDS BEFORE 1945

Two points may be made concerning the forestry programme in the Highlands in the inter-war period which are of considerable geographical interest. The first concerns the management of the Forestry Commission properties themselves and the striking of the right balance between different land-users. For the Highland area, while ripe for development by the Commission in the 1920s and 1930s, nevertheless makes for difficulties in deciding precisely what land is most suitable for forestry. It is easy to justify planting a large area of land by pointing to the extent of forestry in past ages, yet an opposite point of view could be taken by those who consider that the encroachment of forestry on to good agricultural land is most undesirable. Supporters of the agricultural interest do not deny the favourable employment position in forests, but insist that agriculture could employ more people, given the same levels of capital investment, and suggest that only the poorest land, that least valuable for agriculture, should be planted. Since most of the land most suitable for forestry is at the same time very suited for agriculture, it is clearly unreasonable to expect forestry to restrict itself to poor land, especially in view of what has already been said about forestry as a national policy and the need to strive for a satisfactory economic return on capital invested. Today the Forestry Commission has a vast accumulated experience after some forty-five years in existence and may be able to cope with certain

types of difficult site, but in the 1920s financial and technological considerations made the planting of valuable grazings inevitable.

What may be regarded in retrospect as particularly unfortunate, however,
was the exclusive nature of planting on the lower slopes of glens. Rather
than attempt to balance forestry and farming in an integrated pattern, trees
were frequently planted in an unbroken belt along the whole length of the
estate, thus isolating the 'tops', the high and exposed rough grazings, from
the arable land below. In certain cases, moreover, the whole of the arable
was earmarked for forestry workers' holdings and nurseries, in which
case the 'tops' were left as an entirely separate unit and could only be let
to a neighbouring farmer as a temporary grazing or else treated as a small
deer forest. In either case it was of very limited value, since it was divorced
from the sheltered grazings and arable which are an essential component. It
has been calculated that for every acre (below, say, 1,500 ft) abstracted from
agriculture, some 10 acres above are rendered of little value for stock. Not
only is access important but there must be adequate sheltered ground
retained to allow proper management. If cut off from lower ground by
high fences, sheep are driven along a lateral path and may easily become
trapped in a 'pocket', with consequent high mortality in bad weather.
Deer for their part are of course more mobile and will find access to low
ground at either end of the Forestry Commission property, but this means
that farmers who are next-door neighbours of the Commission will bear
more of their fair share of depredations by marauding deer as a result of the
protective fencing placed only around woodlands. Fig. 9 illustrates the
impact of forestry in the southern part of the Great Glen at Glengarry,
South Laggan and Clunes.

It is of course necessary to protect young trees which could be easily
uprooted, and it could also be stressed that the Commission is a specialised
body with a remit to plant trees rather than develop agriculture. Nevertheless
the pursuance of another exclusive land-use policy after the sheep farming
and deer afforestation of the nineteenth century was most unfortunate.
The practice of the Forestry Commission taking the 'eye' out of an estate
was deeply resented by farming interests, and in areas where there are
feelings of bitterness and mistrust of Commission intentions there is usually
a correlation with heavy planting in the inter-war period. With this in mind,
it is interesting to turn to a survey made by a team headed by Lord Lovat
before the First World War (Lovat, 1911) into the possibilities of planting
trees in the Great Glen area. Large areas were considered suitable, but it is
significant that only a quarter of the land was to be dealt with at a time.

It was recommended that further planting should go ahead only after the first section had established itself and the area could be thrown open to grazing. In this case the other interests, farming and deer, would not be compromised and indeed might well benefit from the shelter value of the trees.

That this line was not in fact followed after the war may be partly explained by the weaker economic position of competing interests, which did not represent the same proportion in the rateable values of local authorities, but this is not all. The Scottish Land Enquiry Committee (Scotland, 1914, p. 253) did not support landlord interests but nevertheless recommended a similar integrated approach by suggesting that 'belts of the low grade pasture land served for afforestation should be selected by the Board of Agriculture in the neighbourhoods of smallholdings and not required for smallholdings'. Both schemes were conceived to suit Highland conditions, which are, of course, very different from the national average to which the Forestry Commission was geared. If regional interests matter, then a way must be found of reconciling national interests with those of the Highland environment. Forestry is admittedly but one of several facets of the local economy, but it affects all land-users. Since land is perhaps the most valuable resource in the Highlands, and since the committal of land to forestry is long-term, great care is required in deciding the nature and extent of planting programmes.

The second theme concerns the location of forestry estates. While the national interests requires a timber reserve, one of the tangible benefits of this for the Highlands is the employment which this creates. This employment is all the more valuable since it is essentially local and rural, with the result that not only is Highland depopulation retarded but the people are 'held' in rural communities rather than in the main towns. Frequently forests are situated so close to main villages and towns that to develop a separate small community would be socially unrealistic as well as costly in terms of providing services such as electricity, water and drainage. But elsewhere the small groups of forestry houses are a valuable new component in the landscape, and especially in the north and west where depopulation has tended to be heaviest. Island districts in particular could derive great benefit from afforestation, since their land resources are clearly limited and there is consequently a strong case for advocating the form of land use which will provide the greatest number of jobs.

Unfortunately the same considerations which prompted discrimination between different parts of individual properties, concentrating planting

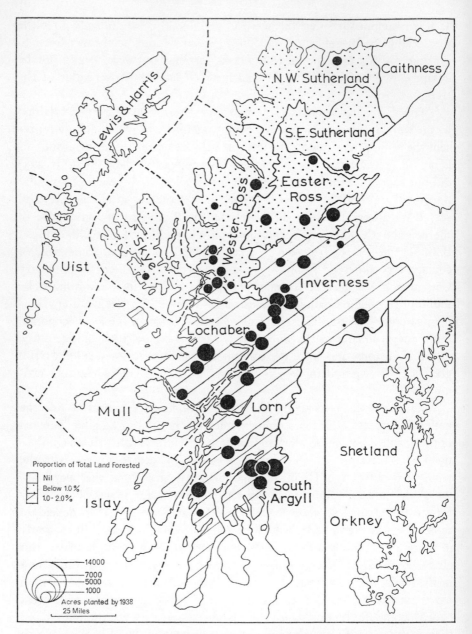

Fig. 10 *Forestry Commission plantings up to 1938*

Within the figure:

Caithness

N.W. Sutherland

S.E. Sutherland

Lewis & Harris

Easter Ross

Wester Ross

Skye

Uist

Inverness

Lochaber

Mull

Lorn

South Argyll

Islay

Shetland

Orkney

Proportion of Total Land Forested
Nil
Below 1.0 %
1.0 - 2.0 %

14000
7000
5000
1000
Acres planted by 1938
25 Miles

on the sheltered grazings, tended to make for the heaviest planting in the south and east of the Highlands. Within the crofting counties Inverness and Argyll stand out with a large area of woodland, whereas the peripheral and island counties were largely ignored, since the land was often unsuitable and there were problems of exposure (Fig. 10). While a concentration of forestry grew up along a belt down the Great Glen and along tributary glens into Argyll, the windy west-coast and island areas with a salt-laden atmosphere were relatively ignored, although these were precisely the places where the employment would have been most acceptable (Plate 1).

PLANTING AFTER 1945

Throughout Britain, however, the effective woodland area in 1939 was still less than it had been in 1914, and further losses during the war called for an acceleration of the planting programme. The Forestry Act of 1945 made provision for a planted area of 3 million acres in Britain, half of which was to be in Scotland. This was followed up by the 1950 programme of Highland development which outlined a long-term policy to extend afforestation to at least 750,000 acres of effective forest, giving employment to 7,500 people in the woodlands themselves, quite apart from contractors and employment in timber-using industries. The Highlands are therefore destined to play a very prominant role in the national programme, and that in itself is encouraging. Yet this cannot fail but create further difficulty over the allocation of land between different uses, since good land forms such a small proportion of the total. Bearing past problems in mind, it will be useful to examine post-war planting to see if any contrasts emerge in management and in the locational pattern of woodlands.

After the war there were two important differences in the process of land acquisition. First, the Forestry Commission lost its independence under the 1945 Act and in Scotland was placed under the Secretary of State. This meant that there was scope for adjudication in any plan to acquire and plant land, and the Department of Agriculture and Fisheries has been able to thwart attempts to plant good agricultural land in large continuous blocks. Secondly, however, the government support for hill farming which was introduced during the last war was carried on in peace-time, and these hill-cattle subsidies have had a welcome stabilising effect on the industry generally, which has been reflected in the smaller number of properties coming up for sale and a general increase in land prices. The Forestry Commission has therefore experienced difficulty in acquiring sufficient land, in particular whole estates, but then these are of less value anyway, since permission to plant the whole area to the exclusion of farming is unlikely to be forthcoming.

Acquisitions have therefore tended to take the form of blocks of roughly 500 acres which can be fenced and planted throughout and then offer shelter to the surrounding agricultural land. There is clearly a lower limit to the size of a block, for while agriculture might benefit most from a large number of small blocks, the cost of fencing the circumferences and providing access to these tiny units would be disproportionately and prohibitively high. As a result of this practice many of the older forests have acquired a number of satellite blocks or outliers, though occasionally new forests are created where integration is not feasible. It follows too that the Forestry Workers' Holding Scheme has not been operated in respect of land acquired since the war; even when a large estate unit is acquired, the practice is now for the Department of Agriculture to look after the sections not earmarked for planting. Fig. 9 indicates how Glengarry and Clunes forests have been diversified by the addition of small blocks, but contains evidence of planting by private landowners too.

Now that the beginnings have been made in developing a pattern of integration, other imaginative schemes have been launched to increase the number of blocks available. One very fruitful line is private planting, which has been conspicuous by its relative absence in the past in the crofting counties themselves, apart from amenity woodlands in various forms. Some notable pioneering work may be mentioned, however, such as that on Rannoch Moor by the late Sir John Stirling Maxwell. He acquired the Corrour estate, and though his attempts to drain part of the moor in 1927 were a failure, largely because of the difficulty of perfecting a suitable plough, the 1,400 acres of forest around Loch Ossian and Loch Treig are an impressive memorial of his foresight. The work of the British Aluminium Company in Glen Spean is also very notable. The company is naturally interested in developing the water-retaining capacity of its watershed area, practically the whole of which it owns, and they are well over half-way towards their target of 6,000 acres of woodland to be planted in large blocks. Since 1947, however, the interest of private landowners in general has been attracted by planting grants of £22 4s per acre offered by the Commission in respect of woodlands which are 'dedicated' to them and managed in an approved manner. Money is also available in the form of annual maintenance grants thereafter, and there are alternative schemes to attract landowners who are interested in planting but who do not wish to be tied to the 'dedication' scheme. By making money and technical knowledge available, and also by smoothing over some of the difficulties relating to estate-duty charges, it is hoped that private planting will cover 3,000 acres each year in addition to the 20,000 acres which the Forestry Commission plan to deal with itself.

A number of attractive developments have been initiated, and the enterprise by the Duke of Westminster at Kinlochbervie in Sutherland is well known. Also notable is the organisation known as West Highland Woodlands in Lochaber, which owes much to the initiative and capital of Lord Dulverton. A property was acquired at Eilanreach in Glenelg in 1947 and some 450 acres have been planted since 1949 with a variety of species, including oak, fir and spruce along with beech, sycamore and larch. A later scheme at Fassifern on Locheilside deals with two 500-acre blocks on either side of a burn; the woodland will provide shelter and the fencing has been laid out so as to avoid trapping sheep on the higher grazings. Provision has been made for reseeding a large lamb enclosure close to the home-farm steadings, thus producing a very attractive integrated unit. Since the Forestry Commission is a specialised body, it cannot be expected to initiate integration itself, though integrated management of its properties has been suggested, yet private landowners are now well placed to combine a number of activities.

Incentives to private planters are particularly valuable, for, as the Zuckerman Committee point out (H.M.S.O., 1957, p. 32),

> forestry requires a certain degree of specialisation, even within the estate. The break-up of large estates and the increase of owner-occupancy of farms have made it difficult for skilled forest workers to find a place in private enterprise and such men are all too rare. While estate owners and their agents in previous days frequently had a great personal interest in forestry, small landlords and owner-occupiers today are almost bound to concentrate their attention and financial resources on the day-to-day problems and increasingly heavy capital requirements of farming.

Another expression of this encouraging trend is the planting of parts of crofting township common grazings. The security of tenure accompanying croft status has prevented the Forestry Commission from developing these grazings in the past, and the exclusive planting policy followed originally was hardly conducive to the crofters voluntarily countenancing any resumption of land, even though it was frequently underused. But crofters, many of whom are forestry workers anyway, are growing to appreciate the benefits of woodland integrated with sheep grazing. Since landlords are naturally anxious to develop an asset which was formerly of doubtful value to them, and the Forestry Commission is keen to acquire more blocks, a formula has now been worked out whereby development funds and compensation are payable to crofters who allow the Forestry Commission to take part of their grazings. The money may then be invested in the improvement of other parts of the grazing, which along with the shelter from the trees will increase the carrying capacity of the remainder. Since this land development grant can be supplemented by Crofters Commission grant schemes, £400 paid to the crofters by the Forestry Commission could finance £800 worth of fencing or as much as £2,500 worth of surface seeding. Such development schemes administered by the Crofters Commission are thereby attractive to all parties, and several such schemes have been launched.

This is another way in which forestry is beginning to play its role in a broad-based policy of land development to reverse the long process of degeneration. For long frustrated by financial uncertainties and a lack of technical knowledge, a growing momentum is being built up with this present pattern of co-operation which is certainly in keeping with the principles of 'conservation, integration and multiple use' advocated by the Scottish Council's Committee on Natural Resources. Greater publicity has been advocated, and it has also been suggested that tenant farmers should be brought within the framework of forestry grants, for experiments by the North of Scotland College of Agriculture and the Department of Agriculture at Dalchork farm show that the level of sheep stocking can be largely maintained despite the loss of some 5,000 acres to forestry out of a total of 23,000. With such measures the Advisory Panel on the Highlands and Islands considered an annual planting target of 20,000 acres to be attainable by the Forestry Commission, quite apart from an additional 3,000 acres each year by private landowners (Scotland, 1964, p. 38). This figure may be compared with an actual average of 12,650 acres per annum planted by the Commission between 1959 and 1964. Of considerable assistance should be the wealth of information which has been accumulated on the planting of poor moorlands and mountainsides through continuing experiments on land on the borders of profitability. An outstanding example here are the experiments carried on at an altitude of 1,050 ft on Rannoch Moor since 1957, where planting is handicapped additionally by rocky knolls and boulder-strewn land.

THE SOCIAL ARGUMENT

It is clearly government policy to sustain the forestry side of land development. Plans were announced in 1963 to plant 450,000 acres in Britain in the decade 1964–73. Though this represents a slightly lower annual target than that attained in the previous decade, government policy is to continue to concentrate on acquiring land in the upland areas, particularly in Scotland and Wales, where population is declining and where the expansion of forestry can bring considerable social and employment benefits. At the end of 1963 the Commission employed 1,779 full-time (including nearly 200 crofters) and 20 part-time workers, while employment given by contractors and timber merchants amounted to well over 300. Even so this number is small compared with some 9,500 employed in agriculture, but the ratio is by no means the same throughout the Highlands, since planting still tends to emphasise the eastern and southern districts where the bulk of the employment is concentrated (Fig. 11).

It was with the needs of the crofting area in mind that the government in 1955 authorised the Forestry Commission to undertake a special programme of planting in the crofting areas even if it meant planting on land that would give a smaller return than usually anticipated. A programme of 25,000–35,000 acres was provided for, but this has been only partly realised. As a result of research the Commission has been able to plant on exposed and peaty land which previously would not have been regarded as suitable. Experimentation is progressing and trials are being undertaken at various places in the northern Highlands, at Fiag, Lybster and Syre, to see if satisfactory results can be obtained from the more difficult types of land. Yet even though the necessary technology may gradually accumulate, the economics would seem to become progressively more doubtful, and marketing such timber may eventually prove an embarrassment. It could be argued that even though the first crop of trees might show a loss, the fact that the necessary infrastructure was installed would make subsequent crops more remunerative. Nevertheless, on the whole it would seem that any sustained programme of 'special' planting for social reasons in the crofting areas of the north-west mainland and Hebrides will have to be separately financed.

Not that this is all, for the problem is more intractable. A number of rural development surveys have been carried out to see how much land could be planted in certain districts in the north-west, and the results are not encouraging (Scotland, 1964, p. 77). In the parish of Assynt in Sutherland, with a total area of 119,000 acres, it was found that even at the cost of virtually extinguishing the agricultural use from the better land only 3,339 acres would be secured for forestry. This would provide a net increase in employment of only seven. If a compromise between farming and forestry were arranged, as would be almost inevitable since much of the suitable land is in fact croft land, then 2,100 acres might

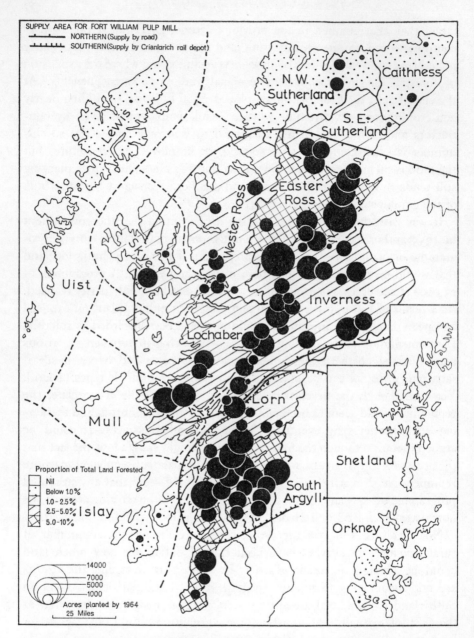

Fig. 11 *Forestry Commissio plantings up to 1964*

be made available with a net increase in employment of five. Other studies reveal roughly similar results: a survey in the north of Sutherland around Loch Loyal and Strathnaver revealed that 3,400 acres were plantable with an employment potential of seven men, but even so only at the expense of agricultural and sporting interests. The problems of Mull and the ability of forestry to solve them constitute another interesting local study, but discussion will be deferred until Chapter 11.

One is forced to conclude, therefore, that even with moderate progress in the west and in the Hebrides, progress which will nevertheless go some way to bringing about stability locally, the disparity between these exposed places and the more sheltered sites in Argyll, Inverness and Sutherland is bound to grow, since the scope in these more favoured counties is still very great; even in Argyll only 9·8 per cent of the county is under trees, compared with 16 per cent, for instance, in Kirkcudbright. In mid-Argyll alone the planting programme is currently growing from 1,360 acres to 2,500 acres per annum by 1971, and a new forest has been inaugurated at Raira to deal with recent acquisitions of land between Kilmelfort and Kilmore. This ties in with the view that forestry, burdened in Britain by high capital costs, can only be competitive if large-scale units are managed. Moreover forests in this area are well placed to play a role in the interests of tourism and recreation, and although there are no national parks in Scotland as yet, certain forests such as Inverinan on Lochaweside have made arrangements for visitors to explore the forest paths and study a variety of ecological aspects with the aid of brochures and exhibitions. Further afield, a new drive-in forest park has been opened at Aros, near Tobermory, Mull.

The role of forestry is a fundamental and complex one – fundamental because it must be a major component of any land-use plan which may be devised in the interests of Highland development but complex too, since ecological, economic and social criteria can all be brought in to broaden the discussion. Forestry cannot be taken on its own, and that this has been accepted in all quarters constitutes a major breakthrough, marking the end of the exclusive policies which affected not only forestry but the deer-forest and commercial sheep economies which preceded it. The dangers inherent in the neglect of legitimate interests have been appreciated, and the mistrust and suspicion which have tended to introduce an element of rigidity into Highland affairs, especially when backed up by protective legislation, are gradually giving place to restrained optimism. There are still problems, but the machinery for dealing with them is becoming sufficiently sophisticated and sensitive for reasonable solutions to be reached.

CHAPTER SIX

Highland Farming and Crofting Today

AGRICULTURE has always played a fundamental role in the Highland economy. The waves of afforestation, first for deer and later for woodlands, merely removed or depressed the agricultural interest from certain localities; in the Highland area as a whole agriculture has always been the most important form of land use. But the industry has rarely achieved the stability which its own interests and those of the Highlands as a whole demand. With a very low proportion of the land in arable, occasionally less than 1 per cent, hill livestock farming is inevitably the main interest. There is some inflexibility of land use and little scope for variation in the type of farming, and hence the industry is exposed to the vagaries of market prices for sheep and cattle. While Lowland farms can concentrate on other enterprises if the profitability of livestock is low, a change from rearing to fattening or dairying on any scale would not be appropriate to Highland conditions, since there is so little good grazing. Moreover, short-term trends can be highly damaging: a hard winter followed by a drought in spring is bound to bring heavy losses amongst the ewes and lambs, losses which are felt for several years after in view of the depletion of the breeding stock.

It is perhaps for these reasons that Highland agriculture has at times found itself ill-equipped to meet its competitors for land on favourable terms. However, following the outbreak of war in 1939 it was deemed expedient to support hill farming by offering subsidies for hill sheep and hill cattle at rates commensurate with conditions over the country as a whole each year. These were continued under the Hill Farming Act of 1946 and have been embodied in all subsequent legislation. They provide a welcome buffer for Highland farmers, but it is worth pointing out that since the rate is fixed with average national conditions in mind, a bad year in the Highlands is not necessarily reflected in the level of subsidy. The coefficient of variation in average income per farm has been calculated at 0·30 for hill sheep farms, compared with 0·14 for dairy farms, and even when the hill sheep subsidy is taken into account, the coefficient still remains relatively high at 0·24. This is an unfortunate situation, for it discourages Highland farmers from planning and investing on a long-term basis. It could be argued, by contrast, that above-average returns are desirable to enable farmers in hill areas to provide individually an infrastructure which it may not be practicable for local authorities to provide overall.

SHEEP FARMING

With these points in mind it is proposed to look a little more closely at the nature of farming practices. Very few farms indeed are without a sheep stock, as it is only on small crofts with no sheep soum or on small dairy units that sheep can reasonably be excluded. The dominant breed is the Blackface, and much discussion has taken place as to its merits and demerits compared with those of its main rival, the Cheviot, which it outnumbers by a ratio of 3:1. According to Brownlie (1949, p. 32) the Cheviot was more popular in the early nineteenth century, but the severe winter of 1860 marked the turning point. The same writer found this breed superior to all others introduced experimentally on the hill farm of Ardslignish in Ardnamurchan. The Blackface Breeders' Association argue that their sheep

can stand up to the worst of the snow storms on the open hills with only a minimum of hay and shelter to help them survive the blast and can produce a lamb crop and wool clip. They recover very quickly after a bad winter and they have great courage, which keeps them foraging for the best spring growth available. Their natural inclination is to range to the highest elevations in the summer, keeping to the lower slopes in winter and thus effectively utilising all the grazing throughout the year. No other breed excels the Blackface in this ranging ability.

Moreover their adaptability extends to herbage, with varying proportions of heather being acceptable, and the Blackface ewe has the added advantage of the homing or 'hefting' instinct, for stock will not voluntarily leave an area once settled and acclimatised.

With Highland sheep farming the emphasis is on the sale of surplus ewe lambs, castrated wedder lambs, cast ewes and wool, which is used in the mattress, upholstery, carpet and heavy cloth trades. On the east coast ewes are generally cast at five, but in the west they are generally kept on the hill for a further year since there are insufficient good lambs to maintain the stock otherwise. At one time it was fairly general practice to keep the male (wedder) lambs for two or three years before selling, but this has been discouraged by the growing popularity of smaller lamb joints and also by the payment of subsidy on breeding ewes only, which inevitably makes for an emphasis on rearing rather than fattening. Hence only land which is too rough for ewes or too remote for thorough shepherding is still given over to wedders. A fairly popular practice in areas where low ground is ample is to retain the cast ewes for a further year or two and cross them with a Border Leicester or Cheviot ram. The cross lambs (Greyfaces) are in considerable demand for breeding purposes further south, where they are crossed with a Down ram. Only the richest farms are suited physically for this, since all the low ground is normally required for the hill stock in winter. On the fertile island of Lismore, however, Blackface ewes of normal age are crossed with Leicester rams as a general practice, the higher prices for the lambs being sufficient to justify forgoing the hill sheep subsidy, which is not payable in such circumstances.

Carrying capacity and lambing percentages vary enormously according to the quality of land. In Lochaber (Fig. 12), as might be expected, the highest lambing percentages are recorded on the small farms along the Great Glen and the west-coast fringes, Lismore especially, while performance falls off on the larger farms of the interior. Figures show considerable variations from year to year, however, and for this reason an average for 1961 and 1962 has been taken in drawing up the map. But local conditions are so diverse that results may vary greatly on different sections (hirsels) of the same farm; on one farm in Glencoe in 1962 the overall lambing percentage was 67, but individual figures for the three hirsels were 59, 69 and 76. It should also be stressed that comparisons cannot be made too finely between farms, since the lambing percentage is not always accurately calculated and the standard convention of relating lambs counted in the spring to ewes present at the previous summer's dipping is not always adhered to.

Occasional bad weather can make for heavy setbacks, as was the case in 1947 and again in 1962, when a hard winter and spring drought followed the poor summer in 1961. Ewes were in a poor condition at lambing and the drought meant that there was little grass available for the young animals. Losses were therefore heavy; in north Argyll and Mull it was estimated that of the 53,000 ewes put to the ram only 43,000 were accounted for in the summer following. Moreover the lamb crop dropped from the usual 37,000 to approximately 25,000 and a quarter of the hoggs outwintered died. In addition there was less wool in the autumn. The susceptibility of the industry to bad weather cannot be overemphasised, nor can the desirability of adequate low, sheltered ground for wintering and feeding stuffs.

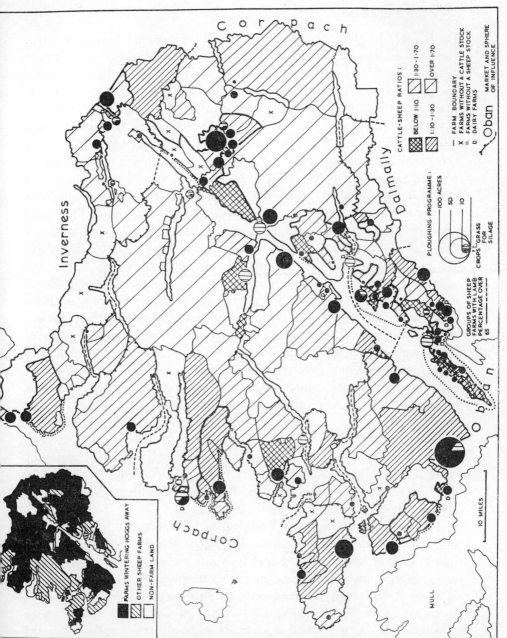

Fig. 12 *Farming enterprises in Lochaber and north Argyll*

CATTLE REARING

Cattle comprise the other major element in the livestock farming pattern. Once the dominant component of Highland agriculture, they have generally been relegated to second place since the introduction of the commercial sheep economy. There are no doubt many reasons for this, one of which is that cattle fitted in better with a labour-intensive subsistence agriculture, making the fullest possible use of the arable potential and the high grazings. Thus the remains of the old rigs visible on so many hillsides are a legacy of the traditional farming pattern before improvement, for Gailey (1960a, p. 249) comments that 'all available evidence points to a maximum extent of cultivation while the clachans still existed as viable settlements and social entities and before run-rig had been abolished in most areas'. Thus even after the '45 almost every available patch of land up to about 1,400 ft was diligently cultivated, and the ridge and furrow pattern shows to what extent the present-day arable is but a shrunken remnant of the old.

Moreover the shieling system made maximum use of the summer grazings; writing on north Skye, for instance, MacSween (1959b) considers evidence to suggest that every clachan of run-rig cultivators possessed and made use of shieling grounds. So great was the pressure of population on resources that boundary disputes frequently occurred between adjacent communities. Even so the problem of maintaining the cattle through the winter was always present, for the beasts required shelter and hand feeding. Hence as many as possible were disposed of in the autumn, but there are tales of the few that were retained being carried from the byre to the pasture in spring on account of their weakness. With a more extensive farming pattern and a big drop in the arable cattle became increasingly marginal, for imported feeding stuffs immediately compromise profitability. This was unfortunate, however, since conservation of grazings can best be achieved with a healthy balance between sheep and cattle.

The question of feeding stuffs remains a critical one still, for the cost of imported hay can quickly absorb any profit which the hill cattle subsidy may sustain. Accordingly cattle are sometimes completely absent from some high grazing units, and on others, similarly sited in exposed positions without sufficient low ground, the summering of cattle may be the only alternative to sheep. Conversely, however, on the best land cattle may exclude sheep altogether, as on some small dairy units and on certain crofts where the arable and common grazings are too small for an efficient sheep stock. Fig. 12 illustrates the variations in the sheep–cattle ratio on different farms in Lochaber and shows cattle to be relatively more prominent on the better farms with plenty of low ground. Perhaps the best-known example of cattle farming in the Highlands is that of the Great Glen cattle ranch between Fort William and Spean Bridge. It owes its existence to the late Mr J. W. Hobbs, who came to Lochaber in 1944 and carried out a spectacular programme of land improvement and reclamation on the Inverlochy estate. Sheep were excluded and breeding cows kept in top condition by feeding silage made from oats, peas, beans and tares grown on reclaimed land. A number of underused crofts at Brackletter were bought out and merged with the enterprise, which employed a large number of people and won for the owner the respect and appreciation of the population of Lochaber generally.

Why then are such farms generally conspicuous by their absence? Let it be said that few people could match the enthusiasm, initiative and resources which Mr Hobbs possessed in full measure. Many other farmers with similar land resources could hardly match his dedication or move as quickly in response to the possibilities offered under the Hill Farming and Livestock Rearing Acts, which allowed 50 per cent refunds for improvements to land. Furthermore, the combination of the ranch with a distillery enterprise increased efficiency in the use of labour and provided a local supply of distillery draff which was useful for feeding. Nevertheless Mr Hobbs showed what could be done in the land improvement sphere, even though the actual degree of intensification is very much a matter for the individual farmer and this high level would not be appropriate in every case. Significantly the new owner, a farmer with other estates in Ayrshire, has cut down heavily on the arable and introduced sheep, with consequent reductions in labour. Moreover the map of cattle–sheep ratios in Lochaber shows, unlike most other patterns, a lack of any pronounced regional trend, indicating that this is primarily an individual farm matter.

The traditional breed of cattle is of course the Highlander, but numbers are decreasing and pedigree animals are comparatively rare. They are still bred on a small number of farms such as those owned by the Department of Agriculture and certain companies (the Ardslignish estate of Boots Pure Drug Company is an example) for crossing and show purposes. Local opinion has it that the Highlander does not go to the hill readily enough, has a low calving rate and is slow to recover from bad conditions. The commonest breeds tend to be Aberdeen-Angus, Shorthorn and Galloway, but since much depends on individual preference it is impossible to associate particular breeds with certain areas. A system recently recommended is to cross Highland or Galloway pedigree heifers with Shorthorn or Cumberland bulls, the first crossed calves being marketed at nine months for finishing or crossed again to produce second-cross calves by Aberdeen-Angus, Hereford or other beef bulls. This in fact accords closely with practice on the Great Glen cattle ranch, where a small pedigree Galloway herd maintains a stream of pure Galloway cows which are served by a Shorthorn bull to give blue-grey calves. These blue-greys are then served by a Hereford or Aberdeen-Angus to produce top-quality beef calves, the main end-product. However, the use of pedigree stock is not as prominent as might be considered desirable, for although the initial outlay is high there are advantages by way of better calves, freedom from disease and a long productive life.

Hill breeds are, however, generally dominant, for payment of subsidy on hill cattle and calves has had the effect of cutting down the numbers of dairy cattle and of encouraging a concentration on breeding. At Swordle farm in Ardnamurchan, as on many others, the practice was to rear heifers for sale as dairy cows when three years old, but the operation of the subsidy has led to a complete swing to beef with an emphasis on calf production. Indeed replacement heifers are normally bought in rather than keep young beasts on the farm for two years without subsidy. Thus in Lochaber, whereas only 41·7 per cent of the cattle were classed as 'beef' in 1945, the proportion was 91·9 per cent in 1961, though the basis of calculating the statistics gives a rather exaggerated picture. On crofts especially there is a tendency to produce an all-purpose animal which is capable of suckling calves and which, at the same time, qualifies for the hill cattle subsidy. Only rarely is the milk from crofters' cows destined for human consumption, and specialisation in dairying on such holdings is small.

THE USE OF LOW GROUND

By comparison with livestock enterprises, arable cultivation is not nearly as important in terms of value of production or acreage. For Scotland as a whole crop sales on hill sheep farms amounted on average to £36 in 1960-1, compared with £2,378 from sheep sales and £551 from cattle. Yet although the proportion of the total farmland in crops and grass is very small, it constitutes a vital accessory to the hill and its importance for wintering and feeding stuffs cannot be too strongly emphasised. Farms without a reasonable acreage of arable are at a grave disadvantage, for the cost of imported hay may reach £40 per ton, the cost of delivery being an increasingly expensive item as one goes further west and towards the islands. Feeding stuffs grown on the farms consist mainly of grass, grazed or cut for hay or silage, and oats, bruised or cut green for silage. Now that the subsistence element is slight it is hardly surprising to find that oats and grass constitute the main crops. A number of other crops, including turnips, kale and rape, are grown for feeding but in relatively small quantities.

Generally speaking arable land is cultivated on a five- or six-year rotation of potatoes, oats (undersown with grass or rye grass) and three or four years in grass, but there are many variations to suit local conditions. A growing trend is to devote all, or practically all, the arable to grass, now that silage is becoming more popular and is being strongly recommended by the Agricultural College advisers. Haymaking is a traditional but hazardous occupation in the west Highlands, where rain can mean a 35–40 per cent loss of dry matter. Several farms, after losing their hay crop, have come round to silage, which can be made in any weather and also makes for a saving in labour at a time when there are heavy conflicting demands from the sheep. There may be a future for hay drying by extraction units, and experiments have taken place at Ormsary in south Argyll. Ploughing arable land devoted to silage would then take place only occasionally to rejuvenate the grassland. A more striking case, however, concerns the island of Luing, where all the 160 acres of arable on the 4,500-acre estate are devoted to silage. Two cuts are taken annually and the silage forms a base for an intensive stock-rearing unit with 500 Shorthorn–Highland cross cattle and 1,400 Blackface ewes. Such intensification is assisted by the mild climate and gentle slopes, which make possible outwintering on grazings regularly fertilised and reseeded.

Such then is the broad pattern of Highland agriculture. A general emphasis on livestock applies throughout, although the balance between cattle and sheep varies regionally and locally, Orkney for instance being particularly prominent for cattle (Plate 8). But everywhere the demands of the hill restrict the uses to which the arable can be put, and irrespective of quality it is only when the requirements of the hill have been satisfied that specialisation in, say, dairying, vegetables or poultry can be contemplated. Indeed such specialisms are generally restricted to small farms where the hill component is practically absent, as is the case on a number of crofts where bulb growing, pig rearing or vegetable production may be carried on, often under contract to a local grocer or butcher. For the most part, however, concentration must be on hill farming, and the search for stability, long-term and short-term, inevitably moves forward in this context. Some relevant points have already been mentioned, namely the possibilities of silage for feeding and of pedigree cattle for breeding, and some other themes will now be considered.

A new innovation is that of inwintering sheep at home. This is particularly relevant to hoggs, ewe lambs retained for the breeding stock which are too young to withstand the rigours of the hill in their first winter. Hoggs are often sent over to the Black Isle and Strathspey for wintering, but this is becoming an increasingly expensive process and may cost some 50s per animal. Consequently some farmers are attempting to winter the hoggs in sheds at considerably lower cost; Brigadier I. Stewart of Achnacone, Appin, estimates his costs as low as 25s to 30s per hogg, but since subsequent performance on the hill is of critical importance it will be some years before a reliable assessment can be made. Inwintering may also enable a farmer to keep some of the lambs that would normally be sold in the autumn, when the market is unfortunately saturated, and then realise a much higher price in the spring, when they may be sold as fatstock. The gain is particularly worth while if the poorer lambs are retained, since they are likely to make relatively greater progress through the winter. The same arguments may be applied to cattle. At Achnacone Brigadier Stewart has been inwintering calves on slatted floors for some years. The higher prices obtained for the stirks in spring, compared with their value as calves the previous autumn, were found to give a satisfactory margin over feeding stuffs.

Other experiments have been conducted by British Oil and Cake Mills on their farm at South Cathkin, Rutherglen, Lanarkshire, to establish the profitability of inwintering lambs which will not fetch more than 1s per lb. on the store market and fattening them on barley and mixed concentrate. A further possibility has been examined by the Cadzow Sheep Company of West Lothian on their farm at Glendevon; inwintering under full electric lighting may allow lambing every seven months. Such levels of intensification may not be appropriate to Highland farms, but in many cases some progress along these lines might be beneficial and have the advantage of assisting the integration of farming and forestry; the low ground would be used for winter feed, the high grazings could be used in the summer, and since the sheep would be inside for the rest of the year the lower grazings could then be planted without harming agricultural interests.

LAND IMPROVEMENT

Another prominent practice is land improvement. It is important to distinguish between the several kinds of land improvement. First there is the land improvement which aims at reclaiming land from the sea in areas like the Kyle of Tongue and the Beauly and Cromarty Firths, or reclamation of large areas of peat moss as at Claish and Kentra in Ardnamurchan (Plate 16). As a more specific example, the scheme suggested by the Department of Agriculture in 1949 may be cited. It was proposed to reclaim an area of foreshore extending to 400 or 500 acres on the sands of Cockle Ebb in Lewis at an estimated cost of £12,500 in order to provide valuable grazing for Tong farm and enable 100 dairy cattle to be kept. This would have been an important asset not only to the individual farm but also to the economy of Lewis as a whole, since local milk production is small and dependence on mainland supplies is thus necessitated. Scope exists on Grimsay, a small Hebridean island, where £10,000 is needed to rebuild old sea dykes and reclaim 100 acres of arable and grazing which have been encroached on after the destruction of the sea defences during a storm. Such a scheme would also allow access to common grazing, which is isolated at high tide and consequently hazardous to cattle, which are in the habit of swimming home with consequent danger of drowning in the case of young beasts. A smaller 20-acre scheme at Badnabay, Sutherland, has been suggested to provide valuable winter feed, but like the others it has been shelved in preference to reclamation schemes involving the improvement of existing rough grazings. With the introduction of machinery capable of use on the hill (such as the caterpillar tractor), reclamation and reseeding has become common. In the case of old arable, ploughing is usually the first operation before the land is sown out to permanent grass with a nursery crop of oats or rape. On rougher ground, however, surface dressing with lime and basic slag is the most effective method, since ploughing peaty ground usually leads to infestation with reeds later on, as was found on the Great Glen cattle ranch where heavy machinery was used to reclaim rough land. The process of land improvement has also been accelerated by government support; the Hill Farming Act of 1946, following the Royal Commission of 1944, continued the hill sheep and hill cattle subsidies which had started in 1941 and also provided a fund of £4 million to be used for making 50 per cent grants towards the cost of comprehensive improvement schemes on hill sheep farms. These Marginal Agricultural Production (MAP) grants have been hailed as the greatest boom to post-war hill farming, and the Livestock Rearing Act of 1951 made a further £16 million available, though following legislation in 1959 the scheme closed at the end of 1963 and was replaced by the Winter Keep (Scotland) Scheme, with provision for ploughing grants and grassland renovation but not for reclamation.

It is possible that public attention has been directed for the most part to the land improvement schemes on crofting townships, notably those in Lewis where the rough grazings are extensive and accessible and where a progressive and youthful element still exists amongst the crofter population to take advantage of the funds which the Crofters Commission can invest in such schemes. The 9,000 acres improved in Lewis have meant an improvement in the quality and quantity of cattle and increased numbers of fat lambs, with better lambing from ewes in sound condition. There is, however, a certain winter-keep problem through the need to keep pace with the increased summer carrying capacity. A high rate of grant (85 per cent) is allowed to cover the cost of carting the 10 tons of shell sand from the nearest beach required for each acre, the cost of fencing, fertiliser and grass seed, which amount to about £4 per acre, and a labour input of forty-eight hours per acre. Progress has also been made on some of the 'scattalds' of Shetland, following the allocation of sections of these township grazings to individual crofters, and in townships throughout the crofting counties as parts of integrated farming–forestry schemes. All this good work should not obscure the efforts of individual farmers, whose piecemeal schemes do not attract the same attention. Examples here include Killichronan in Mull and Lephinmore in Argyll, where the West of Scotland Agricultural College has shown that capital invested over a ten-year period has been retrieved through extra income from increased ewe stocking and higher lambing rates. Very often land may be improved to increase the viability of the farm and justify the retention of a second worker on a unit that theoretically requires one and a half men to work it efficiently. Alternatively a small acreage may be reseeded as a lambing enclosure or to lower the amount of imported feeding stuffs necessary. An area of hill may be improved to develop the grazing potential in conjunction with a forestry project.

Great importance is attached to the need for greater intensification, which requires more development capital and a long-term price policy. Sheep may be remarkable animals, and with ordinary management can be left to make a modest return, but this approach is showing signs of breaking down and is unlikely to be adequate in future if a flock is going to stand as a profitable enterprise. The financial position of Highland farmers compared with their Lowland counterparts is examined in Table 3. Inwintering and land improvement would go a long way to reducing the Highland farmers' dependence on the store market for their livestock, where there is always a risk of unrealistically low prices if bidding is slow at auction marts. Fatstock production would be feasible, and the organisation of the selling on a

Table 3. FARM INCOMES IN THE CROFTING COUNTIES AND
THE REST OF SCOTLAND

Type of Farm	Net income (£ per acre)		Production grants as percentage of net income	
	Crofting counties	Rest of Scotland	Crofting counties	Rest of Scotland
Hill sheep	0·2	0·5	66	60
Upland rearing	3·0	3·2	123	110
Livestock with arable	7·0	8·5	77	48
Dairy	7·0	9·2	52	31

Source: *Scotland (1964) p. 9*

co-operative basis, along the lines already developed by such concerns as West Highland Crofters and Farmers and Kintyre Farmers, might be particularly helpful to island farmers, since large consignments could be arranged. But fatstock production needs good grazings, a consideration which places a premium on development capital for land improvement. If farmland received the same rate of investment as land planted with trees (£40 to £70 per acre), agriculture would be in a much better position to rival forestry as an employer of labour.

THE PATTERN OF LANDHOLDINGS

In all these cases, as with the crofting schemes, improvement makes sense strictly in the context of the individual farm unit. 'Any person owning or using rural land is more vitally concerned with the margin of profitability than the physical margin between different types of cultivation. A profitable farm or estate may well have large areas of uncultivated land on it' (Wibberley, 1959, p. 141). As the Zuckerman Committee went on to say, 'the individual holding has to be taken as it stands. The effect is an almost random scatter of improvement and a proportion of the grants made probably serve only to prolong the separate existence of basically uneconomic holdings.' The Committee regretted that the structure of landholdings inhibited the development of the potential productivity of the land as a whole, and that because of the importance attached to private rights, applied rigidly to particular plots of land, capital subsidies could not be geared effectively to the rationalisation of farm boundaries.

These are very important points for Highland agriculture. Any scheme for developing the industry must obviously accord with the national interest, and if, for instance, livestock products can be readily imported at competitive prices it may well be asked whether or not it is better for the nation to invest in manufacturing for export than to invest in Highland land improvement to increase livestock production which will then be subsidised. Yet when a scheme can be justified the individual farm approach will give a piecemeal pattern of improvement which may not be as fully in the general interest as a co-ordinated regional scheme. When subsidies are considered as well, the extent to which funds should be directed to the protection of basically non-viable units becomes a crucial point for debate. The Hill Farming Committee (Scotland, 1944) argued that subsidies offered no prospect of real improvement in the general state of the industry and that policy should be directed to creating an economically sound industry rather than propping up a decaying one. Should long-term subsidies be abandoned in favour of more liberal grants and loans for land improvement, coupled with attention to the landholding structure?

Certainly the structure of farm units and landholdings needs attention. The estate map of the Highlands (Fig. 13) gives a very uneven distribution pattern, suggesting that several centuries of *laissez-faire* evolution have not produced a satisfactory pattern for present purposes. The process is complex, but for a local example the Lochaber estate boundaries shown on Fig. 4 may be compared with the present pattern. As has already been noted, many estates changed hands and broke up early in the nineteenth century contemporaneous with the improving movement, while other sections were sold as deer forests some decades later. In the twentieth century some other large properties have been sold in separate lots, such as Glencoe, Glengarry and Ardnamurchan, while purchases by the Forestry Commission and tenant farmers have all helped to double the number of landholdings from 60 in 1900 to 137 in 1960.

The pattern of farm units is still more varied and is very dependent on estate policy in each case (Fig. 14). On the best agricultural land where farming has always been supreme the tradition of tenant farms, dating back to the beginning of commercial sheep farming, still persists, although a number are now owner-occupied. By contrast, in more mountainous districts where deer forests were popular the agricultural interest has tended to remain in the landowner's hands, and in these cases a whole estate, apart from small sections which may be let because of the difficulty of integrating them with the rest of the estate, is managed as one farm. The

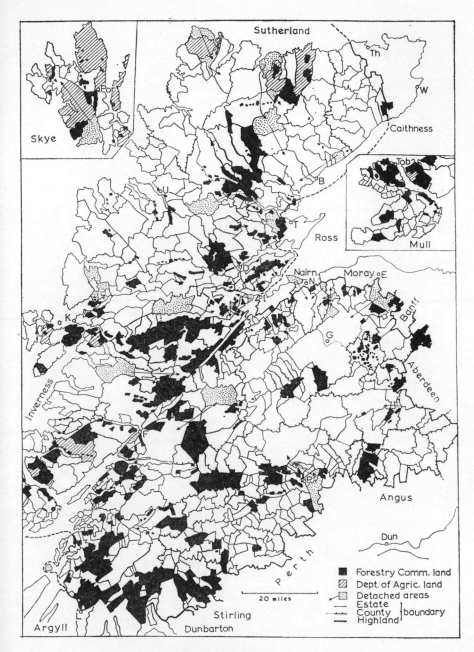

Fig. 13 *Highland estates*

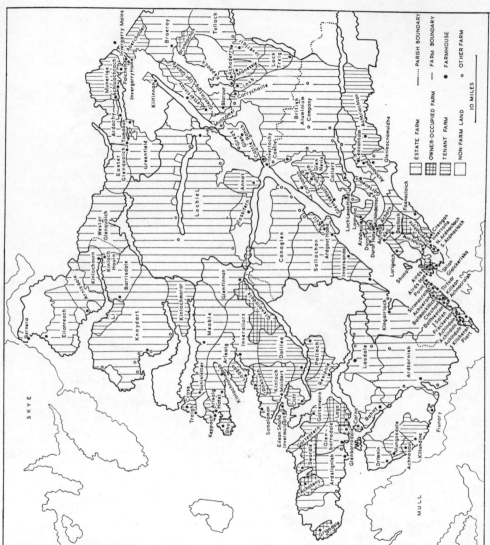

Fig. 14 Classification of farms in Lochaber and north Argyll

largest estates in Lochaber are in this category, namely Knoydart, Lochiel and the British Aluminium Company. In all cases the home farms cover areas exceeding 50,000 acres and are managed by shepherds stationed at strategic points with a small nucleus around the home farm itself, including a tractorman, cattleman, handyman and the farm manager. Peripheral sections are let: Li, loch Hourn is stocked by a tenant at Arnisdale, on the Lochiel estate Annat farm on the south-eastern corner is let, while other farms along Lochielside have been sold, notably Drimsallie and Fassifern, and on the B.A.C. estate farms in upper Glen Spean and on the edge of Rannoch Moor are let. However, on estates owned by the Secretary of State for Scotland on behalf of the Forestry Commission or Department of Agriculture tenant farms, are the general rule on all land outside forestry and crofting.

To mention these contrasts is not to criticise any section of the farming or landowning community but merely to illustrate variation in the size of farms and ask whether this accords with the optimum pattern. This poses a further question in itself, since the concept of the optimum farm is difficult to define; while the smallest farms should be absorbed, the desirability of the large family farm as opposed to the large estate farm is debatable. While family farms may produce more, especially on poorer types of land, efficiently run estate farms should allow a better return provided land is not being seriously underused. If the land is not making a true contribution – and on some sporting estates agriculture may be dangerously run down in an effort to maintain a wilderness for sport – there may be a case for division into smaller units as well as a change of management. In other instances consolidation of fragmented holdings is called for, and the landholdings on the island of Lismore (Fig. 15) are a case in point. Most farms now take in pieces of land, comprising former farms or crofts, which are not adjacent, and this situation, in addition to the small total size of each agricultural unit, reduces efficiency. Should the problem be left to solve itself through a dwindling population, or would a co-ordinated reorganisation and development plan be justifiable?[1]

THE CROFTING PROBLEM

If it is considered desirable to eliminate the extremes of small units on the one hand and underdeveloped large units on the other, then the crofting problem (Collier, 1955) enters prominently into the picture. Because of the generous legal definition of the size and rent requirements for croft status,

[1] The H.I.D.B. have powers to take over land which is being improperly used, but a case is difficult to prove in practice.

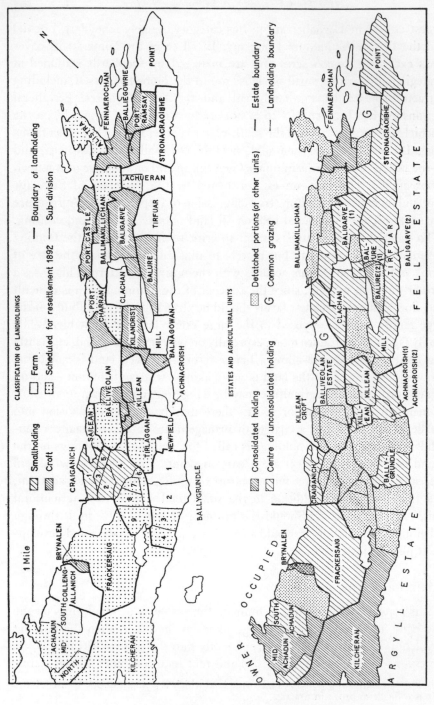

Fig. 15 Fragmented holdings on the island of Lismore, 1963

the bulk of the small tenant farms in the Highlands are inevitably crofts and as such enjoy a number of statutory privileges, including security of tenure, the right to a fair rent and compensation for agricultural improvements carried out. It has been argued that these benefits have perpetuated what may be described as a *Reliktlandschaft* by giving rigidity for social reasons to smallholdings lacking economic viability to varying extents. Some of the holdings laid out by the Department of Agriculture in the inter-war period are quite large, and some enjoy the added benefit of having grazings apportioned to each holding instead of the common grazing (Plate 18). However, the nineteenth-century townships, crofter–fishing settlements especially, where viability was never the aim at any time, are often placed in difficulties with declining employment in estate farming, fishing and stalking deer, industries upon which many crofters once depended (Plate 17). Inevitably, therefore, the crofting population has declined, with emigration as a voluntary process increasing after the improvement in communications by way of reliable steamer and rail services to the south. But that is not to say that those who remain have adequate resources; over-population is still a feature of the crofting system, and hence some reform and development is indicated. In view of its legal distinction, however, the crofting component of the Highland agricultural problem is looked after by a separate government body.

How prominent is the crofting element in Highland agriculture? This is clearly a basic question and one which has been largely answered by the work of Mr H. A. Moisley (1962*b*). The crofting population has been estimated at between 64,000 and 80,000, that is, roughly a quarter of the total population of the crofting counties or two-fifths of the rural (non-burghal) population. But the distribution of crofting within this area is very uneven; if rented smallholdings smaller than 50 acres, which are practically synonymous with croft holdings, are taken as a percentage of the total number of farm units, then figures of over 90 per cent are obtained for the Outer Hebrides, Shetland and the north-west mainland. In parishes north of the Great Glen the proportion seldom falls below 70 per cent (except in parts of Caithness and Easter Ross), but south and east of this line there is a gradual falling off to below 30 per cent in some cases. There is a very low figure of 21 per cent for Orkney, because here, although 80 per cent of the agricultural units are smaller than 50 acres, some two-thirds of them are owner-occupied and therefore do not enjoy legal croft status. If the actual amount of land in crofting is considered, then the same broad pattern emerges which allowed Moisley to conclude that 'crofting land dominated the landscape only in the Outer Hebrides, Skye and Tiree, and to a lesser extent, in the west and north coastal parishes from Ardnamurchan to (but not including) Caithness. Elsewhere the agricultural structure is predominantly one of substantial single farms' (Moisley, 1962*b*, p. 87).

Crofting, therefore, tends to be most prominent in those areas where limited land resources and remoteness ensured the late and partial introduction of agricultural innovations. The agricultural revolution was never fully effective in the north-west mainland, Hebrides and Shetland, and hence remnants of traditional techniques still persist along with Gaelic speech and culture. Moreover it was these areas, where depopulation was least marked at the end of the nineteenth century, which were declared 'congested districts' and benefited most from the land settlement schemes initiated in the early twentieth century. Where crofting had largely disappeared there was no attempt to revive it. Legislation has therefore served to accentuate the distinction between east and west within the Highlands, and in 1964, of the 19,276 crofts mentioned in the Crofters Commission register, less than 40 per cent were on the mainland, 30 per cent were in the Outer Hebrides, 15 per cent in Shetland and 20 per cent in the other islands (mainly Skye and Tiree).

Throughout much of the mainland therefore crofting now represents only the relict core left by long-continued processes of reorganisation. This legacy moreover transcends the boundaries of the crofting counties, for in parts of the north-east there is a tradition of small farms or crofts representing the attempts of small farmers to reclaim marginal land on the periphery of the large estate farms which emerged after the improving movement. In these cases, however, common grazings were rarely a characteristic and it is noteworthy that the original intention was to discriminate between the individual smallholdings and the crofting communities with a township organisation and the existence of common grazings. The crofting counties were merely a comprehensive context adopted in 1886 within which certain areas were to be declared 'crofting parishes'; to claim this status the existence of common grazings, or proof of their former existence in the recent past, was essential. However, the subsequent extension of the provisions of the Acts to all rented smallholdings below 50 acres in the crofting counties has removed this distinction and at the same time arbitrarily deprives many Highland smallholdings of the benefits of legal croft status simply because they lie outside these seven counties. It must also be remembered that within the crofting counties there is an important distinction between crofting communities in the north and west, generally with a small average croft size, and the individual smallholdings created in the early twentieth century, which are generally much larger and are functionally small farms but which then qualified for croft status because their arable was less than 50 acres. It is unfortunate that this contrast receives no legal endorsement, for it renders the problem of sustaining genuine crofting communities more difficult; the bulk of any funds set aside to support crofting agriculture on an acreage basis will automatically go to the larger, richer crofts in the east and south.

Crofting constitutes a complex problem and one which has received considerable attention during the last fifteen years. The Taylor Commission was appointed to inquire into crofting conditions and reported in 1954 to the effect that crofting 'as now organised is fighting a losing battle against the social and economic forces of the day' (Scotland, 1954, para. 10). They recommended legislation to secure the reorganisation of townships. Under the Crofters (Scotland) Act of 1955 the Crofters Commission was reconstituted with powers to reorganise, develop and regulate crofting. Moreover a considerable number of academic and other studies have been made on crofting conditions in various parts of the Highlands, the greatest contribution coming from the Department of Geography at Glasgow. By making detailed inquiries on every croft in a number of parishes in the Outer Hebrides a comprehensive picture has been built up, and these methods have also been used by other workers in different parts of the crofting counties. It is proposed to examine the results of a crofting survey in one area (Lochaber) as a preliminary to discussing ameliorative measures.

A CROFTING SURVEY OF LOCHABER

Fig. 4 sets out the extent of the croft land in Lochaber and attempted to discriminate between the different types of croft, separating the resettlement townships of the early nineteenth century from the various later attempts at land settlement. Lochaber is marginal to the main crofting region as discussed above, but smallholdings are very prominent in certain parishes, notably in Ardnamurchan and Sunart where the valuation of croft land exceeds that of farmland (Plate 16). Areally the amount of land in crofting has probably changed little in the last eighty years as a result of the protective legislation enacted in 1886. Indeed the land settlement which was prominent in Glenelg and Ardnamurchan especially has probably sustained a considerable increase. A number of communities have disappeared, however, notably on the Ardnish peninsula of the Arisaig estate, Eilean Shona and

Eigneig in Moidart, the North Morar townships east of Kylesmorar, Skiary on Loch Hourn and some small groups in parts of Morvern. In all these cases there was little land, no alternative employment and no road access which would make a journey to work feasible.

Altogether some 741 holdings were noted in 1962, but only 440 of these could be classified as agricultural units, for 180 had no stock or crops and were either completely derelict or used only for hay. The remaining 121 were sublet, legally or informally, to other crofters or farmers. Subletting was officially discouraged for a long time because depopulation might thereby be encouraged. But subletting is generally the result rather than the cause of dwindling, and is now encouraged in preference to the croft lying derelict. Of the 440 agricultural units only 198 have sheep stocks while 372 keep cattle, a reflection of the limited grazings in many nineteenth-century townships, where provision was often made only for summering cattle. Arable is prominent in that 376 units have some arable cultivation, but only in 196 cases was this sufficient to justify application to the Crofters Commission for cropping grants; on many crofts the area cultivated does not exceed one-eighth of an acre, and those crofters applying for cropping grants were cultivating on average only 2·5 acres.

But there are some interesting contrasts within Lochaber, examined in Table 4. There is a high proportion of derelict crofts in Arisaig and Moidart (33 per cent), Ardnamurchan and Sunart (30 per cent) and Lismore and Appin (25 per cent), a feature which, along with the high rate of subletting in the latter parish (33 per cent), reflects the prominence and inadequacy of tiny holdings which are suitable only for cattle. The other parishes show up well, in that Glenelg and Kilmonivaig have a high proportion of holdings with sheep stocks – 54 per cent and 48 per cent respectively compared with only 8 per cent in Arisaig and Moidart. This is due to the large common grazings allocated in Kilmonivaig in the nineteenth century, and in Glenelg to common grazing extensions and the establishment of smallholdings. Ardgour, Kilmallie and Kilmonivaig show the greatest interest in cropping, with 56, 40 and 39 per cent respectively of the crofts in these parishes applying for cropping grants, whereas in Glenelg and Lismore and Appin this falls off to 14 per cent. Parishes around Fort William therefore enjoy relatively healthy crofting conditions, with an increasing element of decay further away.

In Lochaber only 10 per cent of the crofters are working on their holdings full-time. But even this low figure may be unrealistically high, because some tenants of working age may well obtain part of their income from

Table 4. A CROFTING SURVEY OF LOCHABER AND
NORTH ARGYLL, 1962

Parish	Croft holdings	Agricultural units						Crofter tenants				
		(a)	(b)	(c)	(d)	(e)	(f)	(a)	(b)	(c)	(d)	(e)
Ardgour	50	41	40	34	13	4	5	46	5	31	9	1
Ardnamurchan and Sunart	211	117	110	99	53	64	30	194	18	72	64	40
Arisaig and Moidart	73	44	42	41	6	24	5	59	5	37	15	1
Glenelg	106	66	48	56	57	21	19	95	13	40	30	10
Kilmallie	124	81	72	71	19	21	22	123	7	71	26	–
Kilmonivaig	66	45	39	29	32	16	5	58	4	27	22	5
Lismore and Appin	102	42	21	38	17	26	34	102	11	44	34	13
Morvern	9	4	4	4	1	4	1	5	1	3	1	–
Total	741	440	376	372	198	180	121	682	64	325	201	70

Key

Agricultural units: (a) Total agricultural units
(b) Total with arable cultivation
(c) Total with cattle stock
(d) Total with sheep stock
(e) Number of croft holdings which are lying derelict or used only for hay
(f) Number of croft holdings sublet.

Crofter tenants: (a) Number of tenants
(b) Number working full-time on their croft
(c) Number working part-time on their croft
(d) Number of tenants who are retired
(e) Number of absentee tenants.

Source: *Field survey*

interests in tourism and business which the survey did not reveal. Again, it must be appreciated that the difference between the number of crofts worked full-time and the number of viable holdings is quite considerable; some full-time crofters may well be underemployed. Not surprisingly practically half the crofters are working permanently or periodically in another job with the British Aluminium Company, the Forestry Commission, the Post Office, the county council and so on. Another 30 per cent are retired people, and the remaining 11 per cent are living away from their crofts, often permanently. But interesting again are some of the variations within Lochaber. The proportion of full-time crofters is slightly higher in Ardgour and Glenelg than in other parishes, but overall the differences are slight and the small numbers involved do not make the figures here very meaningful. More significantly the proportion of part-time crofters is highest in Kilmallie (69 per cent), Ardgour (67 per cent) and Arisaig and Moidart (64 per cent), falling to 37 per cent in Ardnamurchan and Sunart. On the other hand the proportion of absentees is highest in Ardnamurchan and Sunart (21 per cent), Lismore and Appin (13 per cent) and Glenelg (11 per cent) and the proportion of retired tenants is as high as 38 per cent in Kilmonivaig and 33 per cent in Ardnamurchan and Sunart, Glenelg, and Lismore and Appin.

These figures tie in to some extent with conclusions already noted. In parts of Lochaber, notably Ardgour and Kilmallie, crofting is relatively vigorous, with a good average size of holding and a fair level of agricultural activity (82 per cent and 65 per cent respectively of the crofts are agricultural units), and the young tenantry is supported by a wide range of ancillary employment offered in the Fort William area. In much of Lismore and Appin opportunities are good but croft land is just too limited in extent to support agriculture on any scale today. Less than half the crofts are farming units and many crofters are retired or absentee. On the island of Lismore especially crofting has largely disappeared, and the majority of the crofts are grazed in conjunction with one of the many small livestock farms there, as illustrated in Fig. 15. In Ardnamurchan and Sunart the small size of many holdings, coupled with remoteness and limited ancillary employment apart from the forestry in Sunart, makes for a similar picture of decay in spite of crofting's impressive areal extent in this parish. However, there are eighteen full-time crofters in this parish, which suggests some local variations. In Glenelg and Kilmonivaig generalisation is also difficult, for a prominent sheep economy on the crofts is evident yet many of the tenants are retired or absent, pointing to the limited opportunities in parts of these far-flung parishes. In Arisaig and Moidart, however, there is a substantial element of dereliction but the age structure of the crofters who remain is good, with 64 per cent of the tenants working in other jobs. Morvern is omitted from the discussion since crofting is today restricted to a few holdings at Drimnin.

Much, therefore, depends on the availability of other employment in each locality, and much depends on the size of the crofts. In many cases it is not practicable for the crofter to follow a reasonable rotation, and for that reason, and also because the main interest of many crofters lies necessarily outside agriculture, the standard of cultivation is low and little advantage is taken of agricultural grants available through the Crofters Commission. On the other hand improvement of common grazings has in some cases increased the agricultural capacity. Clearly even parish figures are misleading generalisations to some extent, for every township is different. Some case studies are therefore mentioned in Table 5. In the case of the

Table 5. SOME CASE STUDIES OF CROFT SETTLEMENTS, 1962

Township and type	Parish	Holdings			Agriculture			Labour				Common grazings	
		(a)	(b)	(c)	(d)	(e)	(f)	(g)	(h)	(j)	(k)	(l)	(m)
Crofting township													
Blaich	Ardgour	25*	10	10	10	9	7	5	5	–	–	2,936	293
Bohuntine	Kilmonivaig	27	13	13	13	8	12†	–	7	6	–	6,000	461
Bunacaimb	Arisaig and Moidart	7	7	7	7	7	–	–	5	2	–	550	79
Corriebeg	Kilmallie	4	1	1	1	1	1	1	–	–	–	1,000	1,000
Carnoch	Lismore and Appin	35	32	14	1	14	–	–	26	4	2	1,940	61
Fishing township													
Camusbane	Glenelg	23	17	4	3	3	2	–	3	8	4	960‡	56
Port Ramsay	Lismore and Appin	13	13	–	–	–	–	–	–	9	4	47	4
Sanna	Ardnamurchan and Sunart	32	20	2	1	2	1	1	1	7	12	496	25
Individual croft													
Dalnatrad	Lismore and Appin	1	1	–	–	–	–	–	–	1	–	13	13
Rhemore	Morvern	1	1	1	1	1	1	1	–	–	–	135	135
Smallholdings													
Beolary	Glenelg	7	7	6	6	6	6	–	6	1	–	6,000	857
Drimnatorran	Ardnamurchan and Sunart	5	3	3	2	2	2	2	–	1	–	9,500	3,167

(a) Number of holdings
(b) Number of tenants today
(c) Number of agricultural units
(d) Agricultural units with arable cultivation
(e) Agricultural units with cattle stock
(f) Agricultural units with sheep stock
(g) Full-time crofter tenant
(h) Part-time crofter tenant
(j) Retired crofter tenant
(k) Absentee crofter
(l) Size of township grazings (acres)
(m) Grazings per tenant.

* Now 11 holdings after reorganisation
† Club sheep stock
‡ This figure includes 660 acres added as a sheep grazing in the late nineteenth century.

Source: *Field survey*

orthodox township the existence of sheep grazings at Blaich and Corriebeg has much to do with the viable crofts which these townships support. Most of the crofts are in agricultural use, but this is clearly not the case at Carnoch (Glencoe), where the availability of employment in tourism and the Kinlochleven aluminium factory tends to restrict interest in agriculture to cattle, with only one holding having arable cultivation. By contrast, at Bunacaimb (Arisaig) there is similarly a prosperous community but an admirable combination of crofting agriculture and tourism. Dwindling, however, is evident where other employment is limited: Corriebeg consists now of only one holding, albeit a viable one, and Bohuntine, tucked away up Glen Roy, is declining in spite of its extensive grazings. Even on the newer smallholdings which generally allow a substantial sheep stock there has been some amalgamation, and many smallholders have other jobs.

Much more serious and consistent, however, are the problems of the old crofter–fishing communities, where holdings remain very small indeed even after considerable amalgamation. There are few agricultural units relative to the number of tenants remaining, and the number of tenants shows a big reduction from the number of holdings in 1886, when most of the crofts were visited by the Crofters Commission and their 'fair rents' recorded. This situation is a response to the local employment difficulties in Arnisdale, Lismore and west Ardnamurchan, which means that most of the tenants are retired or live away from their holdings. The single croft holdings, small pieces of land probably once lotted here and there for shepherds and other estate workers, are in very much the same position, as shown by the case of Dalnatrad in Appin. But there are exceptions, and at Rhemore in Morvern a high degree of intensification secures a marginal viability for this slightly larger holding.

A DEVELOPMENT PLAN FOR CROFTING

It is clear that a considerable amount of croft land is being underused, a surprising situation in view of the heavy pressure on limited resources which is still typical of parts of the Highlands. But crofting is symbolic of the incompleteness of the agricultural revolution in the Highlands and the failure to make a clear distinction between the agricultural and industrial population. Crofting legislation ensures that this distinction will remain blurred. Hence the crofting problem is only partially an agricultural one;

Plate 1   *The Great Glen*

Looking north from Fort William and the estate of Caol, a clear impression of this natural routeway can be gained. Although it is not aligned to the best advantage for north–south movement in Scotland today, it was important in the prehistoric colonisation of the north by people from Ireland and was of great strategic importance in the unification of Scotland. Note the Caledonian Canal and evidence of afforestation.

Plate 2 Glenmore–Glenelg

Glenmore opens on to the Sound of Sleat and exhibits a profile which is typical of west Highland glens. However, around Glenelg the grazings are relatively rich and support Cheviot sheep as opposed to the more usual Blackface breed. Afforestation has taken place higher up the glen and there are signs of nucleated settlement at the mouth.

Plate 3   Loch Leven

The view looks eastwards from near the confluence with Loch Linnhe towards Glencoe and Ballachulish, where the old slate quarries can be seen. The small raised beaches are most important for agriculture and also for settlement, which is particularly considerable on the 'Gold Coast' (North Ballachulish and Onich) as well as at Ballachulish and Kinlochleven. A bridge across the narrows, replacing the ferry, would be a great help to north–south communication.

Plate 4   Sound of Mull

Morvern, on the northern side of the Sound of Mull, is an extremely favoured area, with a mild climate and fertile soil derived from basalt. The Forestry Commission has made extensive plantings at Fiunary, but inaccessibility has discouraged many forms of development – Morvern is one of the few mainland districts still largely dependent on sea transport. Lochaline village, at the mouth of the loch, was built following the clearances and is supported by a prosperous silica-sand mining industry.

Plate 5   Ross of Mull

There is a great contrast in scenery between the mosses around Bunessan, partly colonised
by crofting settlement, and the rugged surfaces of the Ross of Mull granite. In the background, beyond Loch Scridain, the scenery is dominated by the basalt with its more
tabular appearance.

Plate 6   Isle of Staffa

Here the basalt rock exhibits a remarkable columnar form, the result of rapid cooling. Although a key tourist attraction, Staffa suffers, like

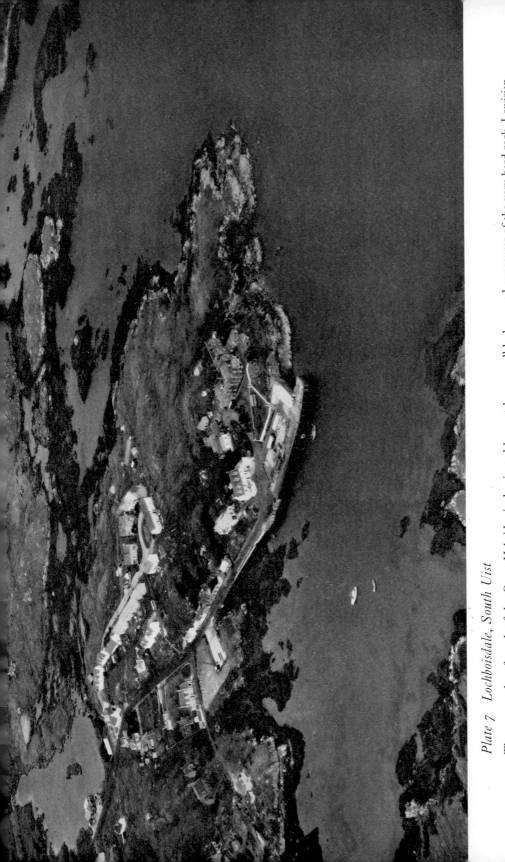

Plate 7   Lochboisdale, South Uist

The topography of much of the Outer Hebrides is dominated by peat bogs, small lochans and exposures of the very hard rock, Lewisian gneiss. Resources for agriculture are much better on the Atlantic coast, where the machair sands provide excellent grazing. Lochboisdale lies at the end of the steamer route from Oban.

Plate 8   Orkney

The superior land resources of Orkney give rise to a prosperous agriculture and a high density of dispersed rural settlement. Featured here is part of the causeway system linking the mainland with the southern isles of Burray and South Ronaldsay.

Plate 9 Callanish, Isle of Lewis

A typical crofting settlement in the Outer Hebrides. There is great variation in housing conditions, although many of the thatched houses are now used only as byres. Contrary to what might be supposed, the 'lazy beds' represent a massive effort to overcome the limited depth of soil by the creation of artificial gardens. Visible in the distance are the standing stones of Callanish, a Bronze Age megalith which was cleared of accumulated peat in 1872.

Plate 10   Jarlshof, Quendale, Shetland

An excellent site near Sumburgh Head offering a sheltered anchorage, sandy soils, water supply, fishing resources, and local stone and clay. It was used in Neolithic times, as well as in the Bronze Age and in Viking and medieval times. Movement of sand away from the site has revealed many cairns, huts and enclosures.

Plate 11   Iona

The cathedral is part of the Benedictine Abbey founded in about 1200, which became the high church of the diocese of the Isles in the early sixteenth century. The island is associated with St Columba, whose monastery lay just to the north of the cathedral; for missionary activity in the sixth century Iona offered seclusion on the fringe of the Scottish kingdom of Dalriada.

Plate 12   Dornoch, Sutherland

A small town important as the seat of the bishopric of Caithness, established by David I.
Lacking a good harbour, it was unable to maintain its importance in the field of commerce;
Tain became the principal port on the Dornoch Firth, until its harbour silted up, while
the attraction of the main lines of communication around the head of the Dornoch Firth
has left the burgh in a backwater position compared with Brora and Golspie further north.

Plate 13   Fort George, Inverness

Still used as an army barracks, Fort George was built after 1745 as part of a chain of garrisons holding the line of the Great Glen. It was linked to the south by the military road from Coupar Angus through Braemar and Corgarff, and built in a position such that troops could easily be moved across the Inverness and Cromarty Firths in the event of trouble in the north.

Plate 14   Dunrobin Castle, Sutherland

The estate mansion is still a prominent feature in the Highlands, although the fragmentation of properties has left many of them redundant. Some have been adapted as hotels or private residences, but others lie derelict or have been demolished. Dunrobin is still associated with the Sutherland estates, although these are now relatively small.

Plate 15   Durness, Sutherland

One of many crofting communities established on the north coast of Sutherland as a result of the clearances from the straths inland. The settlement pattern is typically linear. Although the ruthlessness with which the changes were carried out has tended to be exaggerated, through the publicity which Patrick Sellar attracted when factor on the Sutherland estates, the fact remains that the coastal sites offered for resettlement were some of the poorest and most exposed in the north.

Plate 16   Acharacle, Argyll

With the introduction of commercial sheep grazing, small areas of peat moss along the
coast offered some scope for the resettlement of the displaced small tenants if periodic
employment could provide an income to supplement the produce from reclaimed land.
The land on the edges of Kentra Moss at Acharacle was taken in by tenants on the Ardnamurchan estate.

Plate 17   Scorraig, Little Loch Broom, Wester Ross

Here the long, narrow arable holdings of the crofting township show up clearly since they are separated by dykes, in contrast to the many cases where crofts are not even fenced. However, Scorraig lies on the northern shore of Little Loch Broom, where lack of road access makes a combination of crofting agriculture and regular employment elsewhere almost impossible; dwindling has now reached an advanced stage.

Plate 18   Burravoe, Yell, Shetland

The crofting landscape in Shetland is distinct in that the usual west Highland form of township settlement is absent and crofts are functionally more like small consolidated farms. The result of this is only a very small village settlement, with shops, churches and council houses forming a rather loose and incoherent focal point for the area.

Plate 19   Castlebay, Isle of Barra

A Hebridean service centre and steamer terminal where the proprietor encouraged a more compact and regular layout of buildings in the centre of a group of crofting townships. Offshore is the recently restored Kishmul Castle, seat of the MacNeil of Barra.

Plate 20   St Kilda

Village Bay is the only section of the island's coast where steep cliffs are absent, but there was inadequate shelter for a safe anchorage and boats had therefore to be hauled on to the sandy beach. The island is now uninhabited apart from a small service establishment, but the old main street is clearly visible, as is the hill dyke and the various dry-stone structures formerly used for storage.

Plate 21   Inverness (pop. 31,278)

The largest town in the crofting counties and one which must play a key role in any programme of Highland development. With the river crossing point guarded by the castle, Inverness had a strategic location at the northern end of the Great Glen and also at a point where the coastal plain is limited by a tongue of high ground. In spite of early sea contacts with the continent of Europe, the main growth awaited the opening of reliable transport routes south across the Ness–Spey watershed.

Plate 22   Fort William (pop. 3,236)

Originally the site of the garrison of Inverlochy, rebuilt as Fort William, a vigorous urban community has developed providing services for the Ardnamurchan and Lochaber districts. Lack of good building land has forced development along a linear axis around the head of Loch Linnhe, but planning is also hindered by a separation of the burgh from the rest of the urban unit for local government purposes.

Plate 23   Oban (pop. 6,738)

Oban lies in a nodal position for shipping movements, at the focus of the Sound of Mull and the Firth of Lorn. The realisation of its potential for tourism in modern times was accelerated by the arrival of the railway from Glasgow in 1880, after which Oban became known as the 'Charing Cross of the North'. Fishing is important, as are Oban's service functions, which include stock marketing.

Plate 24   Invergordon (pop. 1,839)

Invergordon has an excellent site on flat well-drained land adjacent to the deep water of Cromarty Firth. These resources found their main use in the past as a naval base, in connection with which the oil-storage tanks were built. But as similar sites in more accessible areas become congested, industrial growth is becoming feasible and an aluminium smelter is under construction.

Plate 25   Lerwick, Shetland (pop. 5,860)

Lerwick is the main urban centre for Shetland and an important port for white fish and the summer herring fishing. Its recent growth has been wholly at the expense of the rural areas, as the population of Shetland is falling. There is a need to establish more viable village centres, but although this constitutes an attractive physical plan the economic base is difficult to find, since forestry and tourism have made limited headway.

Plate 26   Stornoway, Isle of Lewis (pop. 5,202)

The main town on the island and the base of the local tweed industry. But the fabric of rural life is still strong in the large townships which are within commuting distance of Stornoway and where domestic weaving can be efficiently integrated with factory-based spinning and finishing. Stornoway has benefited from recent schemes to expand island fishing fleets.

Plate 27   Crinan Canal, Ardrishaig

The canals cuts across Kintyre and by avoiding the often stormy passage around the Mull of Kintyre shortens the distance between the Clyde and the west Highlands by some ninety miles. Opened in 1801 after several financial difficulties, the increasing size of vessels reduced its scope as a major routeway, although for some time connections with canal boats at Ardrishaig and Crinan gave a passenger route to Oban. 'Puffers' still use the canal en route to the Islay distilleries, and pleasure craft are important.

Plate 28   Mallaig

As the main transport routes to the islands shifted back to land routes coupled with the shortest sea crossings from the mainland, the need arose for new steamer terminals at the railheads. Mallaig lies at the end of the West Highland Railway from Glasgow and Fort William and has steamer connections with Skye and the Outer Hebrides. It is also an important fishing port for the South Minch. The site is very limited, however, and settlement has been forced to spread discontinuously around Mallaig Bay.

Plate 29 Lybster, Caithness

A small fishing community which has lost ground in modern times to larger ports such as
Wick. A striking feature in contrast to the morphology of many west-coast settlements is
the level site and regular, planned layout of buildings.

Plate 30   British Aluminium Company, Fort William

Lochaber was the third of a series of reduction works built in the Highlands when hydro-power resources were adequate to cope with the scale of aluminium production needed at the time. Even so adequate power could only be obtained at Fort William by linking three catchment areas. Changing technological conditions can now justify larger smelters drawing electricity from the grid, as will be the case at Invergordon.

Plate 31   Pulp and Paper Mill, Fort William

The nodal position of Fort William as a collecting centre for Highland softwoods, together with good water supplies and land and sea transport, account for the location of this new industrial development, one of the largest in the Highlands.

Plate 32   Loch Luichart, Easter Ross

Although less steeply graded than their west-coast counterparts, the eastern glens have the advantage of a higher and more regular discharge and the main catchment areas have now been exploited for hydro-electric power. Undeniable economic benefits have followed, but the 'amenity lobby' has frequently criticised the design and layout of the main installations and, perhaps with more justification, the erection of pylons.

though there may be a continuing agricultural activity, the quality of the soil in many cases is poor, and the crofts are largely used for housing accommodation and to provide a base from which the crofter can engage in non-agricultural activities. Indeed an agricultural solution to the crofting economy would be tantamount to further depopulation and resettlement. Simpson (1962, p. 64) has calculated the crofting population at 59,212, but considers that only 10,863 could be supported by agriculture alone.

This was the situation which faced the newly reconstituted Crofters Commission in 1955. They quickly insisted that 'it is the essence of our mandate to maintain the crofting population' (Report for 1955–6, para. 110), and went on to assert that 'agriculture by itself cannot support viable communities' (Report for 1959, para. 63). In view of this they were forced to discourage the policy of producing economically viable units by amalgamation, because 'each amalgamation means the elimination of a potential crofting family' (Report for 1957, para. 110). However, although on the whole it can be no more than a palliative, agricultural improvements have been made where practicable; in addition to hill cattle and hill sheep subsidies administered by the Department of Agriculture, crofters can apply for cropping grants and improvement grants. These latter cover regeneration schemes for common grazings, fencing and other forms of equipment. In 1961 over £250,000 was paid out to crofters for improvements. In certain areas, therefore, agricultural development can make a major impact; the land improvement scheme in Lewis is important, as is the scheme launched by the Highlands and Islands Development Board for a local bulb industry on croft land in North Uist. This follows the experience gained by Hebridean Bulb Growers, a co-operative which was based in Tiree from 1957 until its operations were wound up in 1967.

But in spite of certain successes, progress in other fields has been disappointing. The Commission has been successful in regulating crofting, but reorganisation and development have been less conspicuous. The Taylor Commission recommended that an active and imaginative use should be made of land settlement powers in the crofting counties as a contribution to the solution of the crofting problem, and advocated a free use by the Secretary of State for Scotland of his land settlement powers to acquire land for crofters. However, this was not taken up seriously by the government, who no doubt felt that existing economic conditions in farming could not justify the heavy expenditure which would be involved in forming new smallholdings. They were no doubt aware too of thinking on land settlement at the end of the nineteenth century, when it was argued that there was insufficient land of a suitable nature for smallholdings to make any substantial impact on the overpopulation problems.

But the rejection of land settlement has meant that reorganisation of existing croft land, on which the Taylor Commission laid great stress and which the Crofters Commission was empowered to foster, has been practically a non-starter. Crofters are naturally unwilling to lose their land even if they are not making full use of it, and it is rarely possible to annex sufficient non-croft land to create viable holdings for every crofter. Hence reorganisation is only possible in townships where there is plenty of land and where there is a small enough number of tenants for all to benefit by consolidation.

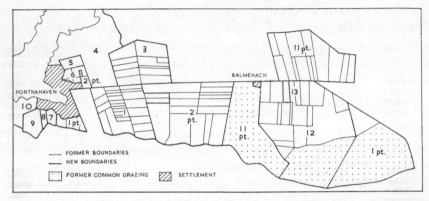

Fig. 16 *Reorganisation of crofts at Portnahaven, Islay*

For these reasons schemes have gone through at Blaich in Ardgour and at Portnahaven in Islay (Fig. 16), while on the island of Fetlar in Shetland reorganisation has been greatly assisted by the incorporation of 2,000 acres of non-croft land. Without such incorporation reorganisation on most townships is unlikely, since the total land in the community is frequently inadequate for even one viable holding to emerge. In Lewis, where practically the entire land in the island is already in crofting, the scope is even more limited.

It is generally accepted, therefore, that the potential of the majority of the crofts and part-time farms cannot be assessed purely on agriculture, for only on the larger crofts can agricultural viability be a realistic aim. The essential requirement is to ensure that there is employment outside agriculture for the crofting population. Speaking of the trickle of government money which has found its way into crofting agriculture, Sir Robert Urquhart, former Chairman of the Crofters Commission, argues (1964, p. 190) that it 'has been dispersed without significant benefit because the attempt to revive the agricultural sector of the economy in isolation could not and cannot now succeed'. He suggests, moreover, that 'if Parliament used surgery impartially on all the sickly members of the Highland economy the crofters would submit willingly to their part of the operation' (p. 189). Very much the same points were made in Parliament by Highland M.P.s when the Crofters Acts were being debated: 'No Bill will ever succeed unless marching alongside with agricultural development we get industrial development' was the comment of Sir David Robertson, M.P. for Caithness and Sutherland at the time (*House of Commons Papers*, vol. 536, p. 476).

Academics have made much the same point. Simpson (1962, p. 66) argues 'if the economy of the crofting district is to be placed on an eventually self-supporting basis without destroying the crofting communities the only feasible investments are to be made in non-agricultural industries, either in services or manufacturing'. The aim for a small croft must be to find a young tenant with another job. But the large-scale development of manufacturing and tourism throughout the crofting counties is very unlikely, and it would be unwise for all communities to rely on them in planning a stable future. Some progress was made in 1961 when for the first time crofters could claim compensation for buildings erected in connection with their ancillary occupation provided these do not interfere substantially with the use of the croft as an agricultural subject. This legislation has important implications for tourism, since housing improvements can be made and chalets built for tourists as a means of supplementing croft income. Where crofting can be combined with work in manufacturing and tourism, an opportunity is provided in the Highlands to work towards a new form of industrial society which could be healthier and more stable than any community which is completely urbanised.

A major change in the status of crofters is likely under the Commission's proposals to enable crofters to become owner-occupiers instead of tenants paying rent to a landlord. The holding and house could then be bought and sold without the consent of the Commission and land could be resumed for non-agricultural purposes without the authority of the Land Court; in this instance too the full development value of the property would pass to the crofter. Most important, however, the crofter would be able to raise a loan from private sources on the security of his land and buildings and could sink capital into croft developments in the knowledge that the full market value of the improvements could be recovered instead of compensation being payable by the landlord only for improvements suitable to the croft. Agricultural and housing grants would continue and controls would be introduced to prevent excessive purchases of crofts by outsiders at prices higher than competing local buyers could afford. While this issue is still under discussion, it can be recognised as being in keeping with the trend towards freeing crofters from the more restrictive aspects of earlier legislation.

But in the least accessible townships it is not possible to be so optimistic, and here it is necessary, as was the case with forestry, to introduce the social argument to justify a development programme. However it is far easier to justify on social grounds the allocation of funds to protect a flagging economy than it is to develop along basically uneconomic lines, and hence the stalemate is likely to continue in the remoter crofting areas, where population has still not been satisfactorily balanced with the local resources. It may well be that further emigration is inevitable even though it cannot be officially encouraged. Limited progress can, however, be expected in the agricultural sector, the most notable project at present being the Valley Strand land reclamation scheme in North Uist, where 1,000 acres of land may be taken in for bulb growing which could provide as many as 200 jobs for the island, thus following up the pilot scheme referred to earlier.

Thus the crofting landscape may be considered to be as dynamic as most other elements in the Highland economy, despite popular association with its more conservative aspects. It was to be expected that with past injustices in mind crofters would guard their privileges and greet the Crofters Commission (as a representative of remote southern authority) with suspicion. But the formation of the Federation of Crofters' Unions in Inverness in 1962 has helped to promote co-operation to allow the provisions of the 1955 and 1961 Acts to be implemented in the most constructive way possible. The scheme for planting trees on sections of township common grazings already discussed is one of the most promising results. It may well be one aspect of a policy of reorganisation and development which may ultimately see the rural population of the Highlands regrouped into fewer nucleations, each dependent on an integrated agricultural and forestry economy.

CONCLUSIONS

This is perhaps an appropriate moment to close the section on land use. It has appeared on several occasions that land, which is one of the most valuable Highland resources, is being misused and underused. It is clear that with greater investment and reorganisation greater numbers could be employed, and with this in mind the setting-up of a Land Use Commission has occasionally been advocated. This would seem appropriate in view of the various uses to which so much land in the Highlands can conceivably be put. Good agricultural land in the south will find a purchaser who is an efficient farmer, even though a more deserving and younger farmer may thus be excluded because he is less affluent. But in the Highlands good agricultural land is often valuable for forestry and sporting purposes as well. Agricultural estates may thus be purchased for the sporting value of the land, and if so then deterioration in farming standards and underuse of land might follow. The consequences of this running-down process are particularly disturbing when small island communities are affected, as in the case of Mull. What is the best way in which these competing interests can be reconciled?

Radical change might seem necessary and is by no means infrequently advocated. While farmers call for massive schemes of land reclamation and improvement, crofting interests may be heard demanding the annexation of underused non-croft land. During the Second Reading of the Crofters (Scotland) Bill, 1961, Mr Malcolm MacMillan, M.P. for the Western Isles, spoke of the 'sterilisation of hundreds of thousands of acres of Highland soil' by 'sporting landlords who have no interest in the Highlands except as a pleasant retreat from their city interests', and advocated 'an extension of crofting into the neglected estates of the Highlands'. At a meeting of the Federation of Crofters' Unions in 1962, the representative from Lochaber called for an immediate survey of land to be rehabilitated and made into economic holdings. Forestry interests are similarly concerned in extending the acreage under trees, and the Scottish Landowners' Federation would favour a big Scottish forestry programme as an answer to depopulation problems. But local vested interests in all sections of the economy and financial limitations ensure that change will come only slowly, by evolutionary rather than revolutionary means, with the present pattern as the necessary starting point. The careful consideration of the needs of all land-users is fundamental.

Moreover it is probable that change and development on the land in general will not come about quickly enough to maintain the whole of the present population. Rural depopulation is a characteristic of all developed societies and the Highland area is no exception, though the extent to which it has occurred there and the implications for the viability of the communities which remain have tended to give particular grounds for concern. The initiative must necessarily pass to the industrial areas, whose location and extent will be increasingly influential in moulding the future pattern. It is to these large centres of population that the discussion now turns.

CHAPTER SEVEN

Growth of Communications and Services

EVEN today a large number of small settlements in the Highlands and islands have a function which is entirely related to local primary resources, notably agriculture and forestry. This characteristic was even more striking before improvement, when an agricultural settlement pattern of small clachans was common throughout. The subsistence economy of the time did not require focal points to act as local centres of distribution and industry. The ports were obviously important, but since any of the creeks which indent the coast of the Highlands and Hebrides were adaptable to the small scale of commerce, there is little marked nucleation evident in the early maps which are still extant. The development of towns came late and was largely imposed on the landscape to meet the military requirements of central governments, at either end of the Great Glen especially. The clan chiefs also had their strongholds, but these had little significance in the settlement pattern since the clansmen themselves were heavily land-based and their habitations reflected the agricultural potential of the land in each locality.

The years after Culloden saw the further integration of the Highland subsistence economy with the wider national economy of Britain as a whole. Economic interchange with the south increased, and this growing trade, not to mention the more peaceful and stable conditions which now prevailed, made for the greater emphasis on certain distribution centres, some of regional importance and others of more local significance. It is perhaps rather ironic to note that at this time the plans of many proprietors worked in defiance of these trends, for the resettlement of small tenants in planned crofting townships often took place on peripheral parts of estates which even in the early nineteenth century may well have been considered remote. This was no doubt unavoidable in the nineteenth century, given the heavy pressure of population on limited resources, but these exceptional circumstances must be remembered when considering subsequent depopulation, since the remnants of an overpopulated landscape of a century ago are not necessarily the most appropriate basis of prosperity today. Population has shown an increasing tendency to nucleate, and while census material accumulated over the last two centuries shows the gloomy trend of overall losses through outward migration, reflecting consolidation at national level in central Scotland, it also reveals significant and continuing shifts in emphasis within the Highlands in favour of local and regional centres which have become popularly known as 'growth points'.

The selection of these central places would seem to be guided by two main processes, first the development of transport and second the growth of industry, which unlike agriculture can only endow a limited number of sites. The aim of this chapter is to trace the development of transport and from this to discuss patterns of distribution networks for various services such as coal, milk and the post. Such services are crucial to even the smallest communities now that local self-sufficiency has largely broken down, and levels of access to them have a very direct bearing on the ability of remote settlements to survive. A subsequent chapter will then deal with the progress of manufacturing in the Highland area and will attempt to show how this has further upset the population balance by favouring, for the most part, a small number of the more accessible centres. After clarifying these trends by a number of long-term and short-term population studies in a further chapter, the discussion will turn to the problems and implications of this imbalance as it affects the rural areas as well as the growing urban settlements. At all times the unique position of the Highlands and islands on the northwestern fringe of Scotland, the United Kingdom and Europe should be remembered, as should the striking variations in accessibility within the Highlands themselves.

THE DROVE ROADS

Highland transport was in a poorly developed state until comparatively recent times and has always lagged behind the standards reached in other parts of the country. Even though very few parts of the Highlands can really be described as inaccessible, the whole area is relatively inaccessible, although the extent varies locally. The export of primary produce from the Highlands has thus always been a tedious and expensive process, and in retrospect it can be seen that one of the most prominent ways in which central governments have consistently found themselves able to help the Highland economy has been by improving communications. The eighteenth century saw the rapid growth of the cattle-droving trade in response to the opening-up of the English market by the Treaty of Union in 1707, and these 'drove roads' have become one of the more romantic aspects of contemporary life as expounded by the annals of Highland history. In effect, however, the routes followed were not along roads in the modern sense of the term but rather followed broad lines of movement which compromised the most direct line by the needs of grazing and security en route.

The activities of cattle thieves and the political situation among the clans whose territory was crossed, not to mention weather conditions, would doubtless determine which of several possible alternative routes was selected by the drovers en route to the main cattle tryst. This was first held at Crieff but later transferred to Falkirk, which proved to be more central for the Highlands as a whole. So necessary was it that the drovers should have effective means of defending themselves that they were exempted from the Disarming Acts of 1716 and 1748 and allowed licences to carry weapons. Lochaber and Badenoch were particularly difficult areas from the point of view of raiding, but their strategic position meant that they could hardly be avoided. Cattle from the Outer Hebrides generally used the shortest sea crossing to Skye, coming ashore around Uig or Dunvegan, and having crossed the island swam over the narrows at Kylerhea to Glenelg on the mainland. From these a choice of routes was available by Corrieyairack, Rannoch or Glencoe, all of which passed through either Lochaber or Badenoch. Badenoch was again necessarily on the route of cattle passing from the northern Highlands southwards through Easter Ross, and also for droves from Lewis which crossed the Minch to Aultbea, Poolewe and Gairloch and then proceeded southeastwards towards Dingwall and Inverness.

Very disrupting also were the uncertainties of the weather, for these could affect the grazing available on the way, a major consideration on a journey which took several weeks and could only be accomplished at a rate of some ten miles each day. Moreover, since one of the chief weaknesses of Highland communications was the general absence of bridges over the main rivers, many of which had to be crossed on a journey south because the route lay transverse to the general grain of the country, wet weather could make for great complications. The military roads had gone some way to improve and construct bridges, but there were still numerous gaps. Across these torrents the cattle were forced to swim, driven on by 'a hideous cry to keep the foremost of them from turning about, for in that case the rest would do the like and then they would be in danger of being swept away and drowned by the torrent' (Haldane, 1952, p. 40). Similar tactics were employed for some of the shorter sea crossings from the islands to the mainland, where boats were not normally used.

Land communications were therefore extremely difficult and remained a most serious matter for government concern. In some districts land communications were virtually non-existent except by rough tracks; the remoteness that this inspired was hardly conducive to the spread of agricultural innovation and economic development generally. Reliable and adequate communications are an essential prerequisite for economic growth. But even in areas where the fishing industry was being fostered and where the military roads were still making a modest contribution, there were problems of unemployment following the resettlement of small tenants on crofts which could not offer complete subsistence. As the evils of emigration were beginning to be loudly enumerated, the situation clearly demanded attention in the early nineteenth century. Moreover the worsening international position made action particularly appropriate, for the empire-building of Napoleon seemed to make Britain once more highly exposed on her underdeveloped western flank in both Ireland and northern Scotland. Navigational difficulties around the north coast were increased by the depredations of French shipping.

THE COMMISSION FOR HIGHLAND ROADS AND BRIDGES

It was in July 1801 that Thomas Telford, civil engineer, was instructed by the government to examine the possibility of developing certain fishing stations on the west coast and of improving communications through the mainland to the islands, including inland navigation between the east and west coasts. Telford wrote of the 'incalculable loss which the public has sustained, and are about to suffer, from want of roads in this country', and mentioned the need to improve commerce 'which must amply repay the pecuniary assistance your committee have thought is their duty to advise' (Haldane, 1962, p. 33). As a result of Telford's report and recommendations, two great projects were launched: a Commission was set up for Highland Roads and Bridges and another for the Caledonian Canal, both under the chairmanship of Lord Colchester. The speedy action involved in setting up these bodies as early as 1803 is indicative of the alarming situation. Work went ahead necessarily slowly in view of the many unforeseen difficulties in building roads under Highland conditions, but by 1828 a fairly comprehensive road network had emerged. From the Great Glen transverse routes ran westwards to the coast; some of these, Loch Carron–Glen Shiel and Loch na Gaul to Kyle and Arisaig respectively, connected with ferry crossings to Skye, which was still an important bridge on the route to the Outer Hebrides. A branch from the Glen Shiel road over Mam Ratagan to Glenelg maintained the Kylerhea crossing to Skye. From Kyleakin, Kylerhea and Armadale roads were built across the island to the northern ferry points of Uig and Stein (Dunvegan).

Other roads from the Great Glen were of more local importance, and it was hoped that the road to Loch Moidart from Corran Ferry and to Loch Hourn from Glengarry, along with the Kishorn branch of the Loch Carron road, would stimulate the development of fishing which the British Fisheries Society was actively fostering at this time. North of Inverness the main development was the road north to Bonar Bridge, with branches from there to Tongue and Thurso, again with fishing very much in mind. East of the Great Glen activity was more concerned with the improvement and maintenance of the existing military roads, but major new schemes were the roads to Aviemore from Inverness and Fort William over Slocht and Laggan respectively. A number of roads were built in mid-Argyll and connections with Islay and Jura improved. This still left many areas without roads, notably the Outer Hebrides and parts of the north-west mainland, but plans for the construction of Parliamentary roads in these areas were abandoned after the death of Lord Colchester. After 1817, therefore, the work of the Commission for Highland Roads and Bridges was solely connected with the upkeep of the existing installations. Road building in Lewis had to await the schemes of the proprietor, Sir James Matheson, who developed the island from 1844 to 1878.

The other great project was the Caledonian Canal, which it was hoped would avoid the heavy losses to shipping off the north coast and, particularly at the time, reduce the danger of foreign attack. The perils of the northern passage were not reduced by the fact that there was no harbour or place of safety for vessels to shelter from the boisterous weather between Orkney and Cape Wrath, apart from the Loch Eriboll and Scrabster roads. The idea of a canal through the Great Glen was not a new one; it was talked of in 1730 and a survey had been made in 1773 by Watt for the Trustees of the Forfeited Estates. However, the anticipated cost of £164,000 was then considered unjustifiable. Telford now recommended the scheme once more to provide a waterway from east to west and work began, though the extension of the scheme to the west coast via Loch Duich or Loch Shiel was abandoned. The canal was opened in 1822 after many difficulties and regrettably never lived up to the expectations of its protagonists. As Haldane remarks in his masterly review (1962, p. 191), 'long before the canal was finished the shadow of France had receded, coastal lights had taken much of its terrors from the

Northern Passage, while above all steam was fast replacing sail'. The depth of the canal had now become insufficient to accommodate ships on the American and Baltic runs.

For a time there were attempts to reconstruct the canal to keep pace with developments in shipbuilding; the canal was deepened and extensively repaired after flood damage in the years that followed, and this increased the total cost to well over £1 million. The great hopes pinned on the canal were therefore never realised, but it was difficult in 1803 to foresee the full extent of the technological breakthrough which was only just beginning at that time with the first steamship trials. In spite of substantial annual deficits, however, the canal remains open, following a recommendation by the Committee on Inland Waterways (H.M.S.O., 1958), and is used mainly by pleasure craft and fishing boats from east-coast ports making their way to and from the west-coast fishing grounds. A number of small cargo boats carrying grain, timber and general cargo also use the canal, preferring the twelve- to sixteen-hour journey through the canal to the detour round the north coast. Some of the locks are still hand-operated, although those at Dochgarroch and Laggan have been mechanised.

Telford was no doubt saddened by the doubts raised as to the viability of the Caledonian Canal, though his death in 1834 spared him from witnessing their confirmation. However, the roads and bridges were and still are an outstanding success, and the era of the Commission for Highland Roads and Bridges, which came to an end in 1862 with the transfer of responsibility to the Commissioners of Supply in the Highland Counties, marks a definite milestone. But it must be regretted that this valuable infrastructure was not paralleled by sufficient economic growth to maintain the population. Certainly growth was encouraged at the main intersections, and the communities which began to grow up at Spean Bridge, Roy Bridge, Bonar Bridge and Invergarry, to mention only a few, were no doubt orientated in part to providing services for travellers. Often the inn was the most prominent building at such places. However, progress was still slow and there was little in the way of regular public transport services. When these did begin to develop, steamships and railways were becoming the last word. This new era in travel was indeed on its way almost as soon as the roads and bridges had been built.

STEAMERS IN THE NINETEENTH CENTURY

Sea transport has naturally always had a prominent place in Highland affairs, but its importance has seen a number of changes of emphasis. In early times, as long as the Highlands were organised as a maritime empire with land transport notoriously difficult, sea transport was fundamental to island and mainland districts alike. This was very much the case in the Scandinavian period, when galleys were essential to the local chiefs. However, the improvements on land, in the early nineteenth century especially, made for some swing to overland routes using the shortest sea passages thence to the islands. Even then, however, bulky commodities were taken all the way by sea for the most part, but the introduction of regular passenger steamers prompted a reversion to the old pattern, with Glasgow the main port for all the west Highland trade. The first regular service began as early as 1812 with Henry Bell's *Comet* sailing between Glasgow and Helensburgh. Services on the Caledonian Canal were started in 1820 by the *Stirling Castle* from Inverness to Fort Augustus, and the sailing was extended to Banavie and Glasgow with the completion of the canal in 1822. Royal patronage in the form of voyages by Queen Victoria from Ardrishaig to Crinan and from Banavie to Inverness, in 1847 and 1873 respectively, further popularised what has subsequently been called the 'Royal Route' to the Highlands (Plate 27).

Steamers in the west Highlands and islands have for over a century been associated with the name of David MacBrayne. The original company was founded in 1851, when it took over the west Highland trade from G. and J. Burns. David MacBrayne himself was left in sole control of the company in 1879 and it was largely under him that the firm developed its fleet from twenty vessels in 1879 to thirty-two in 1907, when he died at the age of ninety-three. The company is still named after him, although the shares are now owned by Coast Lines Ltd and British Railways.[1] Apart from a small number of local services MacBraynes have a monopoly for both passenger and cargo services, but this is largely because Highland shipping does not attract competition. When MacBraynes were temporarily forced to withdraw from the trade in 1928, no other body or individual was prepared to step into the breach, and since then services have been maintained only by a government subsidy which now stands at £421,000 per annum, a figure which includes payment for carrying mails. Government aid is also necessary to finance new tonnage and has been called on ever since the 1930s, when the *Loch Earn* and *Loch Mor* were built to operate services to the Outer Isles. The tendency is therefore for MacBrayne interests to increase as private

[1] MacBraynes are now controlled by the Scottish Transport Group and this allows greater co-ordination with other undertakings, such as the Caledonian Steam Packet Company, who operate in the Firth of Clyde.

operators find their routes uneconomic. In 1948, for instance, the cargo traffic of the MacCallum Orme Company was taken over.

The original pattern of services was made up of major routes from Glasgow to Inverness and Stornoway which called at a variety of mainland and island ports en route (Fig. 17). For a time the sailing was extended along the north coast of Sutherland as far as Thurso in Caithness, a striking reflection on the standard of land communications. Even by steamer the journey south was a long and tedious one and there were many unforeseen delays. Perhaps the following extract from a MacBrayne timetable of 1909 has not yet lost all its relevance: 'The hours noted above are not to be absolutely relied upon. They only show about the average sailing time and calls are made subject to weather and circumstances permitting. The steamer may be earlier or later than what is stated.' Nevertheless the new steamers were a great advance, especially for the Outer Hebrides where inaccessibility delayed the process of people migrating south temporarily or permanently. Indeed in many Outer Hebridean parishes census information does not indicate any net loss in total population until as late as 1911, whereas on the mainland losses through migration exceeding natural increase were evident by 1831 or 1841. Most of the steamers carried passengers and cargo, but a small number of 'swift steamers' maintained a faster passenger service at a higher fare using the Crinan Canal.

HIGHLAND RAILWAYS

It was not long, however, before the steamers found it necessary to co-exist with the railways. Engineers had been convinced for some time as to the practicability of a line over Drumochter Pass between Perth and Inverness, but construction was held back for some time, fortunately perhaps because it exempted the Highlands from the railway mania which was rife in the 1840s. The original idea was for a single main line linking the Highlands with the south, and much controversy lay over whether the route should run direct from Perth to Inverness or take the longer route by Aberdeen. Initially the latter project won the day and the railway reached Aberdeen by 1850, but it was another eight years before the line was completed to Inverness, a delay which increased pressure for a direct line now that the support of local landowners was assured. The Bill for the Highland Railway was passed in 1861 and the railway completed two years later, a most impressive feat. The Highland Railway continued north of Inverness to reach Bonar Bridge in 1868 and carried on through Sutherland, where the

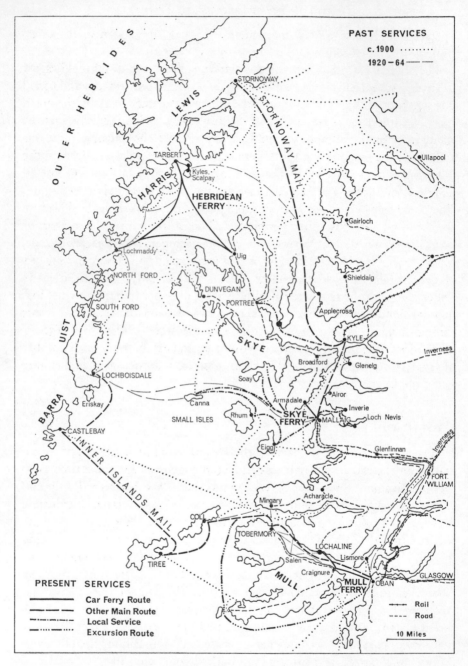

PRESENT SERVICES

———	Car Ferry Route
– – –	Other Main Route
– ·· –	Local Service
· · · ·	Excursion Route

Rail

Road

10 Miles

OUTER HEBRIDES

LEWIS

STORNOWAY

Ullapool

TARBERT

Kyles
Scalpay

HARRIS

HEBRIDEAN
FERRY

Gairloch

Lochmaddy

Uig

Shieldaig

NORTH FORD

DUNVEGAN

PORTREE

Applecross

SOUTH FORD

UIST

SKYE

KYLE

Inverness

Broadford

Glenelg

LOCHBOISDALE

Soay

Airor

BARRA

Eriskay

Canna

Armadale

Inverie

Loch Nevis

SMALL ISLES

Rhum

SKYE
FERRY

MALLAIG

CASTLEBAY

Eigg

Glenfinnan

Inverness

INNER ISLANDS MAIL

FORT
WILLIAM

Mingary

Acharacle

COL

TOBERMORY

LOCHALINE

Lismore

TIREE

Salen

GLASGOW

Craignure

MULL

MULL
FERRY

Oban

Fig. 17 *West Highland transport systems*

railway owed much to the Duke of Sutherland, to reach Wick and Thurso in 1874. Westwards a branch penetrated to the coast at Strome Ferry. In the south a separate initiative by the Caledonian Railway had resulted in construction from Stirling and Dunblane to Callander and Crianlarich, reaching the west coast at Oban in 1880.

It was after this early phase of railway construction that the temperature began to mount. The amount of railway traffic in the Highlands was clearly limited, so the existing companies were unwilling to build additional lines and at the same time were firmly opposed to any rivals attempting to encroach upon their empires. Nevertheless the whole of the west Highlands between Oban and Strome was without rail access, at a time when great anxiety was once again being expressed about the condition of the west Highlands and islands. The Great Glen area and Lochaber were still dependent on the Glasgow steamer, although there had been a scheme to link Fort William with the Highland Railway at Newtonmore in 1863. In 1884, when the Napier Commission was in the process of reporting, a scheme was launched to build a rival line to Inverness from Glasgow by way of the Great Glen, Glencoe and Rannoch Moor, and it was only after bitter debate that the Bill was thrown out by Parliament. Five years later, however, the West Highland Railway was allowed to go ahead with a line to Fort William, roughly along the line envisaged in 1884 but with a wide detour in the north which avoided the difficult section by Glencoe and Loch Leven by approaching Fort William from the north down Glen Spean and the Great Glen from Spean Bridge. This line was opened in 1894 with customary celebration. On this occasion the anticipated opposition of the Highland Railway was overcome by payment of their legal expenses and an undertaking not to promote an extension through the Great Glen for at least ten years.

But the government was now to take a hand. One of the several initiatives which followed the Crofters' Holdings (Scotland) Act of 1886 was the appointment of a special committee in 1892 to examine certain schemes for the improvement of railway communications on the west coast of Scotland. The committee stated that 'none of the suggested railway projects can be regarded as possessing a commercial basis or the element of success as ordinary railway undertakings. If therefore the districts in question . . . are to obtain the advantages of railway communication these must be afforded on grounds other than anticipation of direct financial return.' It was recommended that public money should be used to finance the extension of the Highland line from Strome Ferry to Kyle of Lochalsh and the West Highland railway from Fort William to Mallaig (Plate 28). In the Mallaig case a grant of £100,000 was recommended and a dividend of 3 per cent per annum for thirty years was in fact guaranteed.

The Mallaig line has been described as 'one of these very rare cases in which the electric spark of a common interest flashes between the positive element of commercial advantage and the negative element of a philanthropic undertaking' (Timins, 1901, p. 400). The line, it was claimed, 'will open up a district of the West Highlands of Scotland now devoid of railway communication, provide a harbour and fishery port in immediate proximity to the south-west coast of Skye and the neighbouring isles and be of benefit and advantage to the inhabitants'. But the opposition was considerable; the Caledonian Railway in Oban was incensed that public money should finance a competitor, while the more reactionary local landowners also resented the intrusion. In the opinion of one the area 'had no need whatever of railways' and 'was quite unable to furnish traffic which must be better and more cheaply moved by water carriage'. The railway, it was alleged, would destroy forest land and damage sheep farms, while blasting would choke and destroy the spawning beds in the numerous streams. The development succeeded, however, and in 1901 Mallaig saw a transformation, with the small crofting-fishing community suddenly taking on a new function, like Kyle, as a railhead for the islands. The impact of this new development on the surrounding areas is considered in a later chapter.

A further stimulus to rail construction was the Light Railways Act of 1896, which sparked off a short-lived burst of branch-line construction. Branch lines had been built from Dingwall to Strathpeffer (1885), Wick to Lybster (1892) and Muir of Ord to Fortrose (1894), but the rail network was still essentially a system of main lines which left many communities a long way from a railhead, notably those in the islands and in west Sutherland. The Highland Railway now came out with projects to build branches from the Kyle line at Garve and Achnasheen to Ullapool and Aultbea respectively and also from the Wick line at Culrain to Lochinver and again at Lairg to Laxford Bridge. Shorter branches would link Dingwall with Cromarty, Fearn with Portmahomack, and The Mound with Dornoch, and there were some lines planned in Caithness, Lewis and Skye. None of these materialised apart from the Dornoch branch which opened in 1902, although a start was made on the Cromarty branch and many of the earthworks are still clearly visible around Jemimaville. Further south interest was focused on the Great Glen and attempts were made to fill the gaps between Inverness and Fort William and between Fort William and Oban. However, since these towns were served by different companies, Highland, North British and Caledonian, it was difficult for one to plan without incurring opposition from the others.

In 1895 the Caledonian were refused powers to build a line from Connell Ferry (near Oban) to Fort William, but the following year they were permitted to build as far as South Ballachulish, while the North British was enabled to undertake the northern section from North Ballachulish on to Fort William. This would have left two branches without any physical connection over Loch Leven and only the southern branch was ever built, being opened in 1903. Similar problems were encountered once more in the Great Glen and here the only progress made was a branch from the West Highland at Spean Bridge to Invergarry and Fort Augustus. The Bill for this independent Invergarry and Fort Augustus Railway was passed in 1898, but it was a decidedly ill-fated venture. Capital was exhausted before completion, and when the line was eventually finished in 1901 the company were unable to purchase locomotives or rolling stock. Accordingly the line was run first by the Highland, a most curious situation since there was no physical connection with their system, and later by the North British who eventually purchased the branch in 1914. With no possibility of reaching Inverness there was never sufficient traffic to justify the line and it was completely closed in 1946. Not that the other branches have fared much better, for the Lybster, Dornoch, Fortrose, Strathpeffer and Ballachulish branches are all closed, though alumina traffic to the British Aluminium Company's factory at Kinlochleven maintained the latter in operation until 1966.[1]

The railways had quite a dramatic impact on the pattern of steamer services, for it was now the west Highland railheads which became the passenger steamer terminals rather than Glasgow. But since communications in the islands were poor by comparison – no railways were ever built there – routes did not revert to the shortest sea crossings between mainland and islands. Instead vessels from Oban, Mallaig and Kyle served a proliferation of piers in the islands and changes were often necessary (Fig. 17). Thus the timetable for 1909 shows vessels operating a circular route from Oban and Tobermory (Mull) to Lochmaddy (North Uist) and Dunvegan (Skye), with the outward journey via Castlebay (Barra) and Lochboisdale (South Uist) and the return journey via Bracadale (Skye) and the Small Isles of Canna and Rhum. There were connections at Tobermory for Ardnamurchan, Coll, Tiree and Bunessan on the Ross of Mull, while another vessel could

[1] Even the main railway lines are uneconomic and government grants are made available to British Rail so that services can be maintained. The future of all the lines seems in doubt from about Glasgow to Fort William and Inverness to Wick and Thurso.

be joined at Lochmaddy or Dunvegan for Harris and various other destinations in Skye. The Glasgow to Stornoway service, however, persisted for some time, though the call at Arisaig (Rhu Pier) was dropped in favour of Mallaig and Kyle became more important than Balmacara. Even so it is striking to note just how many mainland calls there still were at this time: districts such as Morvern, Ardnamurchan and Sunart in north Argyll, Glenelg and Knoydart in Inverness-shire and the Applecross peninsula in Wester Ross were still effectively islands in spite of their tenuous physical connection with the rest of the mainland. A number of them are still in this difficult position today.

RETURN TO THE ROADS

Road improvements were on the way. Construction of 'destitution roads' during the famine, and improvement of the tracks and roads by the Congested Districts Board and county councils at the turn of the century, was followed up by black-topping and widening in the post-war period. However, contrasts are still glaring between different parts of the Highlands. While most roads east and south of the Great Glen are well up to standard and many main roads widened and realigned to give an 18 ft-wide carriageway and very satisfactory ruling gradients, further west and north many of the main roads are only about 10 ft wide and vehicles can only pass at the crossing places provided. Improvements are coming slowly, however; the Glenfinnan–Lochailort section of the 'Road to the Isles' was widened and improved over the period 1959 to 1963, but much of the remainder still remains as Telford left it at the beginning of the nineteenth century, apart from the hard surface which was applied between 1930 and 1938. Another important improvement features the A87 between Invergarry and Cluanie, for a new eight-mile section, 18 ft wide, was opened in 1961 to replace the old road from Tomdoun to Cluanie which was flooded by the rising level of Loch Loyne, dammed by the Hydro Board as part of their Moriston scheme.

The problem becomes increasingly serious in the islands, where costs rise still higher in view of the greater transport burden for materials, not to mention labour difficulties caused by high costs for recruitment and accommodation, which must often be provided in mobile bothies. Bad weather can be a serious delaying factor. At the same time it becomes increasingly difficult to justify the expense when only small communities are involved, and this is a heavy burden for local authorities to bear in spite of Exchequer grants which range from 50 per cent of the cost of maintenance and reconstruction in the case of 'C' class roads to 100 per cent for trunk roads. Progress on roads such as the Lochportain road in North Uist which cost £100,000 is necessarily slow. Even with special schemes for roads to remote crofting communities it is necessary to work out an order of priority, although any delay must have adverse implications for the future viability of these settlements. It may be more than fifty years before all townships can be adequately served.

Once again shipping services have had to adapt themselves to changes in land transport as buses began to replace mail-coaches at the turn of the century. One trend has been a progressive reduction in the number of mainland communities served by sea. Thus Gairloch, Ullapool and Lochinver are linked by bus with the railheads of Achnasheen, Garve and Lairg respectively. In Lochaber the steamer service between Fort William and Oban was replaced by the railway from Connell to Ballachulish and by a bus service from Fort William to North Ballachulish which MacBraynes inaugurated in 1906. Similarly a bus connection from Corran Ferry to Salen and Strontian was a replacement for the former steamer link with Oban via Tobermory. In the Great Glen the bus service began in 1912 and eventually ousted the passenger service on the Caledonian Canal. When the road reached Kinlochleven in 1922 a bus service replaced the steamer which MacBraynes had operated on Loch Leven since the aluminium factory opened.

Only where communications by land are extremely difficult and tenuous to maintain, in winter especially, is sea transport still relied upon by mainland communities. Thus in view of the difficult road over the Pass of the Cattle, Applecross is served by a daily boat from Kyle to Toscaig, while the roadless area of North Morar and Knoydart calls for a boat service between Mallaig, Inverie (Knoydart) and the smaller Loch Nevis townships of Stoul, Tarbert, Kylesmorar and Kylesknoydart. North Argyll is a very difficult area to traverse and the deep gashes of Loch Eil, Loch Sunart, Loch Moidart and Loch Ailort, not to mention the freshwater Loch Shiel, give this mainland district of Ardnamurchan a pronounced insularity. Lochaline in Morvern is almost entirely dependent on the steamer link with Oban in preference to the long haul to Corran Ferry over the poorly-maintained A884, and Kilchoan at the 'West End' of Ardnamurchan prefers the link with Oban via Mull to the bus journey to Fort William (Plate 4).[1]

In the islands better main roads have enabled distribution to be handled

[1] Recent road improvements in the Ardnamurchan peninsula have greatly increased accessibility to Fort William, especially from Morvern.

from a smaller number of centres, and hence the number of steamer calls has progressively declined. By 1951 the services fell into a much simpler pattern. In the south the Gourock–Tarbert (Loch Fyne) service connects with a boat from West Loch Tarbert to Gigha, Islay, Jura and Colonsay. From Oban steamers serve Lismore and the Sound of Mull, and the Inner Islands Mail leaves thrice weekly for Coll, Tiree, Barra and south Uist. From Mallaig and Kyle there are services to Portree (Skye) and Stornoway (Lewis) and an interesting circular route to Scalpay, Tarbert, Stockinish and Rodel (Harris), Lochmaddy (north Uist), Lochboisdale (south Uist) and the Small Isles. This run was completed thrice weekly, once in a clockwise direction and twice anti-clockwise. It afforded a connection at Lochboisdale with the Inner Islands Mail for Oban.

As a response to the increasing popularity of road transport, however, shipping timetables have in recent years shown a swing to car ferries using the shortest sea passages (Fig. 17). For some time the limited space for cars on conventional vessels has been a problem, not to mention lack of drive-on and drive-off facilities. But in 1964 car ferries were introduced on three routes: Oban to Craignure (Mull) and Lochaline (Morvern), Mallaig to Armadale (Skye), and Uig (Skye) to Tarbert (Harris) and Lochmaddy (north Uist), operated by the *Columba*, *Clansman* and *Hebrides* respectively. These vessels were built by Hall, Russell and Co. of Aberdeen for the Secretary of State for Scotland under the Highlands and Islands Shipping Services (Scotland) Act of 1960 and loaned to MacBraynes, whose resources are insufficient for them to finance new tonnage themselves. This procedure was first used in 1962 when a new vessel, the *Orcadia*, was built for loan to the Orkney Islands Shipping Company, who could not raise the capital to finance a replacement for the ageing *Earl Thorfinn*.

OVERLAND ROUTES

The route to the islands is thus now once more across Skye, which is linked to the mainland by ferries at Kyle of Lochalsh and Glenelg (summer only) as well as Mallaig. It is thus taking on the bridge function which it enjoyed way back in the days of the cattle-droving trade. However, whereas in those times there were many points used for beginning the Minch crossing, the present need to concentrate pier facilities at one port made for difficult problems of selection, for both Uig and Dunvegan were prominent candidates. Similarly in Mull there was much local controversy over the choice of Craignure as the main steamer terminal for the island, since both Salen

(Mull) and Tobermory stood to lose trade with the withdrawal of the Sound of Mull steamer which formerly served all three places. Tobermory is still a calling point of the Inner Islands Mail, which is not affected by the changes, but is bound to feel its isolation increasingly, located as it is on the northwestern corner of the island and linked with the mainland now by a bus service to the car ferry at Craignure. A number of other services are unaffected, namely the Stornoway Mail and the local services to Toscaig, Mingary and Lismore. The Skye steamer is retained largely in the interests of Raasay, but the vessel concerned, the *Loch Arkaig*, is shared with the Small Isles which were formerly on the itinerary of the Outer Islands Mail, now withdrawn. However, there is understandable apprehension in these islands, since in spite of the provision of adequate piers and the elimination of 'flit-boats' at most islands, the quality of service has declined as compared with the beneficiaries of the car-ferry services. An extension of car-ferry services from Mallaig to south Uist and Barra is under consideration, and additional vehicle ferries are being advocated, commensurate in scale with local requirements. A small ferry is already operating between Scalpay and Kyles Scalpay on the mainland of Harris, and better facilities from Iona to Fionnphort (Mull), Lismore to Oban or Port Appin and Raasay to Sconser (Skye) would be appropriate. Developments in Orkney and Shetland are being considered; in the former case the position of the North Isles in a concentric pattern around the mainland has prompted the novel idea of a local air service to improve links between Kirkwall and the more distant islands (Fig. 18). In Shetland a bridge is being built between the mainland and Burra.

It is likely then that the trend to car ferries will continue as the conventional vessels now at work reach the end of their useful lives. The areas most affected by present planning are Orkney and Shetland in the north and Islay and Jura in the south; in the latter case the vessel at present in use, the *Lochiel*, which runs to the islands from Tarbert (Loch Fyne), will have to be withdrawn by 1970. It is only the very shallow draught of this vessel which enables it to berth at West Loch Tarbert, and its successor will be unable to do this on account of the larger capacity which the growing needs of the islands, notably in connection with the tourist trade, necessitate. The choice of a future route has once again sparked off heated local debate, but to a far greater extent than was the case in Mull and Skye. Discussions between MacBraynes and Argyll County Council in 1964 and 1965 led to a scheme to introduce a large car ferry similar to those operating further north, which would ply between a new terminal at the mouth of West Loch Tarbert and Port Askaig (Islay) and Feolin (Jura), with smaller vessels to serve Gigha and Colonsay. Opposed to this, however, was the Islay Transport Users' Association, formed in 1965 to safeguard island interests; they insisted that a cheaper and more flexible service could be assured by the 'overland' route using Jura as a bridge to link Islay with the mainland not at Tarbert but rather at Keills, as was the case in the days of cattle-droving. Small car ferries would be needed to operate the Keills–Lagg and

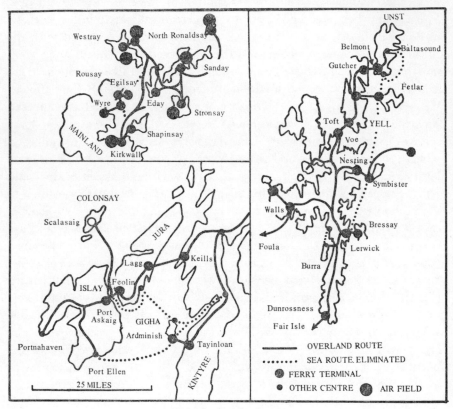

Fig. 18 *Overland routes*

Feolin–Port Askaig crossings, but with a large number of crossings possible daily a greater number of vehicles could be ferried compared with the larger vessel. Colonsay would be served by the Feolin–Port Askaig vessel, while Gigha would enjoy a separate car-ferry service from Ardminish to Tayinloan on the mainland of Kintyre (Fig. 18).

The 'overlanders' were supported by Islay District Council and attracted the attention of the Highland Transport Board, who made a detailed survey of the costs of providing and maintaining the rival schemes and called in the advice of a Norwegian expert. The outcome has been a recommendation by the Board that the 'overland' scheme should be preferred on the grounds of economy, capacity and flexibility. They also consider that the heavy cost of roadworks at Keills and on Jura should be financed separately so that the existing priorities for road improvement and construction on Argyll County Council's lists should not be disturbed. The plan was eventually rejected in 1968 by the Secretary of State on the grounds that heavy initial expenditure would be required on the overland route and the scheme could not be completed in time for the withdrawal of the *Lochiel*. The controversy has now moved to other questions, notably the type of vessel to run from West Loch Tarbert in future and the location of the new pier needed there. Matters have also been confused by the appearance of a private company, Western Ferries, which introduced a small car ferry on the West Loch Tarbert–Port Askaig route in 1968; while the latter was much appreciated in the northern part of Islay, the lack of a similar direct contact with Port Ellen in the south prompted a much greater interest in a new MacBrayne service in that part of the island.[1]

THE TRANSPORT PROBLEM

That such a debate should take place over transport services is understandable, for islanders are all too keenly aware of the costs of isolation. In a purely economic sense these are considerable, and studies in Orkney have revealed that island freight charges may increase the cost of living for an average family by as much as £2 per week. It is appreciated too that since opportunities are almost always better on the mainland the gulf can only be narrowed by the most efficient communications system possible. The viability of any island industry, be it agriculture, manufacture or tourism, is compromised by time and money spent in transport, and since the road is now a faster and cheaper highway than the sea the shortest possible 'bridge' must be sought. In the case of Islay and Jura, however, the 'overland' scheme would have serious implications for Tarbert, for not only would the Islay link be lost but the Gourock–Tarbert link might well be replaced by land transport from Glasgow to Lochgilphead (for Keills).

The Islay case is one illustration of the major transport problem faced by the Highlands and discussed elsewhere by Skewis (1962). In the days of

[1] In January 1970 the *Lochiel* was withdrawn and replaced by the *Arran*, a car ferry from the Clyde, which serves Colonsay, Gigha and Jura as well as Port Askaig and Port Ellen in Islay at rates competitive with the Western Ferries vessel. Moreover, the freight service by sea from Glasgow has been replaced by a road service connecting with the car ferry at Tarbert.

electrified railways, jet air travel and motorways, how can the Highlands and islands enjoy services of commensurate standard? Provision of air services to the Outer Hebrides, Orkney and Shetland has been followed by similar contacts for the Inner Hebrides (Islay and Mull) and certain mainland towns, but heavy reliance will continue to be placed on land and sea transport in the foreseeable future. Here it is evident that not only are communications in the Highlands less efficient than in the country as a whole, but that within the Highlands efforts to date have produced a vastly uneven pattern with growing relative accessibility further north and west. Even with the programmes of road and bridge building going back to the days of the military roads there are still too many ferry crossings on the mainland. Many are well known to holidaymakers, notably Ballachulish, Strome and Kylesku, and others such as Kessock and Corran do valuable work. Strome Ferry is to be by-passed by a new road along the south side of Loch Carron, but it is very desirable that efforts should be made to remove some of the other bottlenecks, notably Ballachulish, where heavy delays are frequently the rule in summer. The deep inlet of Loch Leven has always been a barrier to communications south from Fort William (Plate 3). Difficult terrain makes it inappropriate to follow the old military road, which followed a direct course between Fort William and Kinlochleven over the hills and from there up the Devil's Staircase to Rannoch. The railway, it will be recalled, solved the problem by making a wide detour from Fort William to reach Rannoch Moor by way of Glen Spean, and the use of the railway from Crianlarich to bring timber to Fort William is partly an expression of the difficulties of transport by Loch Leven. The nodality of Fort William for industry and tourism now demands effective action and a bridge is projected. Yet it should not be forgotten that such action at Ballachulish without similar measures at Corran or Corpach would increase the isolation felt by people in Ardnamurchan, where local roads to Kilchoan and Polloch are in great need of improvement. The same point applies even more forcibly for the inhabitants of Bonawe on Loch Etive, whose ferry link with Taynuilt (for Oban) has been completely severed through inadequate usage. Improvements are bound to increase some local contrasts in accessibility as well as reduce others.

Another development which seems very possible is the extension of bridge building in a literal sense to the islands, where such developments have already linked Benbecula with north and south Uist and Bernera with Lewis. In the case of Skye it is thought that a toll-bridge across the narrows at Kyle could be built for £2·9 million (Scotland, 1969). A bridge would provide a more efficient crossing between Skye and the mainland and at certain times of the year would eliminate the bottleneck caused by the build-up of tourist traffic. In view of the removal of the costs of delay at the ferry and all-day access to the mainland for medical services which would follow, the idea has won a great deal of local support. It might make for better prospects in employment and working conditions by emphasising Kyle–Kyleakin as a major focal point on the west coast and would be important too for almost the whole of the Outer Hebrides, since the ferry links Uig at the north end of Skye with Tarbert (for Lewis and Harris) and Lochmaddy, which is a centre for the whole of Uist and Benbecula now that the causeways over the north and south Fords have been built.

Highland interests therefore call for investment in many transport projects to attempt to reduce in some measure the high costs incurred west of the Great Glen in general and in the islands in particular. But how far can a national government go in backing Highland transport, which is never likely to be a paying proposition overall? The argument can be sustained for the maintenance on social grounds of uneconomic but essential services, but how should 'essential' be interpreted? It could be a type of service which affords some sort of reliable contact or it could be a more sophisticated one involving heavy expenditure, allocated in the anticipation of economic growth which may not in fact materialise. Some form of compromise must necessarily be reached to reassure local feeling and at the same time avoid a major miscalculation which the public in general would rightly attack. Already rail, air and shipping services receive government support, as do MacBrayne's bus interests. Moreover special provision has been made for Highland roads over and above the Exchequer grants already mentioned. The Crofting Counties Roads Scheme was launched in 1935 and provides grants for surfacing selected roads in the crofting counties, and Department of Agriculture grants have been available since 1950 for unclassified roads. Thus in 1966–7 expenditure on roads in the Highlands and islands amounted to £20 per head of the population, compared with £6 15s for Scotland as a whole.

A new departure was made in 1959, however, when it was decided to set aside £250,000 each year to build new roads which would open up areas of scenic beauty and assist the tourist industry as well as serve isolated communities. New construction which could not be allowed previously on account of the very limited local interest can now be justified in the wider interests of tourism. Three roads have been completed under this scheme, the Balgy Gap road linking Shieldaig and Torridon in Wester Ross, the Ormidale–Tighnabruaich road in south Argyll and the Moidart road linking Kinlochmoidart and Lochailort in Lochaber and passing the village of Glenuig, which has hitherto been dependent on the ferry boat and track by Loch Ailort. This by no means exhausts the possibilities, for many other deserving cases could be mentioned, such as a link between Glencoe and Rannoch Station or through Glen Affric to Kinlochshiel. Another favourite is the Glen Feshie road, first discussed in Telford's time, which would cross the high watershed between Braemar and Aviemore and be a great asset to the developing tourist industry in the Cairngorms. Some of these are shown, along with the others, in Fig. 19.

As long as local requirements and tourist interests coincide developments may be generally welcomed, but how should any conflict be reconciled? Should a route be selected and a timetable drawn up with local or wider interests uppermost? The car-ferry services introduced by MacBraynes have been criticised for pandering to tourists, and the high rates for vehicles and merchandise are a perpetual source of complaint. Moreover it has been argued that the routes themselves are inappropriate in winter, when the condition of some island roads can cause difficulty. A service from Stornoway to Ullapool has therefore been advocated as a more satisfactory link for Lewis than the Tarbert (Harris)–Uig crossing or even the Kyle–Stornoway link. It is certainly true that the cost of maintaining all the roads suddenly subjected to increased traffic as the result of new car-ferry services places an additional burden on local authorities and ratepayers. The Highland Transport Board was set up in 1963 to give the problem the overall attention it obviously requires, but its co-ordinating role has now been taken over by the Highlands and Islands Development Board and the newly formed Scottish Transport Group.

FUNCTIONAL SYSTEMS

A prominent feature of Highland transport at all times is the high degree of integration achieved. Close co-operation between sea and land transport would of course be expected, but even on land there is little direct competition except south of the Great Glen, where road and rail are occasionally duplicated. Orientation may change through time, as is evident in the discussion over Islay, but at any one time there is normally little choice. Hence the hinterlands of the various service centres can be defined more realistically than is often the case further south under conditions of greater urbanisation and industrialisation, which make for considerable overlapping in the tributary areas around each town. Fig. 20 attempts to portray the pattern of functional regions which has been built up by public transport movements,

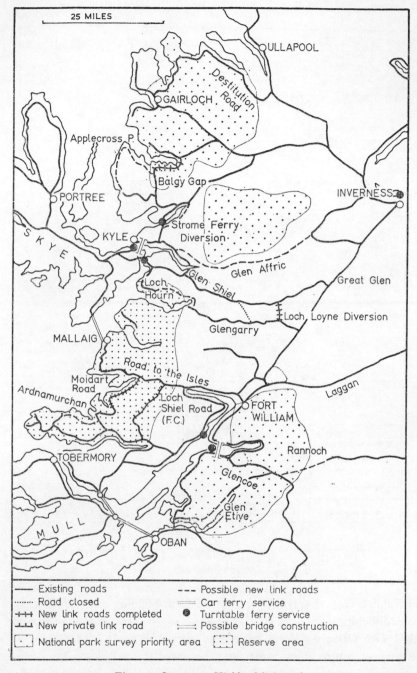

ULLAPOOL

Destitution Road

GAIRLOCH

Applecross P.

Balgy Gap

INVERNESS

PORTREE

Strome Ferry Diversion

KYLE

SKYE

Glen Affric

Glen Shiel

Loch Hourn

Great Glen

Loch Loyne Diversion

MALLAIG

Glengarry

Road to the Isles

Moidart Road

Ardnamurchan

Loch Shiel Road (F.C.)

FORT WILLIAM

Laggan

TOBERMORY

Rannoch

Glencoe

Glen Etive

MULL

OBAN

— Existing roads   --- Possible new link roads
⋯⋯ Road closed   ⚌ Car ferry service
+++ New link roads completed   ● Turntable ferry service
⊥⊥⊥ New private link road   ⚏ Possible bridge construction
⊡ National park survey priority area   ⬚ Reserve area

Fig. 19 *Some west Highland link roads*

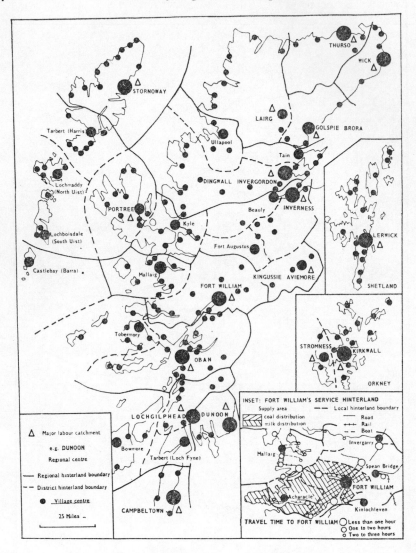

Fig. 20 *Service centres and hinterlands*

and follows very closely the earlier work of Fleming and Green (1952). Some difficulties arise, as in the case of south Uist, which is presently linked with Oban via Barra as well as with Kyle and Inverness via Skye and may in future enjoy a car-ferry link with Fort William via Mallaig. Moreover it must be admitted that the growth of car ownership tends to reduce the value of a hinterland map based simply on public transport, but in this case the scope for individual choice is such that any idea of rigid hinterland boundaries is untenable and the areas tentatively demarcated are functionally unified on the basis of probability rather than certainty.

But allowing these reservations, and also leaving aside Cowal, which is functionally linked with the Renfrewshire coast, eleven functional regions may be identified in Fig. 20. The hinterland of Inverness (Plate 21) extends westwards to the islands, with the mainland areas of Dingwall, Brora–Golspie and Thurso–Wick to the north and Fort William (Plate 22), Oban (Plate 23), Ardrishaig–Lochgilphead and Campbeltown to the south. In the islands, Stornoway (Plate 26) may be recognised as a separate area on the basis of the large population of that town, and the same applies to Kirkwall and Lerwick (Plate 25). For the rest, the small size of the island towns makes it more appropriate to visualise them as the centres of sub-regions within the hinterland of Inverness, except for Barra and Tobermory, which are linked with Oban, and Islay, which is orientated with Lochgilphead through Tarbert. On the mainland it is more difficult to identify sub-regions owing to the proliferation of small village centres on the west coast. Kyle and Mallaig are important, with their island as well as mainland contacts, but Gairloch, Lochcarron and Ullapool in Wester Ross, along with Durness, Lochinver, Scourie and Tongue in Sutherland, have only limited local importance. Only Ullapool is in a position to develop as the centre of a group of villages and hence co-ordination of services can best be achieved by towns on the east, such as Dingwall and Lairg, where the routes from the west converge.

FORT WILLIAM AS A SERVICE CENTRE

It would be tedious to describe the details of the pattern of servicing for the whole of the Highlands, and so the case study of Fort William will be taken. The town is situated at the southern end of the Great Glen in a position which has always enjoyed considerable strategic importance; it was important in the days of the kingdom of Alba in the context of the contacts with Ireland, and again in the context of a unified Scotland when Lochaber was a major objective in the struggle by the government for the control of the Gaelic fringe. Town life was not native to the early inhabitants and was imposed mainly through military necessity but partly as a result of the policy of James VI, who encouraged urban development there in addition to Campbeltown and Stornoway. Fort William, co-existing initially with small agricultural nucleii (clachans) at Banavie and Achintore, was variously known as Maryburgh, Gordonsburgh (from about 1819) and Duncansburgh (after 1834), before taking over the name of the fort itself. After it ceased to be garrisoned by regular troops in 1855 it retained only a very modest industrial and service function through its distillery, herring fishery and limited local contacts. The improving movement saw resettlement closer to the fort on the banks of the Lochy, and as an emigrant port it commanded a number of services. Nevertheless when the railway reached Fort William in 1894 it had only to demolish the fort in order to occupy the valuable site immediately beside the loch and so become the new nucleus of the town.

The appearance of the railway from Glasgow re-emphasised the locational value of the southern end of the Great Glen and the mouth of the Lochy. Fort William was now the undeniable commercial focus of Glen Lochy, Glen Spean and Nether Lochaber, and gradually extended its hinterland further afield. The extension of the railway to Mallaig in 1901 tied in the western areas more closely and placed Fort William once more on the Road to the Isles. Development of road services beyond Corran Ferry attracted local traffic from Sunart and Moidart, areas which had formerly been linked by steamer with Tobermory and Oban. Indeed the extent of Fort William's hinterland and that of its southern neighbour, Oban, is very much a reflection of the changing relative importance of sea and land communications. The position of these two centres is very similar, since both are at the southern end of the Great Glen and its continuation as Loch Linnhe, but while Oban has an obvious nodality for shipping routes, lying at the focus of the Firth of Lorn and the Sound of Mull, Fort William, at the landward end of Loch Linnhe, is a major land route centre. With the great development of steamer services through the Victorian era Oban became the 'Charing Cross of the North', neatly outflanking Fort William, which could attract little sea traffic other than that which the limited capacity of the Caledonian Canal could accommodate. But with the gradual shift in emphasis back to the land routes, in the railway and motor-car eras, the balance has shifted more in Fort William's favour. But as yet Oban's established railhead position and Fort William's difficult road link with the south over Ballachulish ferry have prevented all the implications of this change of emphasis from being realised.

Fig. 20 (inset) illustrates the present balance and outlines Fort William's hinterland as extending roughly from Badenoch in the east to the Small Isles in the west and from Invergarry in the north to Loch Leven and Loch Sunart in the south, thus embracing not only practically all the Lochaber district of Inverness-shire but also much of the Ardnamurchan district of

Argyll. It contains a number of apparent anomalies, however, for the Small Isles are included while a number of closer mainland districts – Glenelg, Ardnamurchan and Morvern – are orientated towards other centres. This is very much a legacy of the days when all mainland communities were served by sea and persists in Morvern because of the very difficult road to Corran Ferry and Fort William. Much the same applies in Ardnamurchan; although road transport will doubtless dominate eventually, as it does already for most of the freight and for mails, the sea journey to Oban 'overland' through Mull is preferred by passengers, as evidenced by the fact that a proposal to withdraw the Tobermory–Mingary service in 1964 and substitute it with a bus from Kilchoan to Lochaline (for Oban) was strenuously resisted. At Glenelg the balance is slightly different again: the road is difficult and is forced to climb steeply over Mam Ratagan to join the main Inverness–Kyle road at Shiel Bridge at the head of Loch Duich, but considerable use is made of it since it provides a far more direct link with Inverness than does the sea journey via Kyle. The withdrawal of all steamer services and the provision of a mail bus from Kyle has recently completed the process.

Such then is the Fort William hinterland for services in general, but it should not be interpreted too rigidly. It is fairly accurate for shopping and professional services, but certain distribution industries indicate important modifications. Postal services are geared very much to public transport; the main railways are the main source of supply for mail from the south and it is most convenient to drop the day's delivery at the various stations en route. Hence almost all the stations on the West Highland line are the centres of G.P.O. delivery areas. The postal area of Fort William covers only those districts which are further down the supply line and also lacking in rail communications, hence necessitating break of bulk in Fort William. The area therefore extends south and west to include Nether Lochaber and much of Ardnamurchan. Mail for a number of Argyll sub-offices is therefore addressed through Fort William, Inverness-shire. The boundaries of the delivery areas show a number of local discrepancies in the road network which maintain various links by water transport: thus Glencripesdale in Morvern where there is a small forest community is linked with Salen across the loch rather than with Lochaline in Morvern. Again the Meoble area on the south side of Loch Morar is linked by water with Morar rather than Arisaig or Lochailort, since only a rough track leads south to the main road. The dependence on water transport along Loch Nevis and Loch Hourn similarly relates Kylesmorar and Knoydart to Mallaig and Barrisdale to Arnisdale.

Mention of milk supplies in this context might seem surprising, since the popular image created by the proliferation of small agricultural units in the crofting counties is one of self-sufficiency in milk at any rate. In fact, however, the operation of the hill cattle subsidy has encouraged an almost complete swing to beef breeds, and much of the milk that is still produced locally goes for suckling calves rather than for human consumption. Moreover inadequate artificial price levels for milk fixed under present conditions of overproduction nationally, and exclusion from the winter keep scheme, mean that many marginal Highland producers are forced out of business and switch to more orthodox practices. This is merely one of many examples in the Highlands of national and regional interests failing to coincide, but the necessary reliance on outside sources inevitably consolidates Fort William's position as a distribution centre. However, the fact that delivery is made by both road and rail from north and south makes for a smaller supply area than with postal services, since a greater number of intermediate centres of demand can be supplied en route. But milk coming by road from Inverness and Nairn is forwarded by rail to Arisaig and by van to Ballachulish, areas which have only a very modest domestic production in contrast to the better grazing areas of Morvern and Appin, where some dairy units continue to support local distribution enterprises.

A still smaller hinterland is evident when coal distribution is considered. Now that the working of peat is going out in view of the high cost of labour, coal is the main fuel, especially in areas not yet connected to electricity supplies. Coal can be easily carried by rail, but when these facilities do not exist sea transport by puffers is still important. Ease of beaching in the case of the smaller puffers enables them to bring a year or half-year's supply to a small coastal locality direct from the Ayrshire coalfield via the Crinan Canal. When the dwindling of population proceeds beyond the critical level the demand may become too small to justify a puffer load, even at two-year intervals; this has occurred at Kinlochourn, where coal has been obtained by road from Invergarry since 1938. But the continued reliance on puffers in Morvern (Lochaline and Drimnin), Ardnamurchan (Strontian, Salen and Kilchoan), Moidart and Glenelg, as well as distribution from the larger railway stations, limits Fort William's area of supply very considerably. Coal distribution must certainly provide the only case of Fort William's sphere of influence extending no further into the Ardnamurchan district than Ardgour. However, petrol distribution shows a tendency to avoid sea transport wherever possible. This may seem surprising in view of the bulky nature of oil, but is understandable owing to the necessity to supply by sea in drums unless demand is large enough to justify a pipeline from a tanker to shore installations. Since the use of drums is expensive, small road tankers penetrate as far as possible and even carry fuel from Fort William to Lochaline (a village which is normally dependent on Oban for other supplies), even though weight restrictions at Corran Ferry make it necessary for loaded tankers to reach Ardgour via the long detour around Loch Eil. This then is a case of greater use of land transport tending to increase Fort William's supply area, although the limits are in this case determined by the location of the various oil companies' adjacent depots.

Fort William is thus becoming an increasingly effective service centre for Lochaber. The distribution of employment in various professional services emphasises this. It has been calculated that retail sales in the burgh of Fort William in 1961 totalled £1·7 million, some £900,000 of which was accounted for by shoppers from the hinterland while a further £400,000 was spent by tourists. Symbolic of the pressure on shopping space in Fort William is the finding that the average retail sales amounted to £22 for each of the 76,000 square ft of retail space and 9,000 square ft of catering and other premises in the burgh. This compares with an average for Scottish town centres of £11 to £13 per square ft. There is thus an impression that trading in Fort William at any rate is a lucrative occupation and that there is much growth potential as well. All parts of the Highlands therefore are not equal: it was emphasised in the section on land use that certain areas were more favourably endowed than others, but now it can be seen that the superimposition of local and regional functional links, as produced by the evolution of transport and other services, enables further discrimination to be made between centre and periphery. Nodality is thus becoming an increasingly valuable resource, and lack of this a growing handicap to development.

CONCLUSION

It must be stressed that the system of central places and hinterlands described is merely a tentative effort, the aim being to illustrate certain characteristics rather than impose a blueprint. A more sophisticated hierarchy must await further research, but of course any system is extremely flexible since different approaches may be adopted and modifications to the generalised hinterland boundaries may follow changes in transport; thus the Islay 'overland' scheme would have the effect of consolidating the nodality of Lochgilphead at the expense of Tarbert, whose sub-regional

6

status might in turn be compromised. What is clear, however, is that while certain towns have important central place functions, only a relatively small area of the Highlands is within effective daily commuting distance of them. Thus as long as opportunities of employment in manufacturing and services remain concentrated, villages and districts situated on the periphery of the various hinterlands will continue to experience a declining population and a deteriorating age structure. Moreover if new industrial growth is confined to a limited number of centres, an element of stagnation may permeate the whole of certain regional and district hinterlands in spite of their significant labour catchments.

These two points help to account for the division of the Highlands into growth areas as contrasted with certain less developed districts, where problems are often seen from a more emotional standpoint. This situation will be examined more closely in the following chapters, with consideration of policies to develop village centres and secondary growth points in addition to the major projects in Caithness, Lochaber and the Moray Firth. The difficulties of decentralisation are great; on regional grounds it could be argued that planning should allow greater prominence to the island approaches, especially Kyle, where road improvements on the routes to Inverness via both Strome Ferry and Glen Shiel are under way. A growth zone to embrace both sides of the narrows has been advocated and a similar case made for Ullapool, especially if a car-ferry route to Stornoway could be opened. Problems arise, however, over the weakness of the local economic potential for future growth and the limited number of good sites on the broken terrain typical of the west coast.

CHAPTER EIGHT

The Development of Power and Industry

PRIMARY industries such as agriculture, forestry and fishing lead on logically to various forms of processing or secondary activity. Originally this form of industry was carried on in a small way in most localities, often on a domestic basis. Technological developments in power, machinery and transport have made it practicable for a large population to be supplied from one large production unit. Similar trends are evident in agriculture and other primary industries, with a concentration on the more profitable mines, fisheries and agricultural zones, although differences appear by way of subtle contrasts in levels of intensification rather than simply by way of presence or absence of activity. Manufacturing, with its greater nucleation, is bound to choose a location where the greatest profits and efficiency can be obtained; that is, where supplies of power and raw materials can be most readily obtained, where access to labour and markets is good and where the costs of building and running the factory are relatively low. Usually, however, there is an element of choice and of subjective judgement, and hence every area cannot expect to have its merits objectively assessed by distant industrialists. A reserve of local capital and initiative is therefore always highly desirable, and bodies such as the recently formed Islay Development Committee and local Councils of Social Service have an important role in assessing and publicising local capabilities.

With the passing of the domestic phase of industry, when local primary production was mostly processed locally, the area has continually suffered from limitations in power supplies, raw materials and accessibility to markets compared with other parts of a country into the overall economy of which the Highlands now found themselves integrated. Labour, initiative and capital therefore gravitated south to areas where opportunities in manufacturing were more attractive, a move which gradually starved the region of wealth and talent, thus rendering a Highland location for industry less attractive still and local innovation more unlikely. But since high levels of employment and high living standards can only be realised by industrial growth – for primary industries can only employ limited numbers and have not as yet secured incomes and returns commensurate with those in manufacturing – it is of fundamental importance for the Highlands that the trend be reversed. The crofting counties must achieve their fair share of the country's manufacturing sector and, equally important, there must be a satisfactory distribution within the area. The following review will bear both these points in mind.

SCOTCH WHISKY

The case of the Scotch whisky industry is a remarkable one (Storrie, 1962*b*), for it concerns a native Highland enterprise which has succeeded in moving from a domestic to a factory base and at the same time has retained its links with northern Scotland. The art of whisky-making, it seems, was introduced to Scotland from Ireland in the fifteenth century, and the earliest direct record of whisky distillation is to be found in the Scottish Exchequer Rolls of 1494. The 'cunning chemists' learnt how to make it from the malt of their barley, the water supplies from local springs and the flames of the peat fires, the only other requirements being yeast to ferment the mash of saccharified cereal grains, including malt, and a copper cauldron and pipe to distil the resulting brew. The spirit was known in Britain as 'aqua-vitae', the water of life, and was translated by the Celts of Ireland and Scotland as *uisge beatha*, from which the word 'whisky' is derived, a word shortened and anglicised from the Gaelic. This was the 'poor man's wine' produced in small pot-stills in the glens of the west Highlands and islands, especially during the winter half of the year when agricultural interests did not demand great attention and when supplies of water, flowing through peat, were most plentiful. The whisky was not taxed but was rough and harsh, with a smoky pungency which outsiders were slow to appreciate.

It is likely that the attachment to the drink spread gradually to the Lowlands, and production began in some suitable places as the market extended south of the border, especially after the Treaty of Union in 1707. Problems arose, however, in the form of tax avoidance on the one hand and blending to suit the southern market on the other. The imposition of excise duties sparked off widespread illicit distilling in unlikely and inaccessible places, with sentries on the lookout for the gaugers. But the smuggling of whisky to the south and the uncertainty of this contraband trade was no secure base for a developing industry, and in the early nineteenth century accommodations were made. Duty was reduced to discourage illicit distilling and at the same time (1823) licences were issued for stills of more than 40 gallons capacity. Among the first to take advantage was George Smith of

Glenlivet, who took out a licence and rationalised his industry of small illicit stills which had flourished in the remoter glens of Speyside. He began the era of the 'whisky lairds', who ran prosperous family businesses in contrast to the one-man distilleries of the crofters and small farmers. The number of legal distilleries in Scotland accordingly rose from 114 in 1820 up to 259 by 1833. Once organised on a commercial basis the industry became a lucrative source of government revenue, and duty has progressively increased so that it now exceeds £10 10s per gallon.

The whisky produced in the pot-stills contained various impurities stemming from the local materials used, especially the water, which, having flowed through peat, is essential to malt whisky. Moreover the enterprise is relatively small-scale and double distillation is necessary, first to produce 'low wines' and secondly to produce the whisky as distinct from other matter, known variously as 'foreshots', 'feints', 'burnt ale' and 'spent lees'. The quality of the spirit and the scale of production were both inappropriate for expanding whisky sales to England and overseas countries, and it fell to Robert Stein in 1826 to produce a patent still enabling distillation by a continuous process known as rectification. Improved and patented by Aeneas Coffey of Dublin in 1830 it gave a high yield of pure spirit, with maize rather than malted barley the important raw material. This new grain whisky could therefore be produced efficiently in bulk and was more acceptable to townspeople, though the whisky taste is still dependent on the inimitable products of the smaller Highland malt distilleries. The blended whiskies therefore contain a body of 55 per cent grain whisky, with the remaining 45 per cent composed of three to four dozen malt whiskies from different distilleries. With so many possible combinations blending becomes a skilled operation: large concerns are inevitable in view of the heavy investment, and a number have pooled their interests to form the Scottish Malt Distillers, a subsidiary of the Distillers Company Ltd. Each concern has its closely guarded 'magic formula' for blending, though a proportion of the malt whisky is bottled straight as the product of one individual distillery.

The distribution pattern of whisky production is therefore an unusual one. The grain distilleries are in the Lowlands of Scotland, often close to the major cities which are the sources of imported raw materials and major consuming centres. Again, since blending is in many ways an assembly industry a central location is essential. Accordingly the whisky industry in central Scotland consists of a small number of large units, each requiring a great deal of warehousing space, for by law whisky must mature for at least three years. Production is therefore always several years ahead of purchase and consumption. But while the maltings may be centralised, as at Burghead and Muir of Ord, the small malt distilleries of the Highlands are still an essential component of the industry, and there were ninety-one of these in 1961 as opposed to eleven in the Lowlands. There is a recognised division of the malt whiskies, however, into Highland Malt, Islay and Campbeltown Malt (with heavy and peaty flavours) and Lowland Malt (made from less highly peated malt), though they do not coincide with geographical conceptions of 'Highland' and 'Lowland'. What is striking is the tendency for distilleries of each type of concentrate into major areas of production, though in all cases good access to roads, railway or sea transport is essential, not only in the interests of marketing but to obtain barley and coal. Even the peat is often brought in. Thus the bulk of the Highland Malt is produced on Speyside and the Moray Firth lowlands, while Islay and Campbeltown Malt is heavily based on Islay, where many of the distilleries are coastal and maintain contact with the Clyde by puffers using the Crinan Canal.

Within the crofting counties therefore it is Islay which has the greatest stake in the industry, and often this is the only source of non-agricultural employment in the island. Frequently distilleries have laid out entire villages, incorporating the distillery itself, warehouses and houses for employees, good examples being Bunnahabhain, Lagavullin and Laphroaig. Fort William can boast two distilleries, one of which, the Ben Nevis Distillery, is remarkable since both malt and grain whisky have been produced since a patent still was installed in 1955 by the owner, the late Mr J. W. Hobbs, whose cattle-ranching enterprise has already been mentioned. This has been done in order to allow blending on the premises and would not have been competitive with southern producers on its own. In view of this the Invergordon distillery is an interesting case, for this is purely a grain distillery (the second one in the Highlands). Since it was built at a time when grain whisky was in short supply, it would now seem to face a difficult future.

TEXTILES

Another industry having a deep-rooted connection with the Highlands and islands is the textile industry, Harris Tweed in particular. The local flocks of sheep provided a ready raw material which could be spun and woven on a domestic basis, and hence the production of woollen goods in various forms was common throughout the Highlands. Even before the introduction of

Blackface sheep there are reports of rents being paid in blankets or 'plaiding', and these articles also entered into trade with the south at an early date. After the improving movement, however, the possibilities increased and the heavier fleeces of the new breeds were in local use throughout the area. The problem has always been to get the industry on to a commercial basis comparable with the counties of north-east Scotland, where the agricultural revolution allowed a clear separation of agricultural and industrial functions. The surplus population was resettled in a number of planned villages, with woollen or linen manufacture as the economic base. In the west Highlands, however, linen failed to take root in spite of efforts by instructors sent north by the government in the eighteenth century, but sporadic progress was made in woollens. A number of mills sprang up which supplied yarn to home industries: thus the Holm Tweed Mills in Inverness sent yarn to producers of knitted goods in Orkney and Shetland, and Oban became a woollen textile centre of some importance on the west coast.

It was not until later in the nineteenth century, however, that the weaving of the Outer Hebrides became widely known, as Moisley (1961*b*, p. 354) explains 'partly for its utility and partly out of philanthropic motives'. For it was in 1844 that the Earl of Dunmore had tartan copied in tweed by local weavers in Harris. The experiment was satisfactory and, with growing contacts with the islands at the time of the deer-stalking boom, outside demand rose to the extent of justifying small depots. Other proprietors fostered the trade, notably Lady Gordon Cathcart in Uist and Barra. Interest spread to Lewis after about 1880, for it had been inhibited up to that time by prosperity in fishing, in much the same way as the industry had been stunted in the early nineteenth century in the Hebrides as a whole through its inability to compete with a local economy in which kelp was then supreme. Interest gradually spiralled, for at a time when Highland textile industries were contracting in face of competition from bigger factories closer to coal supplies, the entirely domestic industry of the Outer Hebrides was able to flourish thanks to its efficient marketing organisation and the high quality and peaty aroma of its product in an era which valued the 'glamour of homespun'.

The momentum was maintained partly by proprietors and partly by the Congested Districts Board. Water-powered carding mills were opened in 1900 at Tarbert (Harris) and in 1903 at Stornoway by local landowners. Non-profit-making marketing groups established depots at Stornoway, Tarbert, Obbe (South Harris), Uig and Balallan (Lewis), Lochmaddy (north Uist), Creagorry (Benbecula) and Lochboisdale (south Uist). The

Congested Districts Board for their part supplied instructors and financed improved looms and other equipment. These stimuli enabled the island weavers to meet the rising demand; growth in Lewis was particularly rapid, for almost 300 looms were reported by 1911 compared with only 55 in 1899. But growing demand created problems and in retrospect the industry can now be seen to have just emerged from a protracted transition period to a sound commercial footing, rather similar to the whisky industry in the early nineteenth century. Carding mills saved some time, but even so local wool became inadequate to support the industry and hand spinning became a burden. Producers were therefore encouraged to use imported wool sometimes of poor quality, and, more particularly, to take mill-spun yarn. Weaving now became the specialist occupation, and because of its heavier nature was often done by men on a full-time basis. But the mixture of hand- with mill-spun yarn and the use of some poor-quality wool tended to lower the former uniformly high standard and create mistrust. Difficulties were increased by the problem of distinguishing between fully hand-spun cloth and the much cheaper mill-spun tweed, which was being used in large quantities in Lewis but to some extent in Harris also.

It was only in 1909 that a trade-mark was sought and the familiar orb stamp used to mark tweed 'hand-spun, hand-woven and dyed and finished by hand in the Outer Hebrides'. Cloth was first stamped in 1911, but this genuine article, fully hand-spun, was still compromised by overproduction of inferior tweed from Lewis. The price of the 'Lewis' tweed was falling and there was a grave danger that the situation would only be saved by introducing power-looms to weave the mill-spun yarn. But if this happened the product would be in no way distinct from other factory woollens and would surely succumb to competition from southern producers. Yet rising demand could never be adequately met on the basis of 100 per cent hand-spun cloth. Compromise was found by way of commission weaving, initiated by the Newall family from Yorkshire who developed the idea after settling in Lewis as agricultural improvers. This practice of mill-spun yarn being handed out to individual crofter-weavers began in 1906 but received a boost after 1918 with the further declines in herring fishing already discussed.

Thanks to the use of good mill-spun yarn, often from England, and efficient finishing, often done on the mainland, the Lewis tweed industry achieved a high level of efficiency and quality while retaining its traditional associations. In 1934 therefore the definition of Harris Tweed was revised to accommodate these new practices: cloth could now be stamped if it was 'made from pure virgin wool, produced in Scotland, spun, dyed and finished in the Outer Hebrides and hand-woven by the Islanders at their own homes in the Islands of Lewis, Harris, Uist and Barra and their several purtenances and all known as the Outer Hebrides'. Backed by effective advertising by the Harris Tweed Association, sales of cloth mounted through the inter-war period. It meant, of course, that to qualify for the stamp cloth had to be carded, dyed, spun and finished in the Outer Hebrides, albeit by mechanised methods. 'A skilful balance was struck between a true domestic craft product, selling in limited quantities at a high price, and a mass-produced article; the resulting expansion of production has been the economic salvation of the island of Lewis' (Moisley, 1961*b*, p. 363). There are some 1,400 weavers at work, the majority of whom combine this steady employment with work on their tiny crofts. In addition there are roughly 1,000 employed centrally in the mills in Stornoway. Production now exceeds 6 million yds and consumes a third of the total Scottish wool clip.

Harris Tweed has therefore placed itself commercially on a sound footing, at least for the time being. Just as Scotch whisky must be produced in Scotland by legal definition, so the orb stamp for tweed can only be used for cloth which satisfies the terms laid down in 1934. But it is worth stressing that while whisky has the additional protection of imitation being wellnigh impossible outside Scotland, and malt whisky is tied closely to the Highland environment, tweed has no such natural defence. There is no real reason why cloth of commensurate quality with Harris Tweed cannot be produced on the basis of weaving in the isles, as at present, with all the other processes carried on in mainland mills. Indeed a cheaper product might possibly result. Consequently, just as the original definition of Harris Tweed was considered outdated and replaced by a more liberal certification, so today there are interests, represented by the Independent Harris Tweed Producers Ltd, which consider greater mainland participation to be economically desirable. The decision by Lord Hunter that the 1934 terms should remain in force was reached after the longest court hearing in Scottish legal history. It has been suggested that 1964 may be recognised as the year in which Harris Tweed was preserved for posterity as the birthright of the people of the Outer Isles. Yet the fact remains that continued Hebridean association is largely maintained by the construction of a legal barrier whose permanence cannot be assured. Since the weaving accounts for only 15 per cent of the total cost of the tweed, the loss of the other processes to the mainland would be disastrous for the island.

An even closer parallel with Scotch whisky lies in the location of the industry. Whisky production in the crofting counties shows a definite tendency to nucleate, and the same is true of Harris Tweed considered in an Outer Hebridean context. It is ironical that the bulk of the tweed is produced not in Harris, as the name suggests, but rather in Lewis, it being deemed expedient to retain the old name in spite of a locational shift of emphasis. As soon as the product ceased to be entirely a domestic industry the small carding and spinning mills exerted their influence. These mills existed only in Tarbert (Harris) and Stornoway (Lewis), as compared with the more comprehensive coverage of tweed depots existing in 1906. Additional freight costs from the mills to Barra, Uist and Benbecula meant that weaving became concentrated in Lochs and Uig in Lewis and around the eastern bays of Harris. Carding mills were proposed for Uist, but nothing was done by 1914 and weaving had practically died out by the end of the war in these southern isles. Later, however, the shift to mill-spun yarn gave Lewis an increasing share of the total production as outside capitalists moved plant to Stornoway once the commission weaving system and new certification were operative. Spinning machinery was installed in Harris, but that island preferred to stick to the genuine domestic home-spun product to which the orb stamp no longer gave particular recognition. The spinning wheel has slowly died out in Harris, but in the absence of any movement to commission weaving with the treadle loom the yarn from the Tarbert factory goes to Lewis, as does the production from the spinning mill on north Uist, opened experimentally in 1947 in an attempt to revive interest in weaving. Thus, except for a limited amount of tweed woven in Uist for mainland mills, all Harris Tweed is now woven in Lewis. Yet within that island the distribution of weaving is not regular, for the emphasis is undoubtedly on the northern and central areas which can be reached most conveniently by vans from the mills in Stornoway. Townships on the roads to Ness and Tolsta and the circular road to Barvas, Shawbost, Carloway and East Loch Roag are well represented, with only a few scattered centres in Lochs and Uig which were the original centres at the turn of the century.

Apart from Harris Tweed the woollen textile industry in the crofting counties is small and scattered. There are small mills in such centres as Inverness, Oban and Portree (Skye), and weaving concerns operate at Lochcarron (Wester Ross) and Kilmuir (Skye). In the setting-up of these smaller enterprises, often combined with a range of other home industries, much has been achieved by Highland Home Industries, a non-profit-making organisation which started up after 1918 to produce and market various hand-made goods. The weaving centre at Kilmuir was one of their first efforts, and this now functions as an independent concern with H.H.I.

concentrating more on marketing, which is done from their chain of shops throughout Scotland. They still retain an interest in the weaving at Morar (Lochaber), which was started after 1945, and the production value, at £12,000, forms a considerable proportion of the total H.H.I. sales, which rose from £3,000 in 1914 to top £70,000 today. The three weavers employed are also crofters and generally suspend activities in summer to concentrate on agriculture. Though small numbers are involved, such enterprises can make an important contribution in rural districts and attempts are occasionally made to launch out on a larger scale, especially since the Scottish Country Industries Development Trust has appeared to stimulate such local effort. However, the market is highly competitive and it is unlikely that a large market would exist for such high-cost quality products. At the same time vigorous local leadership and innovation is most important, and more of it in strategic areas such as the Shetland knitwear trade might achieve much in resuscitating and developing flagging domestic industry.

ALUMINIUM REDUCTION

Textiles and whisky are the two main Highland industries to survive the steam-power era which lay at the root of the industrial revolution. Enterprises like the iron furnaces at Invergarry and Bonawe, which had come to the Highlands in response to cheap and plentiful supplies of charcoal, were forced out of business as the bulk of the nation's manufacturing was attracted to the coalfields of central Scotland, north-east England, Lancashire and Cheshire, South Wales and the Black Country. Such concentration was demanded by the high cost of transporting the large amounts of coal which the relatively inefficient processes of the time consumed. Any manufacturer with premises situated far from the pithead would have his ability to compete thereby impaired. As the momentum continued to build up, the sophisticated infrastructure necessary to support large factories made it more difficult to break away from the narrow confines of the coalfields, where all the necessary services were laid on. The only exceptions were the ports, including London, since it was clearly desirable to process imported raw materials at the break-of-bulk point. In this situation the valuable water-power resources of the Highlands, *neart nan gleann* (the strength of the glens), could not be used.

The Highlands are not completely lacking in coal resources, but they are very small and scattered and have never been the basis of industrial growth.

Development was restricted to Brora in Sutherland and Machrihanish in Kintyre. In the latter case mining originally took place at Torchoilean and Ballygreggan, but the 'Wimbledon' shaft sunk in 1881 was abandoned in 1928. The mine at Machrihanish was opened at the beginning of the century, but after a fire in 1925 and flooding in 1926 it lay derelict until it was re-opened by the Glasgow Iron and Steel Company in 1946, eventually becoming the responsibility of the National Coal Board. Some expansion was attempted, the Kilvillan seam being opened in 1958, but difficult geological conditions were encountered and heavy losses (quoted as £50,000 each year) were sustained as demand declined locally. The mine closed in 1967. At Brora, however, where coal has been dug since 1529, the private mine is still open and produces at a rate of some 12,000 tons annually. After first buying the mine with Highland Fund loans when the Brora Coal and Brick Works Company went into liquidation, the miners have now received a grant of £100,000 from the Highlands and Islands Development Board to drive a shaft into a new seam recently discovered and estimated to contain 8 million tons of coal. The money will provide screening plant, conveyors and hoppers as well as underground works, and annual production may eventually rise to 16,000 tons. With outlets in local distilleries and further afield likely to be supplemented in future following growth around the Moray Firth, there is the prospect of steady progress over a great number of years.

The use of electric power, however, meant an immediate reappraisal of Highland resources. The water-power potential was known to be great, and all that was needed was the finance and technology to exploit it and a market for it on site. Technology was not very refined, and after the experiments of 1882, when a small dam was built at Munich, and 1890, when the monks of Fort Augustus constructed an 18-kW station, only very small sources could be harnessed. Moreover since there was no grid system and no means of transmitting electricity efficiently over any distance, the power had to be used where it was generated. But there was a market opening up in the aluminium industry. This was first produced by reducing aluminium chloride vapour with potassium, a process developed by Wöhler at Göttingen in Germany in 1827 and perfected by Doville in France in 1854. The interest of Napoleon III did much to stimulate development, but although the price came down from about £50,000 per ton in 1856 to £7,500 in 1884, aluminium was still a semi-precious metal. If some substance could be found which would conduct electricity and in which alumina would dissolve, then an electric current passed through the solution would deposit it as a metal. It was in 1886 that Héroult discovered the electrolytic process of reducing alumina in a bath of molten cryolite, a substance found in Greenland. Cryolite proved to be an excellent catalyst, since it was heavier than aluminium, which therefore sank to the bottom of the furnace and could be siphoned off without interrupting a continuous process of reduction. The process was meanwhile discovered simultaneously in America by Hall. It was to acquire British rights in this Héroult–Hall process and in the Bayer process, a method of producing pure alumina from bauxite, that the North British Aluminium Company was set up in 1894. They required a relatively cheap and reliable electricity supply, for 22,000 kW-hours were needed to produce one ton of metal, and a small hydro scheme was the answer.

The company's initial operations were at the Falls of Foyers in Inverness-shire, on the southern side of Loch Ness. The 7,250-acre Lower Foyers estate was purchased in 1894 along with the water rights of five other proprietors to cover a catchment area in Stratherrick. In 1895 construction of the first major hydro-electric scheme in Britain began, to harness a catchment area of some 100 square miles. There was a 'head' or drop from reservoir to power station of 350 ft, and the capacity was 3,640 kW. The factory opened in 1896, when world production of aluminium was only some 2,000 tons, and the output from Foyers represented an important contribution. This amounted initially to 200 tons annually and was as much as could be sold, for the price of £100 per ton still restricted its use in many fields. However, with increased efficiency and widening markets production rose to 400 tons, using all the power available. Previously the surplus power had been used for experimental purposes and also by the Acetylene Illuminating Company for calcium carbide production.

It is interesting to observe that at the time the various installations owned by the North British Company were integrated by sea transport, rather than by land transport as is the case today. The alumina was obtained from works at Larne Harbour in Northern Ireland, where local Antrim bauxite was processed by the method developed by Bayer in the 1880s (though the quality of the local ore was found to be poor and French supplies were imported). The alumina – and the carbon electrodes manufactured at Greenock from 1897 – were taken by sea to Foyers via the Caledonian Canal and the return cargo of ingots and rolling slabs conveyed south to a rolling mill at Milton, Staffordshire, acquired in 1895. Finally soda ash and other necessary chemicals were taken back to Ireland.

The Foyers plant represented a major achievement for the Highlands.

There was no existing settlement or labour force of any size in the area, and all materials had to come in by water to build not only the factory but also a village which eventually housed 600 people. The company recorded that 'the impoverished crofters and fishermen of the Western Highlands acclaim with gladness the advent of this industry into their midst, offering as it does a welcome addition to their scanty opportunities of wage-earning. It inspires them with a genuine hope that the devastating tide of emigration may be stayed, and their beautiful but desolate glens may ere long witness a prosperity hitherto unknown'. The pace began to quicken, however, and world production rose to 7,000 tons by the end of the century. Accordingly production at Foyers was pushed up to its maximum of a little over 1,000 tons per year.

In order to place themselves in a sounder position at the time when the Héroult patents were due to lapse, the company resolved to build a larger factory at Kinlochleven, and in 1904 an Act was passed setting up the Loch Leven Water and Electric Power Company. The work carried out consisted of the construction of the Blackwater Dam, 2,800 ft long and 85 ft high, to provide a storage reservoir of 3,930 million cubic ft draining a catchment area of 55 square miles of hilly country with an average annual rainfall of over 80 in. Also required was a conduit of reinforced concrete nearly four miles long and a six-line pipe-track over a distance of one and a quarter miles to the power house sited with the reduction factory and carbon electrode plant alongside.

By 1909 the factory was open and producing 8,000 tons of aluminium each year, roughly a third of the total world output. It was a big improvement on Foyers, for not only was there a bigger market but some of the technological restraints were removed: downtake pipes, no longer of cast iron, could withstand greater pressure, the 8,000-ampere furnaces at Foyers may be compared with sizes growing from 16,000 to 40,000 ampere at Kinlochleven, and the power-station capacity was many times larger at 23,725 kW. To cope with the greater output an additional fabricating factory was opened at Warrington in 1914 and another alumina factory at Burntisland, Fife, in 1917. Foyers was still supplied by sea transport, vessels entering the Caledonian Canal via Clachnaharry at the Inverness end. Supplies reached Kinlochleven by rail to Ballachulish and then by road vehicle. The choice of Burntisland was to be explained partly by the need to supply alumina to reduction works in Norway, which the company developed at Bergen and Kristiansand from 1907.

Once again there was almost complete dependence on sea transport, and an important part of the scheme was the construction of a harbour at Kinlochleven and the dredging of the 'narrows' at the mouth of the loch. The Loch Leven Shipping Company was formed in 1908 and served the village until a road was opened along the south side of the loch in 1922. Five years later a satisfactory road was built along the northern side too. The population of Kinlochleven (or Aluminiumville, the name first proposed) reached 1,210 in 1910, compared with the tiny crofting population which existed before. The first permanent housing consisted of forty-eight three-roomed flats built in Foyers Road in 1910, a site which proved unfortunate since no sunshine could be enjoyed during the winter months. It has been argued that housing developments at Ballachulish would have been more appropriate, and indeed many employees today commute from that end of the loch, but the transport problems of the time made this a difficult arrangement. Building started on the north side of the river in 1920 at Kinlochmore, after the company acquired the Mamore estate. This is better from an amenity angle but introduces an administrative problem, since the town now crosses a county boundary. A call to extend the boundary of Argyll across the river at Inverness-shire's expense in 1928 was not sustained, and both local authorities are now involved in housing and services. Kinlochleven is still very much a company town, with all the inhabitants directly or indirectly dependent on the reduction works.

But this plant was not enough as world production increased to 43,000 tons by 1911. Contemporary advertising asserted that 'heavy iron pans promise soon to be interesting relics of the past and Cinderella downstairs, who wrenches her back lifting and carrying the clumsy iron stock-pot, will certainly bless the fairy metal that alleviates her laborious task'. But it was not only domestic consumption which was rising, for increasing military use was being found in aircraft, road transport and ammunition; demand rose from 70,000 tons in 1914 to 130,000 tons by 1919. The ceiling had been reached at Kinlochleven, for all that could be done was to build a small extension to draw in the water of Loch Eilde Mor and increase the catchment area by 7 square miles. It was intended to use the water of Loch Treig at an enlarged Kinlochleven plant, but a Bill presented to Parliament in 1918 seeking powers to do this was opposed by Inverness-shire, who objected to the resources of the county being used to benefit the industrial growth and rateable value of Argyll, in which county the Kinlochleven plant was situated. Accordingly the scheme was modified and interest shifted to Fort William.

It was in 1921 that the Bill to establish the Lochaber Power Company received the Royal Assent, and work began in 1924 with the help of a government guarantee covering the issue of £2,500,000 of debentures. Extensive preparatory work was undertaken, including accommodation for 2,000 men, a pier at Fort William, a temporary power station at Monessie Falls and twenty miles of light railway. The catchment area covers 303 square miles, but construction work was carried out in three phases completed in 1929, 1933 and 1943, the latter stage being fulfilled in time of war with the aid of Canadian troops. The first stage was to tap the water from Loch Treig through a pressure tunnel 15 miles long and 15 ft in diameter. From its outlet the downtake pipelines, three-quarters of a mile long, lead to the power station at Fort William, from which a tailrace runs into the Lochy (Plate 30). Eleven side streams are diverted into the tunnel by downtake shafts. In the second stage the level of Loch Laggan was raised to provide storage capacity of 1,401 million cubic ft by means of a gravity concrete dam 700 ft long and 130 ft high. The water is transferred to Loch Treig through a three-mile-long tunnel. Meanwhile the capacity of Loch Treig was increased to 7,370 million cubic ft by a 40-ft-high rock-fill dam. This meant diverting the West Highland Railway but allowed some extension of the power house. The third stage was to dam the Spey in its upper reaches and lead the water through a tunnel to Loch Laggan and on to Loch Treig. The new reduction factory's contribution of 23,000 tons per annum raised the output of the Highlands to some 34,000 tons. To cope with this enlarged scale of operation a new alumina factory was opened at Newport, Monmouthshire, in 1939 and a new rolling mill commenced production at Falkirk in 1944. Complications arose over the supply of bauxite now that French supplies were cut off by the war. Accordingly work on the Awaso deposits in Ghana (then the Gold Coast) was accelerated from 1941, and other supplies came from Guiana, Brazil and India. Even the low-grade Northern Ireland deposits were reworked after forty years' inactivity when ore-boat sinkings became severe, though the Larne factory closed down in 1947.

At Fort William a sizeable nucleus of population already existed, but it was small in relation to the influx which followed the Lochaber scheme. As at Kinlochleven, the company took a hand in the provision of housing at Inverlochy through the Inverlochy Village Improvement Society. The factory draws on other communities in the Fort William area for labour, but limited public transport reduces the radius, especially in Ardgour, where there is no public transport to Camusnagaul ferry and no early morning service at Corran. Even though Fort William has a more diversified economy than Kinlochleven, the British Aluminium Company is still a powerful force employing nearly 600 people. There is a tendency for numbers to decline slightly with increased efficiency in working the furnaces and producing carbon anodes. Difficulties arise at times of prolonged drought, when shortage of water in the reservoirs may mean shutting down some of the furnaces. Such occurrences are rare, the last serious incident arising in February 1963, when fifty men were laid off at Lochaber after a two-month-long drought. Agreements have been reached with the Hydro Board to take power from the grid in case of emergency.

Times have changed dramatically from the conditions obtaining when the Foyers plant began operation, or in 1890, when a mere 172 tons was the total world production of aluminium. Largely unaffected by the depression, world production reached 690,000 tons in 1939 and had rocketed to 1,920,000 tons per annum by the end of the war. The increasing output of the Highland reduction works was therefore becoming at the same time a smaller proportion of the world total. Hydro-power potential was essential, yet while only a few Highland catchment areas had been developed none of the remaining ones was now large enough to provide sufficient power for the large factory, which was then at the optimum size for efficient operation. Even the large output at Lochaber could only be achieved by linking three catchment areas together at considerable expense, and the whole scheme must owe something to the conditions of war which prevailed both at the time of its conception and during the completion of the final stage. There was a desperate shortage then, and all possibilities had to be considered. Indeed the government even went so far as to sanction reduction works using electricity from the grid, factories in South Wales at Port Tennant and Rheola operated on this basis in the later years of the war and produced 12,500 tons of aluminium each per year. But these high-cost plants were both closed down on the cessation of hostilities.

Attention was moving to the larger catchment areas of North America and Scandinavia. In 1926 a 360,000 kW power station came into operation at Saguenay in Canada solely for use by the aluminium industry, with investment running at less than half that needed to install each kilowatt in the Highlands. Even the Lochaber scheme is tiny by present world standards, with its 85,750-kW power station and 40,000-ampere furnaces, compared with the 100,000-ampere furnaces now in regular use elsewhere. Since contemporary aluminium reduction factories were being built with an annual production of some 100,000 tons of aluminium, further development in response to Highland water power is now out of the question. Aluminium smelters using thermal or nuclear power are being considered in Britain, but a Highland location is no longer a unique attraction. Moreover for similar reasons any electro-chemical or electro-metallurgical industry based on hydro power may be ruled out. Thus the thrice-rejected Caledonian Power Bill (1936, 1937 and 1938), which envisaged calcium carbide production from the water power of Loch Quoich and Loch Hourn, cannot be realistically revived, 'a tragic mistake not only for Scotland but for Great Britain' (Scotland, 1943, para. 40). But perhaps more significant is the viability of the existing plants, especially Foyers and Kinlochleven. The tiny Foyers factory found itself in a perilous position in the post-war period but took on a new lease of life in 1954 when it was converted to refine super-purity aluminium. Virgin metal from Kinlochleven and Lochaber, brought over the improved road from Fort Augustus, was used, and the end-product, which was then taken south by rail from Inverness, was of more than 99·99 per cent purity, with properties of durability, ductility, relectivity and lustre making it particularly suitable in specialised chemical plant, reflectors and condenser electrodes. Even so the small size of the plant inhibited economic operation, particularly at a time when the world market for super-purity aluminium was proving to be variable. At a time of sharpening international competition the B.A.C. clearly had to concentrate its resources along the most effective channels. Regrettably, but predictably, the Foyers factory closed in 1967 and the sixty-eight employees either left the industry or moved to other factories. Since Foyers is largely a company village, the closure has inevitably disrupted the community. It would be inappropriate for this to generate alarmist sentiments over the future of Kinlochleven, which is awkwardly located and poorly endowed with sites and amenities for other development. Yet conditions in the industry are clearly very different from those prevailing in 1900, and with the total number of jobs at the factory tending to dwindle still further with the closure of the laboratory, some diversification would be most desirable.

Other technological developments have altered the picture too, for many of the transmission problems which bedevilled the industry in the early days have now been removed. Not only are the Highland reduction factories somewhat anachronistic in terms of size, but their location is no longer necessitated by the need to use the power at source. With efficient transmission along a grid system power can be used far from the generating station. There is no longer any reason to expect industrial growth to follow further exploitation of Highland water catchments; indeed it has been suggested that the main outcome of hydro-electric development has been the expansion of electrical engineering on Clydeside! (Lea, 1962, p. 28). However, technological change is also enabling aluminium smelters to be set up using power from the grid, in view of the increased efficiency of coal-mining and thermal power production. The Highlands no longer offer a special attraction, but although other companies have interests in north Wales and north-east England, the Scottish connections of B.A.C. make Invergordon, with its deep-water anchorage, good communications and extensive sites for development, an attractive location for the new reduction works now under construction with a capacity of 100,000 tons per annum. This factory will obviously have an invigorating effect on the Highland economy as a whole, but will make a special contribution to the Highland and Islands Development Board strategy of Moray Firth development (Plate 24).

THE NORTH OF SCOTLAND HYDRO-ELECTRIC BOARD

Following the pioneer work of the B.A.C. a number of schemes for public supply were launched. The Clyde Valley Company's installation opened in 1926, to be followed by the stations opened by the Grampian Electricity Supply Company at Rannoch (1930) and Tummel (1933). The Ross-shire Electricity Supply Company operated at Loch Luichart from 1934 (Plate 32). But supplies were unco-ordinated and the hydro schemes co-existed along with smaller steam or diesel plants, such as that at Gorteneorn in Ardnamurchan, installed by the proprietor in 1928 to supply part of the estate. Progress was piecemeal and often hampered by organised opposition from landed interests. Well might the Cooper Committee conclude that the whole subject of hydro development 'has become involved in an atmosphere of grievance, suspicion, prejudice and embittered controversy' (Scotland, 1943, para. 13). It was largely as a result of the enthusiasm of Mr T. Johnston that the North of Scotland Hydro-Electric Board was set up in 1943 to handle future development and sell surplus power in the south to the Central Electricity Board. Under nationalisation the Board retained a unique position, and discharges, in its district north of a line from the Tay to the Clyde, the functions undertaken in the rest of the country by the C.E.G.B. and the various area boards. Under the same Electricity Act the N.S.H.E.B. took over existing local authority and private company undertakings in the north.

A number of difficulties have arisen in the efficient use of Highland water power, for it is very difficult to achieve heavy discharge at the same time as a good head. West-coast rivers are steeply graded, but the flow is limited and moreover often not regularised by large lochs or snowfields, so that winter flow is many times that experienced in summer. By contrast the easterly flowing streams give a greater and more regular discharge, but an adequate 'head' can often only be achieved at great expense, by building power stations underground or by leading water in tunnels through a watershed to a power station at a lower level. Thus in Glengarry water from Loch Garry is led through the hillside to a power station in the Great Glen on the shores of Loch Oich, while in the adjacent valley of Glen Moriston the power station is completely underground. Capital costs are very high by comparison with Canada and Norway, and further expense is involved in modifying the infrastructure. The damming and enlargement of lochs frequently means the flooding of sections of road, and diversions must be built. There are several examples of short diversions on the Invergarry–Kinlochourn road alongside Loch Garry and Loch Quoich, for instance, but more spectacular is the eight-mile diversion to avoid Loch Loyne, which was enlarged as part of the Moriston scheme. The old road from Tomdoun to Cluanie is now closed, though its original path across the loch and the crumbling bridges can still be seen in times of prolonged drought.

Hydro schemes also complicate the land-use pattern in an area by sterilising valuable areas of low sheltered ground, and arable land too in some cases. The value of hill farms in the vicinity may thus be affected and farm buildings and shooting lodges flooded. The damming of Loch Quoich destroyed both shooting lodges, and all that remain are the stunted remnants of the former policies. A further problem arises over fishing, which has often been damaged irreparably, though the installation of salmon ladders has done much to enable these fish to reach their spawning grounds. Clearly agricultural and sporting interests can command heavy compensation or even prevent a scheme altogether, especially when landed interests combine with the country amenity lobby in opposing what is construed as 'desecration'. Schemes to flood Glen Affric have been consistently rejected (1929 and 1941) and in the end Loch Mullardoch in Glen Cannich was enlarged and water fed into Loch Benevan by a three-mile-long tunnel. Certainly large increases or decreases in discharge along river beds can spoil a beauty spot, but it can also be urged that the installations accompanying a hydro scheme, if carefully built and sited, comprise a positive tourist attraction.

Figs. 21 and 22 indicate the progress made in the electrification of the Highlands, and show the catchment areas developed and the transmission-line system. The bulk of the output of the N.S.H.E.B. consists of power

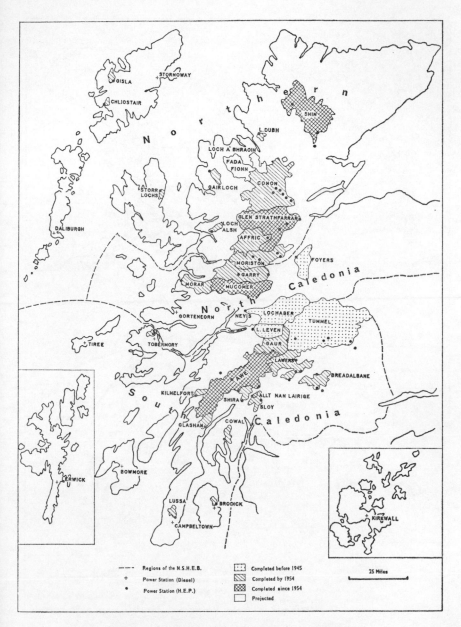

Fig. 21 *Hydro power stations and catchment areas*

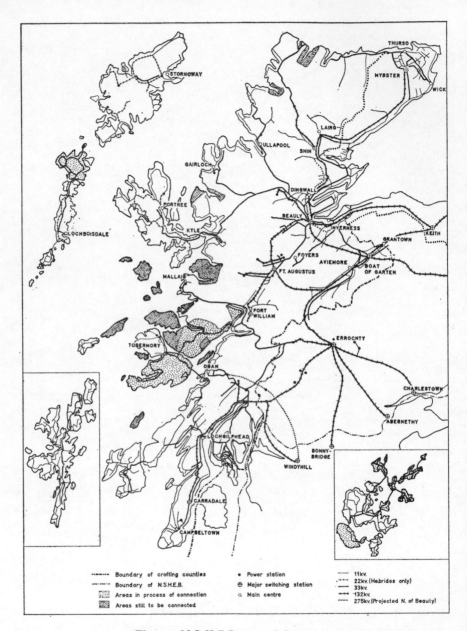

Fig. 22 *N.S.H.E.B. transmission systems*

from relatively large catchments. Various small schemes were also initiated in the early post-war period to supply certain districts in the west not then linked with the grid system. Thus the Morar scheme was completed in 1948 to supply Arisaig and Mallaig; Loch Dubh (Ullapool), Kerry Falls (Gairloch), Nostie Bridge (Kyle) and Storr Lochs (Portree) are some other examples. Where hydro schemes were not feasible diesel sets were installed at various points, especially in the islands (Table 6). Some private diesel plants have

Table 6. NORTH OF SCOTLAND HYDRO-ELECTRIC BOARD:
Installed Capacity, 1949–67 ('000 kilowatts)

	1949	1955	1961	1966–7
Hydro power				
Conventional	86·9	558·8	884·5	1,047·1
Pumped storage	–	–	–	300·0
Steam power				
Oil	–	–	–	240·0
Coal	131·4	102·9	132·9	132·9
Diesel power	32·7	42·4	44·7	49·5
Total	251·0	704·1	1,062·1	1,769·5

Source: *North of Scotland Hydro-Electric Board*

been taken over, as at Ardnamurchan in 1955, but others remain outside the Board's control, such as those at Coll and Colonsay. Mention must also be made of the United Kingdom Atomic Energy Authority's breeder-reactor station built at Dounreay, near Thurso, between 1955 and 1959. Being an experimental reactor as well as a power station the permanent staff is large, and this mainly immigrant labour force has been the mainspring behind the increase in the population of Caithness by nearly a quarter between 1951 and 1961. The population of Thurso burgh rose from 3,200 in 1951 to an estimated 9,012 in 1966. The age structure has been rejuvenated and educational and other services greatly improved. Now, as announced in 1966, a further prototype fast reactor is to be built at Dounreay, thus endorsing the position of Caithness as a major Highland growth point. But it is important that industry should be developed in the area as well.

Although the numbers employed are small once the construction is over, the Board have built nearly 400 houses to accommodate its permanent staff, often in small rural communities. It has also made a remarkable contribution in connecting consumers in all but the remotest parts of the

Highlands and islands, and by 1963 had connected 94 per cent of the total population and 85·8 per cent of the farms and crofts. This includes some 110,000 consumers in 'uneconomical areas' served only at a heavy annual loss. Another £7 to £8 million would be needed to extend supply to other areas, and this is gradually being done through submarine cables from the mainland to certain islands. Once these have been laid certain diesel stations can be shut down. Work is beginning in Uist to provide a network embracing the whole island and extend the existing line from Daliburgh to Gramisdale (Benbecula) and across the North Ford to Lochmaddy in North Uist. Grimsay will be connected en route and other islands will be integrated, Baleshare by overhead poles and Berneray and Barra by submarine cable. Ultimately some 700 consumers may be supplied. Mull has recently been linked with the mainland by a 33,000-volt cable; in 1962 a line was laid, from the main supply line at Lundavra, across Corran Narrows to Ardgour and thence to Morvern, with a submarine cable to Mull in 1965. A southern link with the 33,000-volt system at Tullich, south of Oban, has also been laid to Kerrera and over the Firth of Lorn to Mull in 1966, thus placing the island on a supply 'ring'. The diesel station has gone out of operation and some 250 new consumers in eastern Mull and Morvern have been connected. A line is also to be built to Salen and so link the isolated network around the Ardnamurchan diesel station with the grid and extend supplies to the Strontian valley and crofts near Acharacle. The problem of west Ardnamurchan will remain, however, and this is one of several areas in the Highlands still likely to be dependent on gas and paraffin lighting in the foreseeable future. Coverage, however, can never be complete, for although the Board's functions include the 'social clause' which requires them to 'collaborate in the carrying out of any measures for the economic development and social improvement of the north of Scotland', the Cooper Committee (Scotland, 1943) considered that large parts of the northern area could not, under any circumstances, be given a general supply. It is clearly economically impossible to serve the remotest habitations.

Local people appreciate the value of an authority set up for the benefit of the Highlands and operating exclusively within that area, and there was a storm of protest in 1962 when the MacKenzie Committee (Scotland, 1962) recommended that the N.S.H.E.B. should amalgamate with its opposite number in the south of Scotland. There was instant awareness that amalgamation would automatically mean the subordination of Highland interests to the greater demands of central Scotland. In the words of the Convener of Inverness County Council, Sir Francis Walker, 'the Highlands have different needs from the industrial area and would not get the special consideration they require from one joint board'. Mr J. M. Rollo, Chairman of the Highland Fund, felt that if there was amalgamation 'every penny profit would be squeezed out and spent in the south'. It was with great satisfaction that the Secretary of State's decision to maintain the independence of the N.S.H.E.B. was received.

The connection of more consumers will certainly continue, but the costs of production in the Highlands must be considered alongside those in the south where the Board's surplus is sold (Munby, 1956–7). With refinements in other forms of generation the desirability of new construction schemes in the Highlands is becoming questionable. The potential is still considerable; the estimate of the Water Resources Committee (1921) of 1,880 million units was revised by the Cooper Committee (1942) to 4,000 million, compared with the Board's estimate (1944) of 6,270 million. Technological developments give a current assessment of some 7,250 million units. But it has been argued that further hydro-electric plants 'are not calculated to confer a net economic benefit to the country, either in the short run or in the long run, and expenditure on this object should immediately and finally be terminated' (*Oban Times*, 2 June 1962, p. 1). Accordingly the Secretary of State has refused to sanction a number of new schemes, including those for Glen Nevis, Fada-Fionn and Laidon, on the grounds that none of them will be needed at least until 1975. Greater prospects may lie with pumped storage schemes which use power generated elsewhere at periods of low demand to pump water back into the main reservoir. Power to do this is supplied through the grid from power stations (including nuclear power stations) which operate most efficiently on a continuously steady load, with the result that capacity is higher at times of great demand. Stron Mor (1957) was the first pumped storage scheme to be completed, and this has been followed by Cruachan (Loch Awe). Plans are advanced for additional schemes on Loch Lomond and Loch Sloy and also in the Foyers area, where water could be pumped from Loch Ness to a generating unit at Loch Mhor in Stratherrick. This will involve the acquisition and redevelopment of the B.A.C.'s smaller orthodox hydro plant, which has become redundant with the closure of the aluminium factory there.

NEW INDUSTRIES FOR THE HIGHLANDS

It is disappointing that more industrial growth has not taken place in the Highlands following the provision of electricity supplies. The role of electricity is in some ways similar to that played by coal in the earlier stages of the industrial revolution; factories which were once tied to a coalfield location can now use electricity as the basis of their power supply and on these grounds could be located anywhere. These industries have been described as 'footloose', but this is a misleading title because many of the lighter industries which have grown up in Britain since 1918 are closely geared to supplying the home market and are therefore built in the best position for nation-wide distribution. While many areas in the Highlands have the necessary infrastructure to support industry, the fact that distribution from there is bound to be more costly will normally tend to attract industrialists away to areas closer to the demographic centre of the country, which in the case of Scotland is the Central Valley and for the United Kingdom is the London and Midlands area. These are the regions which have tended to grow most rapidly over the last fifty years, expanding in much the same way as did the coalfields before, when they were concentrating on heavy basic industries such as shipbuilding and textiles to supply a world market which did not begin to shrink through autarkic policies overseas until the beginning of this century. With the changing emphasis on the peripheral regions of Britain they have shown a relative decline, with stagnation in some of the old coalfield areas and continued depopulation in marginal rural areas like the Highlands. The present extent of the development areas illustrates the distinction remarkably well. The Highlands appear in the context of those parts of the country which have been denied prosperity commensurate with that enjoyed further south. All suffer from rates of unemployment in excess of the national average and enjoy various forms of government aid. Highland resources can therefore be appraised in a more sympathetic light.

One example of a successful industry established recently in the Highlands processing local raw materials is Alginate Industries Ltd, a firm which commenced operations in the inter-war period to produce alginic acid from seaweed by means of a process discovered in 1883. The product is used as a stabiliser and thickener in a wide variety of products, including food items like jellies, custard powder and instant desserts and other items such as lubricants, paint and foundry sand. Raw seaweed is gathered by some 500 freelance collectors, mainly in the Outer Hebrides. It is cut from rocks at low tide and then floated ashore on the following high tide. Drying and milling factories exist at Orosay (south Uist), Sponish (north Uist) and Keose (Lewis) which process the seaweed prior to its transfer to mainland factories at Barcaldine (Argyll) and Girvan (Ayrshire), where the alginic acid is extracted. The problem is to maintain supplies of seaweed to the milling factories to keep up production. Accordingly seaweed is collected in the Inner Hebrides, Orkney and Shetland and conveyed in bulk to the Outer Hebridean factories. The annual output of the Keose factory is 800 dry tons, representing 32,000 tons of wet seaweed, but 1,000 tons could be produced if more collectors were available. However, the work is essentially part-time since winter working is impossible with high tides or bad weather.

Another small but flourishing industry, Tennant's Loch Aline Ltd, had grown up around the silica sand of Morvern in north Argyll. It was in 1925 that Sir Edward Bailey drew attention to the 18-ft-thick bed of white sandstone lying under the Ardtornish and Fiunary estates. The sand was valuable for the manufacture of optical glass on account of its very low iron content, but mining did not begin until 1940 when established European sources of supply had been overrun. Leased to Messrs C. Tennant, Sons and Co. Ltd, one of the present owners, the mine met practically all the optical glass requirements for war purposes, but afterwards it had to face competition from Holland and Belgium. However, thanks largely to the unfaltering faith in the mine of the founder, Mr E. W. D. Tennant, production continues at a rate of 70,000 tons annually and reached a total of 1 million in 1962. Carried by sea to Glasgow and Manchester, about half the production goes for optical glass and the remainder for domestic abrasives and similar products. Glass manufacturers in Wick, Irvine and Waterford, Ireland, also use Lochaline sand, and present output may be doubled now that new crushing and screening plant has been installed.[1] This will mean an increase in the labour force over and above the present forty and assure the position of Lochaline as the local village centre for Morvern (Plate 4).

Interest has been expressed in other mineral resources, but often the small scale or poor quality of the material makes mining uneconomical. The diatomite deposits in Skye have remained abandoned for many years, while the once large slate-quarrying industry at Ballachulish which employed four hundred men in the late nineteenth century has been abandoned since 1955. The old quarry face, 1,400 yds long, and huge mounds of waste rock still dominate the village, many of whose inhabitants are now employed at the Kinlochleven aluminium factory (Plate 3). Many of the smaller lime quarries have ceased production; abandoned lime kilns and other installations at Salen in Lismore are a legacy of the once prominent industry in the island, when lime was taken by schooner to various destinations in the

[1] Deliveries to Norway began at the end of 1969.

Highlands. Since the closure of the dolomite mine at Keil (Appin) worked by Cape Asbestos Company for rock-wool manufacture, the main remaining limestone quarries are at Ullapool (Wester Ross), Torlundy (near Fort William) and Kilchrenan (Argyll), which deal mainly with lime for agricultural requirements.

Various attempts have been made to restart operations in the lead-mining area of Strontian in Sunart, north Argyll. The village has given its name to strontium, a substance which was isolated in 1790 after its discovery in the lead mines in 1764. The original company was formed in 1722 by Alexander Murray, proprietor of the estate, and run as an open-cast mine by the Duke of Norfolk and Company. A mining village was established and named New York, after the York Buildings Company who took over operations in 1730 and began smelting the ore from shafts sunk at Bellsgrove, Middleshope and Whitesmith in shallow hearths. The end-product, amounting to some 400 tons per annum, was taken away by sea. Meanwhile lead ore was discovered on the Morvern side of Loch Sunart at Lurga around 1737 and the mine leased from the Duke of Argyll, the ore being conveyed by ponies to Liddesdale for smelting. It appears that operations were run down during the late eighteenth century and completely suspended after 1815. After this the Strontian mines were then worked only sporadically by the proprietor, but over 1,000 tons of lead concentrate was produced between 1852 and 1871, the highest annual figure being 239 tons. Since 1871 there has been no production whatever and the crofting townships of the Strontian valley at Scotstown and Anaheilt remain as a legacy of earlier activity. Temporary interest has been shown at Bellsgrove on several occasions, in 1901, 1917 and in 1957, when a number of samples were taken. In 1963 a new company, Scottish Canadian Highland Development and Exploration Ltd, was formed to conduct mineral exploration there. Diamond drilling is being carried out, but the results of the investigation have not yet provoked other activity.

Interest has been shown in the possibilities of extracting potash from a belt between Loch Eriboll (Sutherland) and Loch Carron in Wester Ross. Although extraction would be difficult, the potential tonnage of potassium is large. Certain shales have a potash content of up to 11 per cent, which could be extracted through a process using magnesia-free limestone such as that existing around Torlundy, near Fort William. The Highland Development Board have been looking into a scheme to extract potash from Sutherland shales at Fort William, at a daily rate of 200 tons of shale yielding 40 tons of potassium nitrate, combining this with cement production at a rate of

600 tons a day. Unfortunately the scheme has proved to be uneconomical, though eventual uses may be found for this material.

The peat bogs of Scotland offer possibilities for commercial exploitation and experiments have been carried out at Altnabraec in Sutherland by the Hydro Board to see if local peat could be used for power generation in the same way as bogs in Ireland currently support a chain of small power stations, mainly in the Irish Midlands. More recently it has been reckoned that Laggan Bog and Monadh nan Cathag near Bowmore in Islay could provide sufficient fuel to maintain the island's power plant (currently running on diesel oil) and supply the distilleries for about twenty-five years. According to information in *Scottish Peat Surveys*, published under the auspices of the Department of Agriculture and Fisheries, 90,000 tons of milled peat could be produced annually from these bogs, which would employ a hundred men during the summer and sixty-five in winter. Surveys of 9,500 acres of bog in Lewis reveal that certain areas could be drained, ploughed and prepared for intensive cultivation and, with suitable pre-cautions, trees could be planted. Similar investigations have been made on Claish and Kentra Mosses near Acharacle in Argyll.

TIMBER INDUSTRIES

The most dramatic progress has been made in the fields of timber-using industries and tourism. The Highland woodlands are a rapidly developing asset as the forests planted by the Forestry Commission in the 1920s begin to reach maturity. The original aim was to create a strategic reserve of timber, but even so the accumulating reserve has begun to act as an economic challenge not only to the state but to private landowners. With some £60 per acre invested and no return for some twenty years after that, it is essential that an outlet should be assured eventually offering prices which will give a fair return. Even with planting and maintenance grants many foresters have been investing as an act of faith. Small factories exist in Inverness and Strachur, Argyll, manufacturing chipboard, but only small amounts of timber are taken (about 25,000 tons per annum), while the N.C.B.'s demand for pit-props is declining. Yet the timber output of Scotland, which was only about 110,000 tons in 1950, rose to 280,000 in 1964 and is likely to reach 567,000 (17 million hoppus ft) by 1970 and 1,130,000 tons (34 million hoppus ft) by 1980. The outlet for small timber (less than 8 in. in diameter) is particularly critical, since this accounts for two-thirds of the total.

Thanks to the efforts of Dr Frankel and others the answer has been found in pulp and paper manufacture, which appears to be economical and able to compete successfully at home against Scandinavian imports. Timber is is being obtained from the Forestry Commission at prices which should match the average paid in Sweden, but even though raw material costs and pulping costs are no keener than in Sweden, economies are achieved by producing paper on the same site. The liquid pulp can be fed straight into the paper mill without the need to dry, transport and reconstitute, and this saving of some £8 per ton or 15 per cent of the total cost of paper manufacture means that the Fort William paper line can be supplied appreciably more cheaply than a factory further south using imported pulp. A large pulp mill simply selling dried pulp to other British paper companies could not match Swedish prices – and could not be supported by Scottish forests either – but the integrated mill can compete. But if the cost of timber delivered at the mill runs too high, because of high transport costs for instance, then Swedish competitors will have an advantage at the wood-pulp stage.

Timing is very significant, for although the demand for paper is always increasing the optimum mill size is also tending to grow, while there is a limit to the wood supplies that Scottish forests can offer and also a limit to the distance over which the timber can be economically transported to the mill. Accordingly when discussions first took place in 1950 it was found that there was insufficient timber to support a mill meanwhile, and Wiggins Teape & Co. Ltd, who have shown a consistent interest in the Highland pulp-mill project, therefore went ahead with new plant for a hardwood mill at Sudbrook in Monmouthshire. Subsequent re-examination in 1957 showed that a large pulp mill would not be feasible until the 1970s at least, but an integrated mill was an immediate possibility. The plans of Scottish (Pulp) Development Ltd, now Scottish Pulp and Paper Mills Ltd (wholly a subsidiary of Wiggins Teape), were approved by Inverness County Council Planning Committee in 1960. Agreement was reached with the Forestry Commission in 1961 and the area of supply was extended to cover forests within a radius of up to 135 miles from Fort William, compared with the 100-mile radius suggested earlier (Fig. 11). This increased the potential and reduced the need for premature clear felling and the use of good saw-log timber for pulping. Work began in 1963 after a special Act of Parliament had enabled the government to lend up to £10 million (repayable over a period of ten years from 1966) to help finance the first phase costing £20 million. This was necessary since the grants normally available in development areas did not apply to the pulp mill on account of its capital-intensive nature.

Construction at Annat followed the cutting of the first sod by Lord Polwarth, Chairman of the Scottish Council (Development and Industry) in July 1963. The Highland contracting firm of Duncan Logan Ltd, of Muir of Ord, Ross-shire, won the building contract for the factory and also for a large number of company and local authority houses in the Fort William area. But the construction of the mill and all the necessary amenities and services, not to mention extensive site preparation and the removal of large amounts of peat, gravel and topsoil, strained the resources of a small area and made it necessary to compete for labour all over the country at a time of shortage. Other improvements needed were on the roads, which in some cases were found to be insufficient to cope with the increased traffic expected after the mill's opening. The bridge over the Lochy near Fort William was widened and the Corpach Basin on the Caledonian Canal was enlarged to accommodate vessels of up to 1,000 tons. Larger vessels, up to 16,000 tons, will have to berth offshore by artificial concrete islands or dolphins and unload their hardwood chips, which Scottish forests cannot provide, with the aid of electro-hydraulic graps and have them blown through a pipeline to the mill. About one-third of the timber needed will be hardwood from Canada, and the first shipment arrived from St John's, Newfoundland, in March 1965. It was at the end of 1965 that production began, although the official opening was delayed until the autumn of 1966. Some difficulty was experienced with the pulp mill, which is only the fifth in the world to use the Swedish Stora process, giving a high wood to pulp yield. The paper mill, however, is standard machinery and was operated on imported pulp so as to be in full working order when the pulp mill was ready.

Why should the pulp and paper mill be located at Fort William? The site at Annat was preferred in the first instance because it was a satisfactory collecting centre for the timber. Some 17,000 trees (500 tons) a day will have to be felled and transported to Fort William to provide the 8 million hoppus ft of softwoods, mainly spruce and pine, which will be needed each year. Fort William is quite central for the whole Highlands and islands and its location should continue to be satisfactory in the long term as further areas of the Highlands are planted. But the road links are not so satisfactory to the south as the detour around Loch Leven means delay and traffic congestion, so the railway can be used instead. Crianlarich acts as a collecting centre for timber from much of Argyll and Perthshire (representing about 40 per cent of the total); this is loaded by day into one of two special trains operating at night between Crianlarich and Fort William and in the reverse direction. Being sited on a tidewater, supplies of foreign hardwood can be brought in direct through the Corran Narrows, and so can softwood from island forests if and when these mature. A tidewater location is also invaluable for discharging effluent, which can be carried straight out to sea (Plate 31).

The other important factor is water, which is consumed in huge quantities. 100,000 gallons of water are needed for each of the 80,000 tons of pulp to be produced annually, and this will come along a three-mile pipeline from the tailrace of the B.A.C.'s power house at their aluminium factory. Up to 50 million gallons can be taken each day, an amount which will be adequate to cope with any future expansion at the mill. Indeed the 80-acre site allows for doubling of both the pulp and paper sections, and these later phases of development may be carried out when local forests can supply the additional wood needed and when the demand for the paper products (which include cartridge, printing, writing and duplicating papers) justifies a second paper machine. It may only be a few years before the second paper machine is installed, bringing the present labour force of 700 to over 1,000, but the additional pulp capacity is not likely before the 1980s. Meantime surplus pulp is sent to other mills in the Wiggins Teape group.

The effect of the pulp mill has been to assure Fort William's position as a major Highland growth point of population and industry. Development may well go further on two grounds: first, the pulp mill is turning out finished paper and hence paper-using industries may be attracted marginally on account of local supplies; but secondly, and probably more important, the largely male-employing pulp mill and aluminium factory mean a reservoir of female labour among the families who have moved into Fort William, mainly from Clydeside but also from within the Highlands and north-east Scotland. One of the greatest attractions a development area can offer an industrialist apart from financial concessions is a ready labour force, and it is entirely for this reason that a small clothing factory opened in Fort William in 1966. The firm of Edward Greenwood and Co., of Hebden Bridge, Yorkshire, wished to extend their production of trousers, and being unable to get labour to staff extended premises at the main factory they have located the new growth in the Highlands. But the growth is controversial, to the extent that it is emphasising an area which was already well placed economically. Other Highland areas could have benefited from growth, yet the current demands for a central position make the more inaccessible places unlikely locations for industrial growth except on a very small scale. But comfort can be taken from the fact that employment in the forests throughout the Highlands will be increased; in fact over 1,000 men will be employed on felling, extracting and transporting trees for the pulp mill, and since only the poorer thinnings will be pulped there will be additional work to cope with the saw-log timber which will also be cut when clear felling on a rotational basis is started. To this extent the pulp mill has an important rural component.

TOURISM

Another prominent 'growth industry' is the tourist trade, which has developed from the Victorian concept of a long vacation at a country house or shooting lodge to touring by a broader cross-section of the population. All counties have increased their tourist industry, though the majority of tourists concentrate on Argyll and Inverness, the two most accessible counties, where centres like Inverness and Oban are particularly important (Table 7).

Table 7. GROWTH OF TOURISM, 1955–65

| County | Number of visitors in | | | Percentage growth, 1955–65 |
| | 1955 | 1960 | 1965 | |
		(in thousands)		
Argyll	347·4	406·8	352·8	1·6
Caithness	41·9	46·4	50·5	2·0
Inverness	332·7	475·8	510·9	53·5
Orkney	15·0	22·3	23·9	59·3
Ross and Cromarty	120·7	181·8	187·1	52·5
Shetland	18·8	17·0	21·8	16·0
Sutherland	47·8	65·3	86·9	81·9
Crofting counties	924·3	1,215·4	1,233·9	33·6
Scotland	4,202·0	5,073·0	5,212·0	24·0

Source: *Scottish Tourist Board*

It is of course unnecessary to dwell on the theme of the beautiful scenery for which the Highlands is rightly renowned, or to mention the romanticism which references to the Young Pretender invariably stir. Holidays in the Highlands have been fashionable ever since Queen Victoria took up residence at Balmoral on Deeside, but the tourist industry cannot flourish on these resources alone. Indeed it has been argued (Scottish Vigilantes Association, 1964, p. A8) that the Highlands are not in a position to appeal to the tourist mass market owing to the limited facilities, and furthermore that to do so would result in visitors in search of quiet and solitude being discouraged. But it is surely a problem of development rather than one of lack of capacity.

7

The case against tourism, on the grounds that it 'adversely affects the character of people and reduces their ability to support themselves in a more constructive and viable way', is countered by experience, which suggests that considerable skill and care is required and that given this the industry can be highly profitable, a point strongly made in connection with the growth of tourism in crofting townships.

Accessibility is still a problem in a relative sense, for although most roads have been greatly improved, limitations in time or money will remove the attractions of remoter mainland or island districts, especially since these do not contain the standard attractions of Culloden, Loch Ness, Ben Nevis and Glenfinnan. The tremendous variations in accessibility within the Highlands will tend to concentrate much of the tourist traffic along the main touring routes. Further points emerge when the Highlands as a whole are fitted into a national context, for while the Highlands compare favourably on scenic grounds, the effective tourist season is very short. Hotels and boarding houses must therefore close for most of the year or stay open with a low level of usage, which in turn suggests that much of the employment offered by the tourist industry is necessarily seasonal. Other holiday areas face similar problems, but many are better placed to extend the season by attracting conferences (a trade which Oban is just beginning to develop now that the new Corran Halls are open) and enjoying better off-season weather. The 'nearness' problem is a big factor, and many people in the United Kingdom can holiday on the Continent more cheaply than they can tour the Highlands. The effect of this is to discourage hotel building and the installation of other amenities in the absence of which tourists will be further discouraged. Winter sports offer some scope, but so far only the Cairngorm area has been able to make great progress. Even here hotel usage is low during certain months, particularly in November and early December before the winter season begins.

The majority of hotels in the Highlands were not built specially for the purpose, and many consist of converted estate mansions or shooting lodges. Others are small, though long-established, inns, and some are merely upgraded guest houses. Limited local capital coupled with a short season and high building costs combine to make new hotel building marginally more difficult in the Highlands. Thus the Scottish Tourist Board comments that 'in rural Scotland where there are vast areas in which tourist facilities must be provided . . . but where initially at least private finance would be unwilling to speculate in the provision of accommodation, practical government investment will soon become essential if development is not to be handicapped and an opportunity lost to restore economic security' (Report for 1962, p. 5). They suggest that 'just as the government assisted industry in post-war years to overcome the financial hurdle by building factories throughout the country, the time has now come when it should build hotels in rural areas like the Hebridean Islands and lease these out at economic rents to qualified operators' (Report for 1962, p. 6). When capital is limited it is debatable to what extent it should be spent on developing growth industries rather than on the protection of declining elements of the Highland economy.

Continuing progress has been made in recent years. The Scottish Tourist Board first received limited funds to the extent of £15,000 per annum to secure the fuller development of the tourist industry in the Highlands, and Sir Hugh Fraser set up a private finance corporation, the Highland Tourist Development Company, from which those interested in providing additional accommodation or other tourist services in the Highlands can borrow funds. For the first time in thirty years new hotel building is under way, and the momentum has now been carried forward by the Highlands and Islands Development Board, whose plan to build a chain of hotels in the islands has been approved by the Secretary of State. The first hotel has been built at Craignure in Mull. Moreover attempts to get local planning authorities to co-operate in the compilation of a national plan for tourism have inspired a greater readiness among local bodies to tackle tourism on a regional basis, and this has been followed up by the establishment of area tourist organisations with a chain of information centres covering the whole of the Highlands and islands.

The most spectacular development of recent years has been at Aviemore. The idea of developing the skiing potential of the Cairngorms arose during the last war, when Glenmore was used for training Norwegian commandos, and passed on to the Scottish Council for Physical Recreation. This in turn led to the founding by Karl Fuchs of the Austrian Ski School at Carrbridge and the setting-up of the Cairngorm Winter Sports Development Board (now known as Cairngorm Winter Sports Ltd). Growth since 1962 has been very rapid, with developments at Aviemore itself as well as at Coylumbridge, where the new Rank hotel has opened, and in Glenmore, where further amenities will be provided. Available accommodation has increased from some 80 beds in 1949 and 138 in 1963 to roughly 1,100, of which 625 are to be found in the Aviemore centre and at Coylumbridge, the two biggest establishments around which smaller private hotels are setting up. Investment has also gone into ski lifts and tows, facilities enlarged in 1961, 1964 and 1966, and road improvements have been made not only to the A9 trunk road from the south but also to the Coylumbridge–Cairngorm road in 1961, with further improvements to Glenmore in 1966. With the application of a tarmac surface to the road the number of persons using the Glenmore camping site trebled from 17,274 in 1960 to 51,053 in 1965.

If the Cairngorm scheme proves to be a viable concern, it cannot fail to act as a major 'growth point' for tourism and will exaggerate the already marked tendency for the tourist industry within the Highlands to coalesce into a number of areas which offer modern amenities and entertainment. Already fears have been expressed that the attraction of Aviemore will draw tourists from their established haunts, to the detriment of these other Highland areas.

Centralisation is unfortunate in a number of ways, but mainly because the basic attraction of the Highlands lies in the unspoilt nature of the countryside and in the relatively uncrowded conditions compared with most other parts of Britain. Rather than channel tourists into limited areas by default or design, should the object not be to disperse visitors as much as possible so that these fundamental advantages are not obscured? The dilemma is clearly seen in Glenmore, where the large Cairngorm tourist development creates problems of land use. In the words of one writer, 'the issue of whether to preserve, partly preserve or abandon the natural landscape presents unacceptably conflicting alternatives'. Will the economic value of scenic beauty be eroded away by over-development? How close and on what scale should tourist services be provided at beauty spots? These are important questions, too often ignored through divided ownership of land in any one area and by a proliferation of interested bodies which may cloud broad but important issues. Yet the inescapable conflicts certainly make co-ordination difficult.

It is important to develop other major tourist areas, and to this extent it is encouraging to see another case of the industry consolidating itself in specific areas in Lochaber and north Argyll. This area has many natural advantages, including Ben Nevis and Glencoe, not to mention Glenfinnan and some fine coastal scenery on the west coast. Lochaber enjoys good communications with the south as well as with Inverness and the Western Isles. This potent combination of accessibility and amenity can hardly be avoided by the Highland tourist, even though the climatic implications of the proximity of Ben Nevis are not always desirable. The potential for winter sports has scarcely been realised, and the momentum tentatively generated by the isolated development at White Corries in Glencoe, where some hotel and ski-tow facilities are available, may be consolidated if action follows the survey presently being conducted on Lochaber's winter sports capability. This area, along with the established tourist centre of Oban to the south, may well prove to be a viable counterweight to the Cairngorms in summer and winter alike.

But this leads to a further difficulty, for concentration within individual tourist areas is very evident. In the Lochaber case the prominence of Fort William as the main point of attraction is well established and the town earns an estimated figure of between £1 and £2 million each year from tourism. The process of local concentration may be studied by using Scottish Youth Hostels Association bed-night statistics, which bring out the interesting pattern of regional differentiation shown in Table 8. As would be expected,

Table 8. GROWTH OF TOURISM IN LOCHABER YOUTH HOSTELS

Hostel	Number of bed-nights recorded in		
	1959	*1962*	*1965*
Garramore	1,790*	5,523	6,955
Glenelg	1,236	1,555	2,085
Glen Nevis	14,609	17,443	17,501
Loch Lochy	6,834	6,204	4,968
Loch Ossian	2,276	1,311	927
Total	26,745	32,036	32,436

* Part season only

Source: *Scottish Youth Hostels Association*

Fort William hostel (Glen Nevis) is the most heavily used of all the hostels in Lochaber, catering for more visitors than the other four together. Garramore, however, shows up well since it combines a situation beside the machair beaches of Morar with one on the route to Skye. But if several years' experience is taken it is evident that the contrasts are widening. Usage at Fort William and Garramore is increasing, while Glenelg shows some small improvement with the introduction of the summer vehicle ferry service across Kylerhea Narrows to Skye. But at Loch Ossian on Rannoch Moor, with no road access, there has been a noticeable falling-off over the years, while Loch Lochy is losing some of its importance as a 'staging post' in the Great Glen. This pattern is only one component of the tourist industry, though it may well be broadly representative.

How can growth be spread more evenly through a tourist area like Lochaber in order to counter the inevitable build-up in the main towns? Planning might aim at some dispersal of the impact by establishing more attractive secondary centres; thus Ballachulish, near Glencoe, has been suggested as a site for local development. But such effort would have to be backed up by plans to put more emphasis on the rural amenities. Already many empty cottages in remoter areas are being taken over for summer use, though road access is normally important. Yet even in remote corners of roadless areas there is some activity, and the centre at the head of Loch Nevis (Camusrory) used by Dr Barnardo's Homes may be mentioned, as well as the pony trekking introduced at Mamore Lodge above Kinlochleven. Other interesting local developments include the crofting museum at Achindrain, the golf course laid out in Ardnamurchan, examples of local initiative without which the remoter districts are never likely to enjoy their fair share of employment from tourism. A tourist report on Lochaber in 1969 recommended transport improvements in Ardnamurchan and the Small Isles, but considered that the country between Loch Arkaig and Loch Hourn should be designated a wilderness area to preserve its wild and remote quality.

On a somewhat larger scale a very attractive idea is to try and create public interest in the forests; the head forester at Inverinan, Argyll, is already planning to open walks through his forest with an explanatory booklet to try and tempt people off the road to learn something of what goes on inside a woodland. The wild life within a forest is a subject of particular interest, and photographs and other exhibits will be put on show. There might well be a case for opening up, in a controlled fashion, national nature reserves and areas scheduled as being of great national beauty. Considerable opportunity may be available with proposals to establish a national park in the Ben Nevis–Glencoe area as well as in the Cairngorms. But great care will be needed to ensure that over-concentration at certain access points is avoided, otherwise the whole idea of dispersal will be contradicted and the local infrastructure grossly overstrained.

The ideal arrangement for the Highlands would thus seem to be a whole series of developed tourist areas, with coherent centres balanced by attractions in the countryside. With this in mind it is interesting to examine the integrated programme once suggested for part of the north-west mainland by the Wester Ross Tourist Association. They advocate the development at Kyle of a hotel, restaurant, swimming-pool, yachting and boating marina, information centre and indoor sports facilities, with appropriate installations

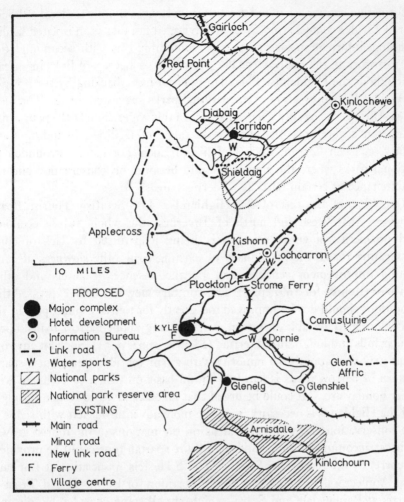

Fig. 23 *Tourism in Wester Ross*

in the surrounding rural areas (Fig. 23). Smaller hotels should be built at Glenelg and Torridon, with 'Continental'-type camping facilities introduced in addition to the improvement of existing sites. The idea is put forward of forming leasehold holiday units in crofting townships. New road links are then advocated from Arnisdale to Kinlochourn, Bundaloch to Camusluinie, Ardaneaskan to Kishorn, Applecross to Shieldaig and Red Point to Gairloch, along with unmanned information points at Glenshiel, Lochcarron and Kinlochewe, key points where secondary roads to the beauty spots take off.

Information centres are of the greatest importance not only for local publicity but in a wider context; they must be envisaged not just as an isolated facility handling information for one area or combining this with accommodation bureau work in the main towns like Kyle, but as a series of links in a chain throughout the Highlands. This plan is given more backing by the position of Wester Ross in relation to the national parks suggested for the Torridon, Glen Affric and, possibly, Glenelg areas. In this wider context the plan would bring out a core area offering a wide range of facilities, including water sports on Loch Carron, Loch Duich and Loch Torridon, surrounded by national parks where the emphasis could be more on conservation and the maintenance of certain parts as wilderness areas.

But what of the rest of the Highlands? The Scottish Tourist Board considers that 'west and north of Inverness the whole future economy and prosperity of entire counties is being jeopardised by lack of communicating roads, the inadequacy of existing roads, the slowness of completing improvement schemes and by the absence of hotels and other services' (Report for 1961, p. 7). The contrary view has been expressed that conditions should not be improved too greatly for tourists, since 'part of the attraction is to be able to return south talking about narrow roads, spectacular hills and long waits at ferries' (Skewis, 1962, p. 51). Such an environment may well appeal to a minority with a flair for adventure, but a sparse pattern of narrow roads is hardly a sound basis on which to compete with other holiday areas. It could be urged that an efficient basic system throughout the Highlands is necessary, with the more adventurous left with scope in the conservation and wilderness areas on the margins of the tourist growth centres; accommodation facilities of a more spartan type could be provided, as currently offered by the Scottish Youth Hostels Association at Lonbain, near Applecross, and Craig, on Loch Torridon, or by the Gatliff Trust in Harris at Rainigadale and Scarp, which are all some considerable distance from the nearest road.

Is the process of development going ahead fast enough? The car ferries to the Hebrides, the proposed hotel chain with facilities for sand yachting, angling and aqua-sports, could do much to develop a popular tourist area in the Western Isles, an area hitherto relatively unknown. But while tourism can revive communities as well as individuals, it is doubtful whether every township can reap a substantial benefit. An interesting case in this context is the development of Tanera Mor, one of the now deserted Summer Isles off the coast of Coigach, Wester Ross. The owner plans to develop the island as a select holiday centre where very high prices will be necessary to overcome the costs of remoteness on this scale. Yet quite apart from the risks of bad weather threatening access to the mainland, it must be asked first whether the further decline of the mainland community of Achiltibuie, on whose facilities Tanera would depend, would not turn the island centre into 'one more Highland folly'? This would imply that it would be more in the long-term interest of the tourist industry of Coigach if development were concentrated on the mainland and Tanera used instead, as at present, as a destination for day trippers, people who would have to be discouraged if the island scheme went ahead so as not to disturb the privacy of the tenants. Thus, by contrast, the shelter provided on Scarp by the Gatliff Trust may well be a more appropriate facility for the small island. Sufficient, however, has perhaps been said to introduce the geographical component as an important factor in the Highland tourist industry.

CONCLUSIONS

The Highlands desperately need jobs in secondary industry. The Highland people, it has been claimed, do not want to fight a purely defensive battle; rather they ask for the chance of turning to more productive enterprises that give them better consuming power and a chance of self-regeneration, instead of the hypodermic syringe from outside. The problem, however, is one of decentralisation not only to the Highlands but within the Highlands, for in spite of a valuable rural component in the labour force, in weaving, pulp and paper manufacture and tourism, there is a definite trend towards concentration in the main centres. The development areas legislation does not help this problem, for incentives apply equally to central and peripheral districts alike. Various new industries have developed in the east-coast zone, such as the Caithness glass at Wick and electronics at Inverness. Moreover a large enterprise can only be accommodated in those areas where the infrastructure is either already there or can be developed at reasonable cost. But small 'mini-factories' are eminently suitable to the limited potential of village centres in the west. Progress in this field has been pioneered by Mr J. M. Rollo, who opened satellite factories at Inverasdale (Wester Ross) and Easdale (Argyll) in association with a machine-tool works at Bonny-bridge. Further projects at Bernisdale (Skye), Campbeltown (Kintyre) and Northbay (Barra) should also stabilise the population of rural districts on the mainland and in the islands, where electrification is removing some of the traditional barriers. This field is now being pursued vigorously by the H.I.D.B., but it must obviously be associated with an investigation to find which village centres are the most effective labour catchments.

CHAPTER NINE

Population Studies

THE HIGHLAND PATTERN

IN 1961 there were 278,000 people in the crofting counties, representing a little over 5 per cent of the total Scottish population of 5,226,000. The distribution within the Highlands is most uneven, however, as shown in Table 9, where the population is classified by area; the Highlands have been

Table 9. ANALYSIS OF THE DISPERSION AND DENSITY OF THE HIGHLAND POPULATION IN 1961

Sub-region	Population in 1961 ('000)			Density in 1961 (per square mile)			Area (square miles)
	Total	Land-ward	Dis-persed	Total	Land-ward	Dis-persed	
ARGYLL							
Islay	4·29	4·29	2·56	10·7	10·7	6·4	399
Lorn	15·16	8·29	4·18	19·2	10·5	5·3	788
Mull	3·49	2·82	2·02	11·5	8·3	5·9	338
South	34·96	17·52	6·98	33·0	16·6	6·6	1,059
CAITHNESS	27·37	11·93	6·01	39·9	17·4	8·8	685
INVERNESS							
Inverness	52·28	21·44	10·37	27·8	11·4	5·5	1,877
Lochaber*	14·24	11·52	3·35	16·3	7·0	2·0	1,632
Skye	7·77	7·77	3·62	11·6	11·6	5·4	670
Uist and Barra	7·39	7·39	2·56	25·2	25·2	8·7	293
ORKNEY	18·75	12·95	11·43	49·9	34·6	30·5	375
ROSS AND CROMARTY							
Easter	28·87	19·30	11·12	25·2	16·9	9·7	1,144
Lewis†	25·22	19·99	3·10	30·5	24·2	3·7	825
Wester	6·82	6·82	3·33	5·1	5·1	2·5	1,313
SHETLAND	17·81	11·90	7·23	32·0	21·4	13·0	555
SUTHERLAND							
North-West	3·96	3·96	2·36	3·4	3·4	2·0	1,135
South-East	9·55	8·61	3·34	10·7	9·6	3·7	891
Total	277·93	176·51	83·55	19·8	12·6	5·9	13,982

* Includes the Ardnamurchan district of Argyll.
† Includes the Harris district of Inverness-shire.

Sources: *Census of Scotland; Scotland (1967)*

divided into sixteen groups, most of which consist of a number of county districts, though in the case of Caithness, Orkney and Shetland the county unit has been taken. For each region the area and total population are recorded so that the overall density can then be calculated. This brings out an average for the Highlands of 19·8 per square mile, but with high densities along the east coast and in south Argyll in contrast to lower figures along the west coast and in the Inner Hebrides. But the Outer Isles, along with Orkney and Shetland, have a remarkably dense population which, even in the case of Orkney, would seem to be in excess of the agricultural potential.

These anomalies may be partly explained by the fact that the most important service centres are situated on the east coast and on the mainland of Argyll and often attract considerable business from west-coast districts (see Fig. 20). The Inner Islands are similarly related to mainland centres, such as Mull to Oban, whereas the Outer Isles have been more successful in generating their own service centres. To try and eliminate this bias, densities have also been calculated on the basis of the landward population only, with all towns of burgh status excluded. The effect of this is to show up the Outer Isles in a still more favourable light, with more than 20 persons per square mile in Lewis, Shetland and Uist and over 30 in Orkney, compared with an average for the Highlands of 12·6. The agricultural resources of Caithness, Easter Ross and south Argyll bring out densities of around 17, with slightly below-average figures in Lorn, Inverness and south-east Sutherland. Again the west coast and Inner Hebrides are the most sparsely populated, although Islay shows up well with its good farmland and scattered whisky distilleries and Skye boasts a large crofting element, though not as numerous as those in the Outer Hebrides. The poorer position and resources of the west are thus emphasised, but this is concealed in the islands by the remarkable density of the crofting population.

With the publication of census figures for individual communities for the first time (Scotland, 1967), it is possible to calculate the degree of nucleation in different parts of the Highlands. Fig. 24 has been drawn up to show the distribution of settlements with more than fifty people resident in 1961, arranged in suitable size groups. The prominence of nucleated settlement in Inverness and Easter Ross along with parts of Argyll might be anticipated, but the extent of nucleated settlement in Lewis, Uist and south Argyll is astonishing and reflects the presence of large crofting townships in the islands and numerous large service villages and forestry communities in the latter. These aspects are reinforced when the density of the dispersed

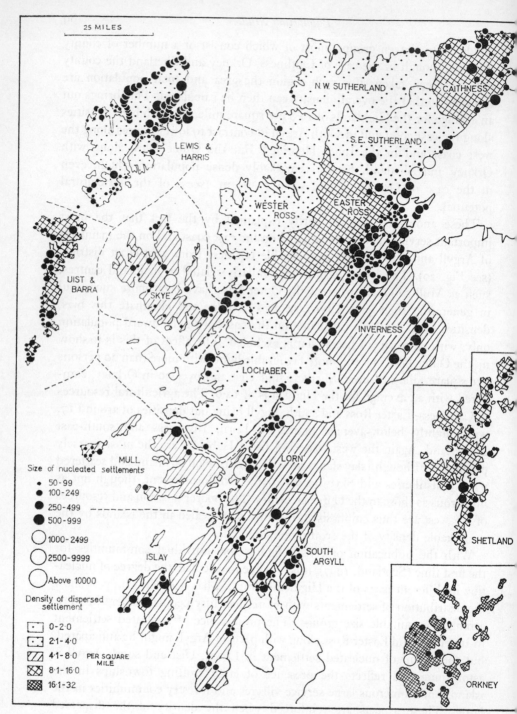

25 MILES

N.W. SUTHERLAND

CAITHNESS

LEWIS & HARRIS

S.E. SUTHERLAND

UIST & BARRA

WESTER ROSS

EASTER ROSS

SKYE

INVERNESS

LOCHABER

MULL

LORN

SHETLAND

Size of nucleated settlements

- · 50-99
- ● 100-249
- ● 250-499
- ⬤ 500-999
- ○ 1000-2499
- ○ 2500-9999
- ○ Above 10000

Density of dispersed settlement

- 0-2·0
- 2·1-4·0
- 4·1-8·0 PER SQUARE MILE
- 8·1-16·0
- 16·1-32

ISLAY

SOUTH ARGYLL

ORKNEY

Fig. 24 *Nucleated and dispersed settlement*

population is shown, with a high figure of over 30 per square mile for Orkney, followed by Shetland (13·0), Easter Ross (9·7) and Caithness (8·8), compared with an average for the Highlands of 5·9. Uist shows a dispersed population density of 8·7 but is not the lowest in the Highlands. The contrasts introduced by the crofting and farming landscapes are clearly demonstrated.

The present pattern is revealing enough, but more interesting still are the variations over time in different parts of the Highlands. The availability of census material from 1801 makes it possible to examine very closely the changes in the population of the Highlands over the last 150 years. The total population of the seven counties was 250,000 according to an enumeration carried out in 1755, and rose to roughly 300,000 at the first official census in 1801. After rising to 390,000 by 1851 the numbers then fell away, declining to 350,000 by 1901 and 280,000 in 1951. There are therefore still more people in the Highlands today than was the case in 1755, but the relative demographic strength of the area in a Scottish context has fallen continuously over the years; whereas, in 1755, 20 per cent of the Scottish population lived in the crofting counties, the proportion was only 13·7 per cent in 1851 and 5·6 per cent in 1951. Similarly the proportion of the total Scottish population born in the crofting counties has fallen progressively from 16·8 per cent in 1851 to 10·1 per cent in 1901 and 6·2 per cent in 1951 (Table 10).

Table 10. POPULATION TRENDS IN THE HIGHLAND COUNTIES, 1755–1966

(*a*) Long-term trend overall

Census year	Population of the crofting counties (millions)	Percentage of the total Scottish population living in the crofting counties
1755	0·25	20·2
1801	0·30	18·9
1851	0·39	13·7
1901	0·35	7·9
1951	0·28	5·6

Source: *Osborne (1958) p. 3*

(b) Recent trends by counties ('000)

County	1951	1961	1966 (estimate)
Argyll	63·4	59·4	58·8
Caithness	22·7	27·4	28·3
Inverness	84·9	83·5	84·5
Orkney	21·2	18·7	18·1
Ross and Cromarty	60·5	57·6	57·1
Shetland	19·4	17·8	17·4
Sutherland	13·7	13·5	13·2
Total	285·8	277·9	277·3

Source: *Census of Scotland*

This pattern is to be explained largely by the heavy rates of emigration, which has often exceeded the natural increase and therefore resulted in a net loss of population to other parts of Scotland, as well as to foreign lands. The overall rate of net migration was −11·1 per cent in 1851, rising to −16·9 per cent in the period up to 1901 but falling off to −7·9 per cent as recorded at the 1951 census (Osborne, 1958). It is interesting to note that Argyll suffered the highest rates in 1851, doubtless the result of its proximity to central Scotland and consequent ease of movement, whereas the lowest rates apply to the most northerly counties, Caithness (−7·3 per cent) and Orkney and Shetland (−4·1 per cent) (Table 11).[1] With better communications and growing overpopulation the rates from the north increase so that by 1951 the earlier pattern is reversed, with heavy losses from Sutherland, Caithness, Orkney and Shetland by contrast with Argyll, which has reached a position of comparative stability.

However, it cannot be claimed that overall the losses suffered by the Highlands are everywhere of the same order, and an interesting trend emerges when the population of each parish in 1961 is calculated as a percentage of the maximum figure to have been recorded since 1801. Very few parishes recorded their maximum in 1961, but those which did fall into a discontinuous line running down the east coast, the Great Glen and its continuation as Loch Linnhe, reflecting the burghs of Thurso, Dingwall, Inverness,

[1] These figures are based on birth-place statistics and cover a period leading up to each census rather than one particular year.

Table 11. NET MIGRATION RATES IN THE HIGHLAND COUNTIES,
1801–1951†

	1801	*1901*	*1951*
Argyll	−21·7	−19·3	− 3·2
Caithness	− 7·3	−25·7	−26·3
Inverness	− 8·7	−13·2	+ 0·5
Orkney*	− 4·1	−14·6	−12·3
Ross and Cromarty	− 8·5	−16·9	−15·4
Shetland*	− 4·1	−11·1	−11·4
Sutherland	− 8·3	−16·9	−15·4
Crofting counties	−11·1	−16·9	− 7·9

* In 1801 Orkney and Shetland were treated as one unit
for migration purposes.
† Calculated from birthplace statistics.

Source: *Osborne (1958) p. 17*

Fort William and Oban (Fig. 25). The only exception to this is Kirkwall in Orkney. Consideration of parishes in the lower orders reinforces this east-west contrast, for while few parishes, either on the east coast or east of the Great Glen, had a 1961 population which was less than 60 per cent of the maximum recorded, hardly any west-coast parish had more than 40 per cent, an indication of both the superior position and resources of the east and the intense overcrowding which was a feature of much of the west-coast areas in the nineteenth century before emigration there became widespread. The only exceptions are certain areas in the east where fishing has declined steeply during the present century or which are mountainous and purely rural in character, and on the west coast the approaches to Skye and the Outer Hebrides, where employment in fishing and services has always been a stabilising factor. The island pattern is roughly a continuation of the west-coast trend, though it has been modified by the tendency for heavy emigration to come only later (after 1911 in much of the Outer Hebrides) and for local island centres to emerge with relatively healthy demographic character-istics (e.g. Stornoway, Portree, Lerwick and Kirkwall). This latter trend is not so evident on the western mainland on account of its closer functional links with the east.

Short-term fluctuations also produce a strong pattern of differentiation within the crofting counties. Table 10 lists the changes in each county over the period 1951–66 and brings out growth in Caithness, stability in Inverness

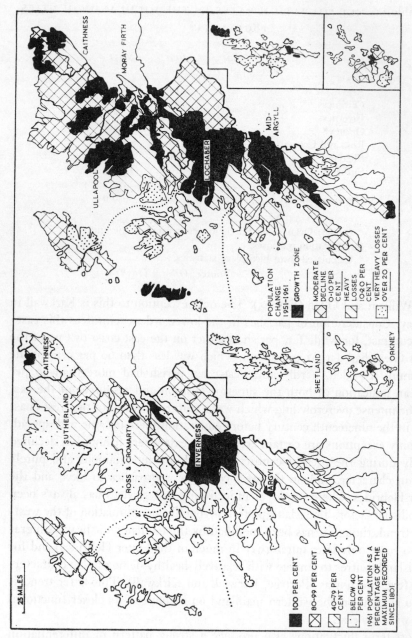

Fig. 25 *Population trends in the Highlands and islands*

and decline elsewhere. An examination of parish figures for 1951 and 1961 is more revealing (Fig. 25). Apart from the special cases of Unst (Shetland) and south Uist, where defence establishments have distorted the picture, all the growth areas reflect the main centres of population and emphasise, with greater clarity, the east–west contrast. The eastern growth zone now appears as a much more continuous belt and is especially prominent in north Argyll, Lochaber, Moray Firth and Caithness, where large-scale growth has been witnessed. By contrast all areas west of the Great Glen are in decline apart from the island approaches (Mallaig especially) and Ullapool, which, though it has no direct links with the islands, has become a popular centre of tourism and fishing since the road from Inverness was improved. Growth here has been partly at the expense of Kyle, whose railhead advantage is now outweighed by its peripheral position in relation to the North Minch fishery. Both on the mainland and in the islands the least accessible communities have lost over 20 per cent of their population; these include Applecross and part of Cowal on the mainland, northern Skye (Duirinish and Kilmuir), Lochs in Lewis, Bunessan in Mull and parts of Orkney and Shetland mainland. Such areas are often adjacent to the centre of growth or stability, but the extreme is reached in the case of small islands such as Barra, Coll, Colonsay, the Small Isles and the North Isles of Orkney and Shetland, where the heavier social and economic costs of insularity call the future viability of such dwindling communities very much into question.

It is clear therefore that while the Highlands are already developing, very rapidly in certain cases, the growth is unevenly distributed. This pattern of zones of growth and decline is of course common to other regions, but probably no other areas exhibit such extremes in accessibility. The very limited areas of flat land are integrated by a sparse road network and an even sparser railway system, and hence contrasts in local accessibility are everywhere great and exaggerated in the west by insularity, which includes a number, albeit dwindling, of mainland communities which are still dependent on sea transport in the absence of satisfactory roads. Hence the growth potential of the Outer Hebrides, or even the west coast, does not bear comparison with that of the Moray Firth. This 'Golden Triangle' is already the main centre of administration and communications in the crofting counties, and has been identified by various bodies, including the Scottish Economic Planning Council, as an area with substantial development potential. The White Paper on the Scottish Economy (Scotland, 1966) endorsed this view, and the H.I.D.B. have since been active in pursuing what has become known as M.F.D. (Moray Firth development).

The resources of this area for industrial growth are substantial, and combine at Invergordon to give a sheltered deep-water harbour (capable of taking very large tankers of up to 200,000 tons and all the biggest bulk cargo carriers likely to be built), ample supplies of fresh water and the existence of suitable areas of flat land adjacent to deep water. Any substantial growth here and under M.F.D. generally would reinforce Inverness as a major centre for the Highlands, with services and opportunities comparable with those available in other parts of Britain, and develop the local market potential for Highland producers and manufacturers. Moreover such large-scale developments would certainly help to balance the overall employment structure of the Highlands, which is generally light on the industrial side. The idea of a university at Inverness is justifiable, in the regional view at any rate, on the grounds that it would add a social and cultural dimension which is currently lacking and, by drawing the Highlands over the 'science threshold' (Drew, 1966) 'provide the application of a greater force of intellectual endeavour to Highland problems from within the area' (Highlands and Islands Development Board, 1967, para. 171). But would not further emphasis both here and in other areas of growth potential such as Caithness (which is to get the prototype fast reactor) act as 'a possible vortex sucking in population from the west and islands'? (H.I.D.B., 1967, para. 28) It will not require growth on a grandiose scale commensurate with generous interpretation of the concept of a 'linear city' around the Beauly and Cromarty Firths to produce this effect, for it is already evident.

THE PATTERN IN THE LOCHABER DISTRICT

As with Scotland as a whole, the regional pattern in the Highlands is one of gains in the centre being made at the expense of peripheral areas. Moreover if local examples are considered it is evident that the same trend of regrouping and concentration is operating; an overall loss is accompanied by growth in the main service centre. Thus the populations of Lerwick, Kirkwall and Stornoway tend to increase, although overall the population of the islands is falling (Moisley, 1962a, p. 196). It would be tedious to take many examples, and here the case of Lochaber will be considered as a local expression of population change. It is an appropriate area for several reasons, exhibiting striking contrasts in resources and accessibility between the centre, Fort William, and certain peripheral areas such as Glenelg and Ardnamurchan which are effectively insular in part. Moreover the industrial growth in Fort William, first in aluminium reduction and recently in pulp and paper production, in addition to its important function as a service centre, has created a major growth point at the centre. Furthermore it is possible to measure past and recent trends accurately using enumeration books and the special tabulations of the 1966 census (which was conducted on a 100 per cent basis in this and certain other parts of Scotland) as well as the published census volumes.

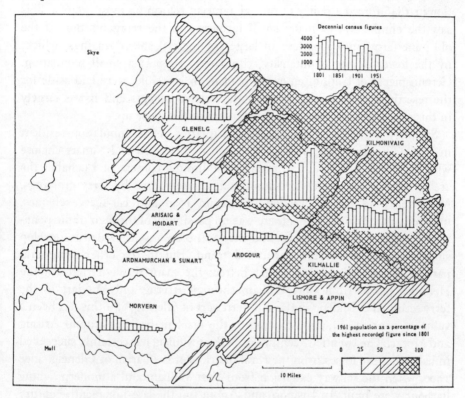

Fig. 26 *Parish population trends in Lochaber and north Argyll*

Published census material is a valuable source in the first instance and provides figures for each parish in the area over the period 1801–1961. There are eight parishes involved (Fig. 26), four of which lie in Inverness-shire (Arisaig and Moidart, Glenelg, Kilmallie and Kilmonivaig) and the remainder in Argyll. Functionally they represent a fairly homogeneous unit, with Fort William the main service centre, and contrasts can therefore be drawn between the central and peripheral parishes. Parishes in the west and south all exhibit a tendency to decline from a mid-nineteenth-century maximum, and this is particularly pronounced in Ardgour, Ardnamurchan and Sunart, and Morvern, where there have been few redeeming factors to make up for the loss of small tenant farmers whose eviction in the early nineteenth century began the downward spiral. The old subsistence economy had for long been propped up by buoyant cattle prices and a sudden demand for kelp (an alkaline substance produced from seaweed) during the Napoleonic period, but conditions of peace after 1815 and severe famine and destitution in 1846 forced a policy of radical agrarian reform on most estates. This saw the elimination of many small farmers and the reorganisation of the old joint farms into a pattern of large commercial sheep grazings, which, by the lower degree of intensity, could only support a small population. Certain pieces of land, often either poor or inaccessible, were laid aside for the resettlement of a proportion of the evicted tenants and it was largely in this way that the present crofting communities grew up.

So today north Argyll has less than a quarter of the population resident in 1841. The deep gashes of Lochs Eil, Linnhe, Sheil and Sunart enclose what is almost an island, and even in the limited context of Lochaber the area is very remote, with circuitous routes interrupted by ferry crossings. Moreover until the completion of certain road and car-ferry schemes, initiated in the last five years, there was no possibility of through traffic penetrating what was a cul-de-sac, and the local economy has failed to develop sufficiently to reverse the downward trend. But in the other peripheral parishes accessibility is somewhat better: the main through route to the Hebrides passes from Fort William through Arisaig and Moidart to the ferry terminal at Mallaig in the southern part of Glenelg, and this has been a valuable asset in attracting tourists to the machair beaches around Arisaig and Morar. The twentieth-century growth of Mallaig has certainly succeeded in balancing the losses from the rural districts of the parish of Glenelg since 1900, when the railway extension from Fort William and a modern fishing harbour were built. In Lismore and Appin too the late-nineteenth-century decline was temporarily reversed by the building of an aluminium reduction factory at Kinlochleven in 1909, though it has not proved sufficient to promote long-term stability.

Finally the parishes of Kilmallie and Kilmonivaig, which include the burgh of Fort William, have grown steadily and both recorded their highest populations ever in 1961. Fort William has become the main centre for the area and attracted distilling, aluminium and paper industries. Moreover smaller industries have moved in to absorb the female labour supply created by the influx of families into the area following the pulp mill's opening, and the upward trend seems bound to continue. Again, since the line of movement from north-east to south-west along the Great Glen and Loch Linnhe is a major Highland routeway, growth is not restricted to the town itself. Parishes are large units, but even the generalised picture presented by such figures reveals the difficulty of maintaining an even growth rate through-out Lochaber. In short, regional development leads on logically to problems of local development, and nowhere is this more evident than within the Highlands.

LOCAL STUDIES

But broad generalisations are not enough, and it is essential to look not only at broad parish figures but also at the individual performances of each community. Detailed information of this sort is not, however, available to the public except for the period 1841 to 1891, when the census enumeration books may be consulted. These are a very valuable source for historical geo-graphy, as Storrie (1962c) has shown, but difficulty is experienced in bringing the picture more up to date. One possibility is to use registers of electors, which give the name and address of each voter with special symbols to denote service voters and normally non-resident property-owners. But unfortunately they omit the population under twenty-one years of age, and by comparing figures calculated from electoral registers with census data it is clear that the proportion of the population under twenty-one varies very significantly between different areas. In Lochaber as a whole the proportion of the popula-tion under twenty-one was 32·5 per cent, but fluctuated locally between the extremes of 14·6 per cent and 46·9 per cent, indicating that the age of a com-munity, as well as its size, is a very relevant factor. However, within these limitations electoral registers do enable detailed studies to be made, and material has been abstracted to support nineteenth-century enumeration book data and build up some local patterns in the contrasting areas of Glen Spean and Knoydart.

Fig. 27 deals with the area of Glen Roy and Glen Spean to the north-east of Fort William, a district often referred to as Brae Lochaber. The 1851 distribution shows very dense settlement spread uniformly along the lower reaches of the Spean and Glen Roy, thinning out in the upper parts of the glens and on Rannoch Moor, where possibilities for agriculture were very limited in view of the lack of arable land. Even then, however, there were certain anomalies, for the emphasis on the Highbridge and Inverroy areas is unmistakable and is the result of reorganisation on the Inverlochy and MacIntosh estates. On Inverlochy small tenants from Leanachan, Corrichoille and Killachonate were resettled around Highbridge and Brackletter, while MacIntosh consolidated the small farmers in lower Glen Roy (Bohuntine and Inverroy) and around the hill of Galmore. This contrast between the crofting townships and the smaller farming communities (who nevertheless held the bulk of the land) is again apparent in 1891, although partly obscured by the large numbers of construction workers employed on the Glasgow–Fort William railway. The 1966 pattern, however, shows a new element, the service villages of Spean Bridge and Roy Bridge which

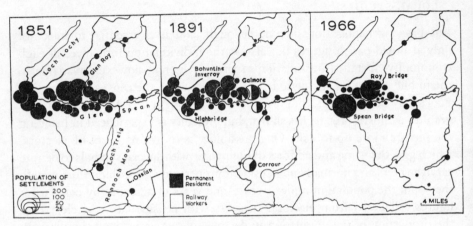

Fig. 27   *Distribution of population in Glen Spean, 1851–1966*

have grown up with increasing road and rail traffic, whereas the rural communities, crofting and farming alike, have continued to decline, although some afforestation has improved the position around Corrour and Killachonate.

Overall the process is reasonable enough, but it is worth emphasising two points: first, there was sufficient land both in terms of quality and quantity to enable the conflicting requirements of small tenants and commercial sheep farmers to be reconciled, and the extent of resettlement was such that widespread emigration did not follow the clearances of the early nineteenth century. Secondly, the relatively prosperous agriculture, coupled with accessibility, has allowed large central villages to flourish offering employment in distribution, transport and tourist services, not to mention commuting to Fort William, which is only ten miles away. The process of rehousing crofters from nearby townships in these villages may be regarded as a second phase of resettlement, initiated this time by local government housing policies rather than by estate management decisions but having the healthy outcome of stabilising the pattern overall.

Glen Spean may be taken as a typical example of the processes at work in the more accessible areas of the Highlands. When a poorer and remoter district is considered it is evident that the same forces have resolved themselves very differently. Knoydart is one such area and lies in the centre of Glenelg parish, clearly separated by Loch Hourn to the north and Loch Nevis to the south (Fig. 8, inset). In 1841 the estate supported a dense population, almost all of which was coastal and the bulk of which lay on the western tip, which is agriculturally the most valuable. In such an area it was more difficult to introduce commercial sheep farming and at the same time maintain the crofting element, since the latter was numerically large in relation to the employment available locally and also in relation to the limited amount of arable land.

Croft holdings were never intended to offer full support to a family, and part-time employment was required in shepherding, fishing or estate work. If other employment was lacking the crofts would have to be larger but this could only take place to the partial or complete exclusion of sheep farming, which demanded some low, arable ground to provide shelter and feeding stuffs for the hill stock in winter. Yet commercial farming could not be discouraged beyond a certain point, since it was often the high rents from this source that determined the landowner's solvency. The dilemma was a critical one and was often delayed so long that many landowners became bankrupt in the process. Thus Knoydart in 1841 shows the farmers of Inverguseran and Scottas pressing against the small tenants' arable in the west. It was not until 1853 that the final solution was implemented when, with the sale of the estate in the aftermath of famine, practically the entire crofting population was evicted and herded into an emigrant vessel anchored in the Sound of Sleat. Only Airor and Skiary survived, the former being then the ferry point for Skye and the latter a small fishing community on the remote northeastern edge of the estate: in both cases there was some employment and no conflict with sheep-farming interests.

By 1891 the distribution pattern was radically altered. It was still scattered, but the main nuclei were now the deer-stalking bases of Inverie, Barrisdale and Kinlochourn. Sporting interests were able to compete successfully against farmers in the difficult times of the late nineteenth century, and very often sheep were entirely excluded in the 1880s until the stalking boom was brought to a sudden halt by the war of 1914. A reaction to afforestation for deer came in the form of a government smallholding policy (which developed from 1886 and lasted until the 1920s), which allowed some increase in the size of the Airor township grazings. Today the contending interests are better balanced, but the population has contracted enormously: since Knoydart has no road access from the surrounding areas and the only internal link is a track from Inverie to Airor, the old ferry point, the entire population has been drawn to this section of the estate (apart from Barrisdale and Kinlochourn, which are now separately managed). At the same time the remoteness of Knoydart has placed limits on the size of Inverie, which can only take on the modest functions of an estate village. It is therefore accounting for an increasing proportion of the total estate population but has also declined absolutely since 1891, in sharp contrast to the rising fortunes of Roy Bridge and Spean Bridge in Brae Lochaber.

ANALYSIS OF A GROWTH POINT

Another line of approach is to use the 1961 census data and the special tabulations of the 1966 census to examine the development of the 'growth pole' in Fort William. To what extent have divergent trends emerged between the centre and the peripheral districts? An increase of 26·8 per cent in Fort William burgh has been achieved over the last five years, but in certain adjacent landward areas of the county the increases are even greater; in Caol the population has increased almost by half (49·6 per cent) and in Kilmallie South, which embraces Corpach and Annat, where the pulp mill is sited, the population has practically doubled (94·1 per cent). Further afield too some growth has been experienced: 23 per cent in Kilmallie North, where there has been some new housing, and 6·2 per cent in Nether Lochaber, where the 'Gold Coast' in the vicinity of Onich and North Ballachulish is attractive to the managerial class. But it is striking that Ardgour–Sunart, immediately across Loch Linnhe from Fort William, has grown only modestly (3·6 per cent). Around this growth centre there is an almost complete ring of peripheral electoral districts with population losses. In certain cases the loss is insignificant (0·01 per cent in Ballachulish) and elsewhere the losses are only moderate, but occasionally, as in Glenelg, Lismore and Appin, Kilmonivaig South and Kinlochleven, the losses of over 10 per cent in a five-year period are more disturbing. In Kinlochleven, however, the change is largely the result of rehousing across the river to Kinlochmore, which lies in Nether Lochaber. The only exceptions to this clear pattern are first Inverlochy, in the centre, a maturing company estate built at the time of the aluminium factory and now showing a decline of 10·1 per cent, and secondly Mallaig and Moidart on the periphery, which have grown through improvements to communications on the 'Road to the Isles' and from fishing and fish farming.

These trends are largely reinforced by other criteria. The age structure of the central districts, with recognisable pyramidal forms, may be contrasted with peripheral areas, which show an exaggerated 'pinching' in the 15–30 age group through necessary absence, often permanent, for educational or vocational reasons, and in some cases an inversion of the pyramid structure. This emerges with particular clarity in Ardnamurchan, where 29·8 per cent of the population are now over sixty years of age, but it also evident in Lismore and Appin, Ballachulish and Glenelg, where well over 20 per cent of the population fall into the highest age bracket. These figures may be compared with those of 17·5 per cent for Inverlochy and 14·3 per cent for Fort William burgh, but also with the still lower figures of 5·8 per cent and 9·8 per cent for Caol and Kilmallie South respectively. These two latter districts are particularly distinct and have absorbed the bulk of the in-migration experienced recently in Lochaber.

An indication of the economic importance of the various districts can be gained from employment data. The percentage of the population in employment is generally between 40 and 50, being lower in districts which have a high proportion of either children (Caol, Kilmallie North, Kilmallie South and Nether Lochaber) or retired people (Glenelg). Inverlochy is again distinct with 54·1 per cent of the population in employment; here the 45–60 age group is well represented and is probably accounted for by people who came to Lochaber in their younger days (when the aluminium factory was built in the inter-war period) and whose children have since left home. Absolute numbers of employed persons and the structure of the local economy are more revealing, however; numerically the superiority of the centre is to be expected, but the structure shows that only in Caol, Inverlochy, Nether Lochaber and Kinlochleven do jobs in manufacturing, mining and construction represent the main category.

THE SEARCH FOR STABILITY IN RURAL AREAS

A study of registers of electors for 1962 and 1967 (with a qualifying date of 1961 and 1966 respectively) can produce a useful picture of short-term changes by individual communities. The growth zone stands out as two

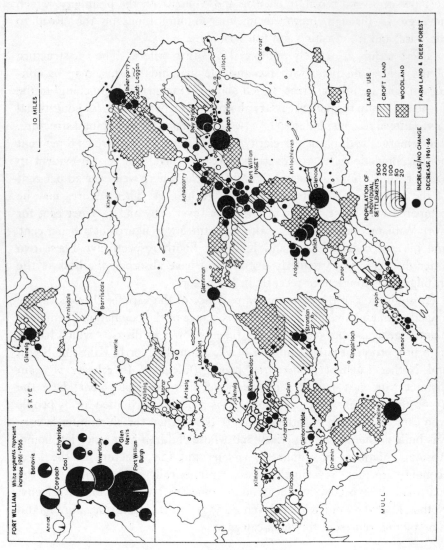

Fig. 28 *Population and land use in Lochaber and north Argyll, 1961–6*

axes crossing at Fort William, one running east–west from Lochailort to Roy Bridge and the other north–south from Invergarry to Glencoe. But in the peripheral areas the situation is often confused, with some stable or developing communities in spite of the general declines experienced overall. The balance is different in each case and can be explained partly in terms of the pattern of land use in each area and the nature of the balance struck between croft, farm and forest land. It is for this reason that Fig. 28 portrays the trend in each community in the context of land use and the estate structure.

Croft holdings in Lochaber only rarely offer viability in themselves, but are valuable as homes and smallholdings provided that employment is available locally. The health of a crofting community can therefore be a useful guide to the state of the local economy, with an aged tenantry indicating stagnation and an active one a sign of local strength. But the security of tenure and the nominal rents enjoyed by tenants since 1886 mean that a crofting population, albeit reduced and elderly, can be maintained without the full support of outside employment. Hence in general the crofting population would not be expected to react as suddenly to changes in the local economic climate as farming communities, where, except in the case of the small family farm, there is no corresponding inertia factor. This is not to say that the short-term fluctuations in the crofting population will necessarily be less than those in agriculture, since an aged crofting community could easily lose a number of its members through natural causes, but rather that there is a better basis for long-term stability than on estates, where even with progressive policies management decisions cannot be guaranteed and cannot be expected to give top priority to the maintenance of the population.

Some attempt to quantify these points is made in Table 12, where the rural section of the landward population of Lochaber has been divided into eleven areas, each of which is large and homogeneous enough in area and population to allow meaningful analysis. The communities are then classified into three categories according to their dominant function, a process which must be arbitrary to some degree since crofting, farming, forestry and tourism are often combined in various ways. However, it is significant that whereas crofting townships in Lochaber have lost marginally less than farming communities (11·2 per cent as opposed to 11·5 per cent), in certain areas – Ardnamurchan, Glenelg and Lismore and Appin – crofting communities have lost very heavily indeed. This is largely accounted for by the rapid dwindling of communities of mainly retired people, which are

Table 12. POPULATION CHANGES IN LOCHABER AND NORTH
ARGYLL IN DIFFERENT TYPES OF RURAL COMMUNITY, 1961–6

| Area | Overall change in rural communities | | | | Percentage change |
	Farming	Crofting	Other	Tota	
Ardgour	− 19	− 4	–	− 23	−13·9
Ardnamurchan	− 9	− 26	8	− 37	− 8·6
Arisaig and Moidart	− 8	− 9	−18	− 35	−13·9
Brae Lochaber	− 4	− 9	−17	− 30	− 9·3
Glenelg	− 6	− 28	2	− 32	−10·7
Glengarry	6	− 4	1	3	1·5
Lismore and Appin	− 18	− 32	− 5	− 55	−16·2
Lochiel	− 29		9	− 20	− 7·5
Morvern	− 18	–	− 1	− 19	−12·7
Nether Lochaber	− 5	− 8	2	− 11	− 3·7
Sunart	–	–	3	3	4·3
Total	−110	−130	−14	−254	− 8·5
	(− 11·5%)	(− 11·2%)	(− 1·8%)	(− 8·5%)	

| | Total rural population | |
	1961	1966
Ardgour	166	143
Ardnamurchan	470	433
Arisaig and Moidart	270	235
Brae Lochaber	332	302
Glenelg	299	267
Glengarry	200	203
Lismore and Appin	340	285
Lochiel	265	245
Morvern	150	131
Nether Lochaber	296	285
Sunart	119	124
Total	2,907	2,653

Source: *Turnock (1967b) p.* 65

very prominent in these areas. But where crofting communities are more active, through younger men finding employment locally, then farming communities may well show a more rapid decline, as in Ardgour and Lochiel, where the majority of estate communities have shown a serious decline.

In short, therefore, the age structure of crofting communities and estate policies are unrelated factors which produce a very varied pattern of population change, though there is generally a downward trend throughout each area.

Estate policy in particular is highly susceptible to sudden change. Although broad regional farming patterns have been established, the fact that most estates combine a number of enterprises, including farming, forestry and deer stalking, means that decisions over the optimum pattern of land use and the optimum degree of intensification can easily change, with consequent changes in the amount of employment available. As in the case of dramatic agrarian change in the nineteenth century, such action often accompanies a change in ownership, when sudden reappraisal is inevitable. Thus on many estates reduced intensification has meant sharp falls, but increases are recorded at Barrisdale (Glenelg) and Greenfield (Glengarry), where there has been some development of the sporting and recreational potential. The farming community at Rahoy (Morvern) has grown and the island population of Eilean Shona (Ardnamurchan) has remained steady through the energies of the new owner.

But one factor which brings some order into this complex of individual cases is that of forestry and tourism, for communities with a stake in these activities lost only 1·8 per cent of their population between 1961 and 1966 compared with 8·5 per cent for rural communities in general. Forestry is today mainly carried out in Lochaber by the Forestry Commission, and the distribution of their estates and those of the main private woodland owners are shown in Fig. 28. The Great Glen area is the most prominent area, along with Sunart, Morvern and the northern portion of Glenelg. All these areas can therefore gain from the pulp mill in Fort William offering a ready outlet for timber, which was originally grown merely as a strategic reserve. Forest communities are likely to grow as the pace of activity quickens, and in the areas concerned crofting communities are likely to benefit as well. There can be no doubt that the stability at present enjoyed by districts like Glenelg, Glengarry and Sunart is at least partly the result of afforestation, and areas without this factor are deprived of a valuable stabiliser.

The overall pattern in the rural areas is one of a declining population, but the varying local strengths of crofting, farming and forestry, coupled with differing levels of intensification, produce extremes varying from a gain of 4·3 per cent in Sunart to a loss of 16·2 per cent in Lismore and Appin. By taking broad zones within this range, Fig. 29 classifies these local trends, identifying an area of stability which embraces Glengarry, Nether Lochaber and Sunart, where forestry is sufficiently prominent to maintain the crofting population and counter the modest losses from farming. Next comes a broad intermediate section where losses have been substantial; this includes Ardnamurchan, Brae Lochaber, Lochiel and Glenelg. The forestry element is present in the last three cases and all have the benefit of some tourist attraction, but any gains here have been far outweighed by heavy losses, particularly from crofting in Ardnamurchan and Glenelg and farming in

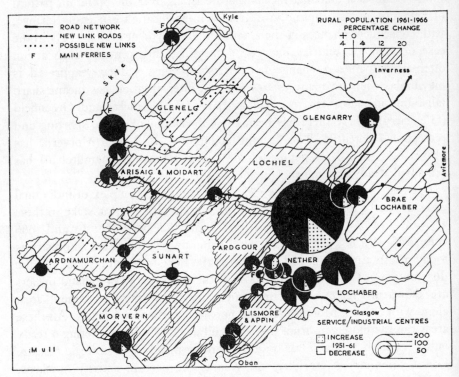

Fig. 29 *Rural population trends in Lochaber and north Argyll, 1961–6*

Lochiel. Finally come Ardgour, Arisaig and Moidart, Lismore and Appin, and Morvern, where rural losses have been in excess of 12 per cent. It appears to be mainly the farming element in Ardgour and Morvern that is losing heavily, whereas in the other two cases the losses are more broad-based, noticeably crofting in Lismore and Appin as has already been mentioned.

Mitigating circumstances can, however, be sought where the population of the main service or industrial settlements, whose performance is shown separately in Fig. 29, has risen in sympathy with rural losses. Rehousing is a major operation, since many of the buildings are becoming substandard and the task now lies mainly in the hands of local authorities, whereas it was formerly an estate responsibility. New houses are being built for the most part in the main villages, and where this is taking place some drain from the rural areas may be anticipated. Consequently much of the rural loss in Brae Lochaber and in Ardgour may be linked with new housing in Spean Bridge–Roy Bridge and Corran of Ardgour respectively. Again the decline in Lochiel is modest compared with the gains not only in Spean Bridge but also in Fort William. Moreover the Forestry Commission has sometimes preferred to house its workers in a central village rather than build a self-contained forest community in a more inaccessible place; thus in Glenelg many of the forest employees live in Kirkton, and much the same applies in Glengarry (Invergarry), Lismore and Appin (Kentallen), Nether Lochaber (Onich–North Ballachulish and Ballachulish–Glencoe) and Morvern (Lochaline). Local authorities and the Forestry Commission are thus in a position to influence the settlement pattern as decisively as the estate-owners a century ago over the question of the location of new housing. Careful co-ordination is very necessary to balance the conflicting considerations of the economies and convenience of concentration and the need for stability in small communities.

Rural losses in Ardgour, Brae Lochaber, Lochiel and Morvern may be offset against growth in the central villages and in Fort William. But this leaves Arisaig and Moidart, Ardnamurchan, Glenelg, and Lismore and Appin as areas still meriting concern, for the main villages as well as the rural areas have lost population, though admittedly not as heavily. In spite of the general prosperity of Lochaber, these west-coast districts have so far been unable to attract any substantial growth. Should the policy be to allow the decline of this marginal zone to continue, or should regional development have a more comprehensive local counterpart?

A striking feature of the problem region as now defined is that it correlates with one of the few sections of the west coast of the Highlands where a coast road is absent. Apart from the 'Road to the Isles' to Mallaig it is only at Glenelg in the far north of the region that access to the coast ties in with a through road system. Not only does this increase the costs of isolation for the local inhabitants, but it discourages tourists whose time is limited. In recent years some striking progress has been achieved, for a car ferry from Oban now serves Lochaline and it is then possible to travel to Mallaig via Strontian, Acharacle and the new link road from Kinlochmoidart to

Lochailort, opened in 1966. Already Lochailort and Kinlochmoidart show population increases contrary to the general local trend, and this sudden improvement in space relationships may provide the stability needed. Significantly small enterprises have begun at either end, fish-farming experiments at Ardtoe (Acharacle) and again at Inverailort (Lochailort). A small size of installation is needed since the local infrastructure could not accommodate a large enterprise, but it is still extremely valuable in creating stability, since a small number of new families can create a basis of confidence.

It is also interesting to note that the Forestry Commission has built a road along Loch Sheil to link Glenfinnan with their Glen Hurich forest. This road provides a link with the Strontian–Pollock road, and since the new link is about to be surfaced some increase in tourist traffic may be anticipated here. But a case could be made for bridging the remaining gap between Arnisdale and Mallaig by building a road first to Kinlochourn, presently at the end of a narrow road from Invergarry, and then across Knoydart via Barrisdale and Inverie. This would then connect either with a car ferry direct to Mallaig or else the road could continue to Kylesknoydart, where a ferry would operate across the narrows to Tarbert (North Morar), and a final road link would then join the existing system at Bracara (Morar).[1] Again, Ardnamurchan could be brought more into the pattern by completing the link along the north coast between Ockle and Gorteneorn, thus allowing a circular tour of the peninsula in preference to the single road to Kilchoan. The expense would be great, but as they are in close proximity to major Highland touring routes there is every likelihood of these new routes attracting sufficient traffic for tourism to become a valuable local industry. Moreover any policy of land development, forestry especially, can only be justified if timber can be extracted and marketed at competitive rates, so that road improvements could be regarded as the necessary foundation of any local development plan.

CONCLUSION

The main theme which emerges from this chapter is the mobility of population, not only over the long term but also over the short term at the present day. The tendency for the Scottish population to regroup and redistribute itself is very evident within the Highland area and also within individual

[1] Quite apart from heavy costs, the tendency to designate the remoter districts as 'wilderness areas' makes road schemes such as that in Knoydart less likely.

districts of the crofting counties. The Scottish Plan already referred to envisages this process continuing, but industrial growth in selected areas may result in the total Highland population being maintained overall in future (Scotland, 1966, p. 53). At the same time, as evidence from Lochaber suggests, the impact of forestry and tourism has considerable local importance in rural areas. These industries 'can utilise a dispersed local population for their labour and resident services which would otherwise be increasingly difficult to obtain', but, as the Scottish Plan goes on to stress, 'they should not be regarded as pretexts for shoring up decaying communities. Rather the reverse. It should make concentration in viable though necessarily still sometimes fairly remote units a good deal easier to achieve' (Scotland, 1966, p. 53). The case of Sutherland is mentioned, where the growth of forestry and the creation of family farms in central Sutherland could make the concentration there of population from some of the very seriously run-down communities of western Sutherland a practical proposition. Whatever changes may be recorded in the Highland population total in the future, it is certain that the settlement pattern will continue to move towards a layout of fewer but larger villages and towns. Planning to guide this process must take careful note of the potential of each district so that the village centres and their dwindling margins can be identified most effectively. Some of the problems involved in rural and urban areas are discussed in the following chapter.

CHAPTER TEN

Planning Problems in the Growth Zone and Rural Areas

THE likelihood that an increasing proportion of the Highland population will in future live in the main urban areas makes it important to assess the potential or capacity of the main towns for future growth. Can the sites accommodate growth indefinitely, or are there likely to be constraints which will at some stage impose a ceiling on expansion? The nodal positions of towns like Fort William in the west or Inverness in the east are becoming increasingly valuable, but are their sites of commensurate quality and do Highland conditions pose special problems of urban growth? To examine this theme it is proposed to study the growth at Fort William (An Gearasdain) in recent years and compare the situation there with the Moray Firth, where growth is being strongly encouraged by the Development Board.

LOCHABER: WEST HIGHLAND GROWTH POINT

Fort William's role as a service centre is both a substantial and expanding one, with most of the firms in the narrow, crowded High Street being partially dependent on custom from the rural hinterland. Yet the population of Fort William itself is considerably larger than that of its hinterland as the result of recent industrial growth. In 1963 there were approximately 6,500 residents in the Fort William urban area compared with 6,750 in the hinterland as defined in Fig. 20 (including Kinlochleven). But the population of Fort William was approaching 10,000 by the end of 1966, and may reach 13,500 by 1980. The relative size of the hinterland will inevitably fall, even assuming there is no further depopulation. This underlines the important function of Fort William as a manufacturing centre, for almost half the 1963 labour force of 2,300 was employed in this way, and this proportion, already very high by Highland standards, will doubtless continue to grow. These industrial developments have already been discussed, but it will be relevant to note some of the factors responsible.

In the case of the aluminium works opened in 1929, it was fortunate that Fort William should have been favoured during the short critical period (1895–1930) during which technological conditions allowed industry to be located in the north based on the hydro-electric power of the relatively small Highland catchment areas. The relatively small scale of aluminium production, coupled with transmission problems and a local planning controversy as to whether Inverness-shire water should be used in the adjacent county of Argyll, where the earlier Kinlochleven reduction works had been located, were factors which favoured a location in Fort William. But later growth, particularly the pulp mill opened in 1966, is much more a response to nodality, with Fort William's location providing a satisfactory focus for timber collection by road and rail from Highland forests coupled with port facilities and an adequate water supply. This positional advantage in a Highland context is proving increasingly valuable in attracting light industries, such as the small clothing concern which opened in 1966. A satellite of a larger parent factory at Hebden Bridge, Yorkshire, the new development springs largely from the availability of female labour in Lochaber, since the aluminium factory and pulp mill employ comparatively few women. The danger of imbalance in the local employment structure is thus being removed, and further developments (possibly in the form of advance factories adjacent to the aluminium factory) should continue this trend. The construction of a mint producing aluminium currency is one of several original suggestions.

The forces making for centralisation are operative everywhere, but they are particularly striking in the Highlands since local contrasts in accessibility and opportunity are so sharp. Distances measured directly between Fort William and the main villages in the hinterland may be compared with those measured for the actual distance by road or sea, which are often much greater. It is clear that the settlements in north Argyll are far more remote than their distance from Fort William, as the crow flies, would suggest. A particular case is Trieslaig on the western side of Loch Linnhe opposite Fort William. The 'forgotten people' there, currently lacking a proper water or electricity supply, are within a mile of the centre of Fort William, where, in the words of one Trieslaig resident, 'they even have central heating!' Yet the distance to Fort William by road is twenty-three miles. Thus the real extent of the growth point is closely circumscribed, especially in the south-west.[1]

These findings may be applied to education, where the special service of secondary education must of necessity seek a central location; hence Lochaber High School draws pupils from a wide area. But the isochrones

[1] Electricity was, however, made available in this area in December 1969.

drawn to indicate the distance from Fort William to other centres of population in terms of travelling time by public transport show that only a small area lies within one hour's journey. Because of the length of journey and infrequency of services, commuting is often out of the question and scholars must stay in lodgings or hostel accommodation. This applies to all secondary pupils in Ardnamurchan, Sunart and Morvern and the less accessible parts of Glenelg, Arisaig and Moidart, Kilmonivaig and Ardgour. As many families are all to acutely aware, even weekends at home are often out of the question. The journey to primary school is also often tedious, for pupils from Kinlochourn must make a daily journey to Kingie in Glengarry by private car, and even so the educational desirability of a system of one-teacher schools in remote areas is being increasingly brought into question.

Unfortunately this process of movement to the nodal points not only affects the depopulated areas by compromising the continued viability of the dwindling communities and increasing the per caput cost of essential services, but also has certain embarrassing implications for the centres of growth. Although the location of Fort William is proving to be gradually more valuable, its site imposes certain limitations. The narrow raised beaches afford a level site for only the railway and the High Street before settlement is forced on to the steep slopes of Cow Hill. Lateral expansion round the head of Loch Linnhe has therefore been a prominent feature of twentieth-century growth. Housing schemes have developed at Claggan, Inverlochy, Caol, Banavie and Corpach, and the last three, which have taken the bulk of the recent population increase (Table 13), are between three and four

Table 13. POPULATION GROWTH AND DISTRIBUTION IN THE
FORT WILLIAM URBAN AREA, 1961–80

	1961	*1963*	*1965*	*1968*	*1980*	*1980–*
Total population	6,350	6,455	7,750	9,130	11,520	13,545
Distribution						
(a) Percentage of population in Fort William burgh	46·3	42·0	41·5	38·2	38·7	39·9
(b) Percentage of population in landward area	53·7	58·0	58·4	61·9	61·3	60·1
of which:						
East of the Lochy	38·7	34·7	30·8	26·3	20·6	17·9
West of the Lochy	61·3	65·3	69·2	73·7	79·4	82·1

Source: *Inverness County Council, Lochaber Development Plans*

miles from the centre of the town. The existence of Blar Mor, a large area of peat moss at the mouth of the Lochy, certainly offered some scope for housing, but the difficulty and expense of draining the central portions and of developing them sufficiently to support construction is limiting building to the fringes. Thus there are plans for an estate of 230 private houses at Lochyside which will go some way to even out the heavy imbalance between this sector and council and tied housing, which currently account for 85 per cent of the total.

The results of this process are twofold. First, by expanding laterally on level sites away from the centre intense competition for land arises, not so much between housing, recreation, industry and services but rather between buildings of any sort and agriculture. It is well known that in the Highlands the relatively small areas of arable land are of inestimable value in supporting the large acreages of marginal hill land by providing shelter and feeding stuffs for livestock in the winter. Consequently the development of arable land for building will have far greater repercussions than its small area would suggest. The problem is additionally intractable since much of the arable involved in Fort William is croft land, where tenants enjoy a number of statutory privileges including security of tenure dating back to the first Crofters Act in 1886. The problem of resuming land is therefore complicated, but it also calls into question the desirability of thus inhibiting the process of adaptation to modern conditions of a distinctive pattern of farming already handicapped by restrictive and protective legislation. Many crofting communities today exhibit the highly unsatisfactory characteristics of underuse of land and a predominantly aged or absentee tenantry, but around Fort William the favourable employment position is reflected in a more vigorous tenantry and a reasonable level of agricultural activity. The dilemma is increased by the existence of a Crofters Commission (set up in 1954) with powers aiming at the reorganisation, regulation and development of crofting. A recent expression of these terms of reference is the provision of development funds to improve rough grazings by integrated farming–forestry programmes, and progress has been made along these lines at Banavie with plans to plant 500 acres of hill and reseed 200 acres of common grazing. In view of this, and also since the land which it is proposed to build on was reclaimed by ancestors of the present crofting population some 150 years ago after moving from more inaccessible parts of the Lochiel estate along Loch Arkaig, it is understandable that the crofters should feel that the urban development plans show a 'callous disregard' of their position. In fairness to the planners, however, it must be mentioned that some

£100,000 has already been spent, at a rate of £500 per house, in providing additional underbuilding on poorer sites so as to limit the amount of croft land needed. Clearly there is a reluctance to spend more money in order to avoid further resumption. Nevertheless crofters cannot be expected to be more public-spirited towards the loss of land than other sections of the population, and further friction may be anticipated in the developing areas in the Highlands.

The second point is that with this pattern of growth the centre of Fort William is progressively losing its geographical centrality; moreover in view of its limited space it is increasingly hard pressed to maintain itself as the commercial centre of the urban area. The unfortunate position of the railway line immediately beside the loch, coupled with an unwillingness to resite the station, adds a further complication. There have been proposals to make further developments at Lochybridge with a view to making this a future commercial focus: already the Lochaber High School is there, and current congestion in the High Street of Fort William burgh and shortage of office accommodation and recreational facilities might well be resolved by continuing this trend. Certainly inertia is always a potent force, but there is no reason to suppose that individual businesses would resist a move if the whole process were suitably co-ordinated. Major difficulties which make this unlikely, however, are first the delicate land-use controversy, already described, between the planners and the agricultural community, and secondly the unhelpful pattern of local government.

Although the urban area of Fort William has grown in impressive fashion in recent decades, the trend has not been followed by a commensurate increase in the size of the burgh of Fort William. Some adjustments have been made in the past at Claggan (50 acres) in 1947 and at Achintore, where the 150-acre Plantation site was annexed in 1963, but even so the greater part of the urban area, in terms of both area and population, lies without the boundary in the Lochaber district of Inverness-shire. This is a situation common to many large centres of population with suburban areas outside the jurisdiction of town councils, but Fort William illustrates this in a very exaggerated form, since the location of the main industrial installations in the landward area means that the burgh's rateable value is exceptionally low. The mere fact that control of the effective urban area is divided makes for difficulty in formulating a Lochaber development plan, and applied to specific issues such as the Lochybridge proposal it means that objectivity is compromised by the natural unwillingness of the burgh to countenance any decline in its present importance as the commercial centre not only of

Fort William but of Lochaber as a whole. Consequently, although planning responsibility lies in Inverness, the burgh has felt itself obliged to act alone, through consultants, over future plans for provision for shopping and car parking.

Housing development is proceeding on the Plantation site, which should ensure that roughly the same proportion of the rising total population remains within the burgh boundary. But more striking is the alternative plan for a new centre at An Aird, within the burgh, a choice which would seem reasonable given the essential prerequisites of a substantial housing programme to ensure that demographic balance between burgh and landward areas is not allowed to deteriorate any further. In the 1980s, therefore, over 50 per cent of the housing may be within the present limits of the burgh, as opposed to 39·9 per cent in the plan. Combined with the new hospital and proposed amenity complex, the case for a new town centre in the burgh is thus made stronger, and it now seems likely that additional facilities will in fact be provided in the present centre, with An Aird in reserve. 60,000 square ft of new shopping space will be needed to cater for the anticipated doubling of turnover from the present £6·7 million by 1981. Such plans must, however, impose great financial strain on the limited resources of the burgh, especially in the difficult interim period between house building and development in the centre, where delay means the loss of increased rateable value. Special financial assistance may be needed, for high rates are not only a burden to existing ratepayers but a disincentive to potential industrialists.

An important question at the same time is the path which should be taken by a new road which will have to be built to supplement the High Street, which is very congested, especially during the summer. Some possibilities were discussed in the 1950s, the key factor to emerge being whether the railway could be cut back about half a mile from its present terminus to free the valuable site at the lochside. If this was achieved, a new road could replace it allowing ready access to the shops in the High Street on the eastern side and possibilities for a promenade by the shore on the western side. On the other hand the retention of the railway would force a relief road over a difficult site along the hillside behind the burgh or adjacent to the railway, standing on stilts built out of the loch. In the latter case the presence of the railway would prevent easy access to the shopping centre and force trade from the burgh, especially during the summer. Moreover by continuing its path with a sweep over An Aird the potential of this site for a new centre might be compromised. Indeed, coupled with the Lochybridge proposal, the burgh would have been completely outflanked and its future prospects compromised. But research showed that the point about access was particularly relevant, since the parking survey commissioned by the burgh showed that at the moment 85 per cent of the traffic emanated from, was heading for, or wished to stop briefly in, the burgh en route. On this evidence a by-pass as opposed to a relief road would seem inappropriate, and it is with considerable local satisfaction that the relief-road concept, with the removal of the railway, is likely to be followed. The road will be primarily a route for the town, with the secondary function of a trunk road for through traffic. The preparation of design plans for this road and the Ballachulish bridge project were authorised in 1969.

In view of the present difficulties it is hardly surprising that there is an element of resentment that major decisions affecting the first west Highland growth point of industry should be taken in Inverness. The call for formal recognition in terms of local government of the functional unit of the burgh and surrounding villages is therefore becoming stronger in order that, in the words of the Provost, Canon G. K. B. Henderson, 'the prosperity brought by industry can be enjoyed in the area to which the industry has come'. Significantly this undoubted need for some sort of revision of boundaries comes at a time when a Royal Commission on Local Government is carrying out investigations. But in working towards a better system it is clear from the foregoing discussion that the rural hinterland must be carefully considered, as well as the Fort William area and the burgh in particular. It may well be appropriate to consider 'Greater Lochaber' as a local government unit at the lower level of a two-tier system which would continue to centralise certain functions at Inverness.[1]

But another line of approach is to argue that the area embraced by the Lochaber development plan is too small. Would it not be preferable to incorporate villages such as Roy Bridge and Spean Bridge to the north and Onich and north Ballachulish to the south more fully into housing development plans? The costs of dispersal would no doubt be high, but might be justified taken in the wider context of spreading growth a little more evenly. For the most remote areas it is unreasonable to expect that the high social and economic costs of isolation can ever be more than partially defrayed, but a larger number of communities in a more intermediate category ought to be able to derive greater direct benefit from centrally placed industrial developments. At present the number of people commuting to work in Fort William is very small indeed: according to figures supplied

[1] The Royal Commission reported at the end of 1969 and Fort William proposed as the centre of a second-tier authority within the Highlands and Islands Region, with a territory extending to Skye and south-west Ross.

by the British Aluminium Company in 1963, only fifteen out of a total labour force of 581 came from outside the Fort William urban area. Some planned dispersal of building, accompanied by an improvement in the currently limited and underused public transport services, might serve to assure the stability of the larger rural communities and ease pressure at the centre. Improvements in transport would have a great influence on the feasibility of dispersion. Thus the building of the bridge at Ballachulish across the mouth of Loch Leven will give considerable new value to the Oban–Fort William road link. This has already been strengthened by alterations to make the Connell railway bridge more suitable for road traffic, and the growth of an airport at Connell would reinforce this and encourage future growth at Ballachulish–Kentallen as well as at Barcaldine and Benderloch. An alternative approach could be to develop a local airfield at Camisky, near Spean Bridge, and thereby increase the attractions of sites north of Fort William.

Fort William is seldom portrayed in literature in a favourable light. In 1809 (1 90–1) Anne Grant wrote of the town: 'I have no spite against this place but I am provoked at its superabundant negatives'. Among these she mentions that 'it is Highland without being picturesque and romantic; it has plains without verdure; hills without woods; mountains without majesty, and a sky without a sun; at least his beams appear so seldom that I wonder the Lochabrians are not dazzled into idolatry when he walks in its brightness'. Some years later MacCulloch (1824, 1 330) seems to have been hardly more impressed by the inhabitants when he wrote of the single street 'crowded with idle men walking about with their hands in their pockets or collected in groups to yawn together or converse in monosyllables, except when roused to louder talk by an occasional sojournment to a whisky house'. More contemporary literature is equally indignant, for M. E. M. Donaldson speaks of Fort William around 1920 as an 'ugly little town, compacted of hideous buildings' which 'incongruously defaces the landscape'. Such statements, if not exaggerated, point largely to the failure of nineteenth-century attempts at development in the model village of Gordonsburgh, built on a cramped site and in an area then unembellished by the work of the Forestry Commission. It could hardly have been foreseen that a site selected for growth as a military installation to be supported from the sea would one day be called upon to support a service centre for an industrial and tourist complex with heavy demands for car-parking space. The limitations of the west Highland environment and Fort William's own local problems make for a very distinctive urban morphology and one which should be overhauled to attain a degree of attraction commensurate with its fine setting and industrial function (Plate 22).

DISPERSAL OR CONCENTRATION?

Urban expansion in the west Highlands is therefore feasible provided the growth potential exists, though the morphology of settlement is likely to be less compact than in the case of the majority of towns elsewhere. Fort William, with its linear pattern of growth, may be compared, on a smaller scale, with Mallaig, the fishing port standing on the Sound of Sleat, whose rocky site scatters development round the bay and may in future force it to Bracara, a township five miles away, although the total population is still below a thousand (Plate 28). A site for a possible fishmeal plant is being sought even further away at Stoul or across Loch Nevis in Knoydart, although this is partly in response to amenity considerations. Again, Kyle of Lochalsh, in a key position slightly further north, is built on a rocky site with a population of less than 700 and should be seen more as the main village at the end of a line of settlement stretching through Duirinish, Plockton and Strome to Lochcarron rather than a coherent point of urban growth. With such places in mind, as well as the more compact nucleated settlements such as Stornoway and Ullapool with their 'model village' origins, it is tempting to envisage the Highlands and Islands Development Board's powers and growing experience in industrial growth being used to develop a range of new centres. Several west-coast and island districts have no real growth point established at present, and although centres in this peripheral zone, such as Kirkwall, Lerwick, Portree, Stornoway and Ullapool, occasionally show some modest growth, it is insufficient to offset losses from their hinterlands.

A new town of between 10,000 and 15,000 people in the Kyle–Kyleakin area has been discussed by Inverness-shire Planning Committee. It would occupy sites at Kyleakin (Skye) and on the mainland side at Duirinish and Balmacara. Transport facilities in the area are already good, but improvements to the ferry service, either by providing a twenty-four-hour service or by building a bridge, would enhance the value of this development as a centre for Skye and Wester Ross. It would become an important tourist centre, but this industry, along with agriculture, forestry and fishing, could only support a centre of some 1,000 people. The scheme would demand substantial employment in manufacturing and a cornerstone of this sort is by no means assured. Moreover the labour supply is currently inadequate, and it is not recognised as a key labour catchment in the Scottish Plan (Scotland, 1966, p. 150).

Other suggestions have been made by the Federation of Crofters' Unions, who are disturbed about the future of the Hebrides and north-west mainland, where the bulk of the crofting population is concentrated, in the light of schemes to develop the Inverness area. Their idea is to develop fishing on a large scale at Stornoway and Ullapool, with a car-ferry service between the two centres. The idea recalls many previous attempts going back to the efforts of the British Fisheries Society in the eighteenth century, and much depends on the rate at which the industry can regain local support. Signs in the Outer Hebrides are encouraging, but it will be many years before expansion will justify new installations on the scale envisaged, let alone create rival centres to Aberdeen. Moreover Ullapool does not have ample room for expansion nor does it possess a populous hinterland, so that, like Kyle, it is not an important labour catchment. More attractive is the re-development of transport links between Ullapool and Stornoway, a route which recalls the droving traffic from Lewis to Ullapool, Gairloch, Poolewe and Aultbea. There were plans to build the railway to Ullapool in preference to Kyle, and with the construction of new car ferries for MacBraynes attention was again focused on the possibilities of the Ullapool–Stornoway crossing. At the moment traffic would scarcely justify an additional service to the Uig–Tarbert route which was finally selected for the car ferry.[1]

Other centres which could benefit from major growth projects are Kirkwall and Lerwick, but in the absence of major industrial growth only fishing can be suggested, and appropriate though this is to Orkney and Shetland it can hardly support a large town. North-west Sutherland is a problem area too and one where there is great local dissatisfaction over the centralisation of secondary education facilities on the east coast of the county. Here attention has been drawn to the value of Loch Inchard and Kinloch-bervie, while another organisation considers that great potential lies in the anchorage of Loch Eriboll. Their resources are considerable, but it would appear that great congestion further south will be needed before major installations in these areas can be contemplated, unless the scheme is of a military nature. With an absence of local raw materials and large hydro-power potential, the search for cornerstone industries of pulp-mill propor-tions is indeed difficult, and smaller enterprises such as satellite factories or fishery expansion schemes are more appropriate for local centres.

The most recent suggestion in this search for new major growth points involves mid-Argyll, and is conceived in the wider context of the industrial development of the Clyde estuary. It is proposed that Crinan Moss, near Lochgilphead, should be developed as a major industrial complex, its 8 square miles being adequate to accommodate, it is claimed, three refineries

[1] Current thinking envisages the opening of the route as a replacement for the Stornoway–Kyle–Mallaig service. This would be serious for Kyle if it were associated with the closure of the railway from Inverness.

the size of the Grangemouth complex, a power station, an international airport and a new town. The flat site is no more than 30 ft above sea level and lies adjacent to sheltered water 50 fathoms deep. Unfortunately communications with the Glasgow area would necessitate the building of a new motorway with tunnel or bridge crossings of the Clyde and Loch Fyne, though it is envisaged that the first stage of the motorway, to Cowal, would also form part of an eventual Glasgow–Inverness motorway linking Oban and Fort William en route. The Highlands clearly do not lack good sites for industry; the problem lies rather in the higher cost of developing them as long as cheaper alternatives exist in the Central Valley.

It is understandable that the recent tide of optimism should lead to local speculation about development prospects, for many would consider that it was the Board's principal function to concentrate on those areas which have been less successful in attracting employment hitherto. It has been argued by crofting interests that the Board will be judged by its ability to hold population in the true crofting areas. However, while social benefits may be made available in all parts of the Highlands, it is impossible to envisage a similarly even spread of industry; not only is there insufficient large-scale industry to fill every available site, but small light industry cannot be introduced so as to support every small pocket of unemployment. Instead the most attractive resources must be concentrated on. The Scottish Plan refers to the tendency in the past to allow the special problems of the Highlands to result in a policy of special treatment, 'justifying its own set of standards and insulation from criteria applied elsewhere in Britain. This tendency has been fed both by Highland feeling itself and hardly less by outside sentiment which would preserve a distinctive way of life. Undeniable benefits have been won as a result of special treatment. But it is arguable that in the long run the Highlands have lost more than they have gained' (Scotland, 1966, p. 52).

The interpretation of this would suggest that in the past this special assistance has not been directed to investments which might be economically most worth while, but rather to the preservation of the established economy which would otherwise founder or decline still further. The realistic appreciation of the advantages of the Moray Firth compared with west-coast and island districts suggests a welcome reappraisal of this policy. But it follows that in turn the Moray Firth must be considered not in isolation but in relation to similar sites outside the crofting counties. Growth there must be shown to be in the wider Scottish interest as well and not only in the interest of the Highland sub-region.

This may be a crucial point. Scotland as a whole, a planning region of singular coherence in Britain in view of her long tradition of legal and administrative independence, is itself a 'problem area' with a declining population due, as in the case of its Highland sub-region, to emigration southwards across the border. The continuance of this process at current rates will remove any hope of the Scottish population increasing at all by the year 2000, by which time the total population of Britain should have increased by 17 million over the 1966 total of 54·9 million, and, by upsetting the age structure, will not only reduce the number of people of working age but ultimately lead to negative rates of natural increase through lowered fertility. The first priority for Scotland must be to modify this general problem, since the success of development plans in the sub-regions, including the Highlands, will depend on whether the overall regional structure is sound or not. In other words, just as the remoter parts of the Highlands need a core area of growth around the Moray Firth, so the objectives for the Highlands as a whole, as a necessary disaggregation of regional policy for Scotland, can only be approached once Scotland as a whole is in sight of the same goals.

The keystone of present development policy is therefore the generation of major growth points involving substantial increases in population whenever the natural advantages of the area seem to warrant it, but for the present only three such areas have been identified. Besides the Moray Firth area, taking in the Highland capital, Inverness, these include Lochaber, already discussed, which saw extensive growth before the introduction of any co-ordinated development machinery, and Caithness, which has considerable capacity following the infrastructural improvements associated with the nuclear power station. To try and accelerate the rate of growth here, factory space is being offered at Wick Airport Industrial Estate at a rental of only 1s per square ft (compared, for example, with a top office rental of £10 per square ft in Central London), and a 6,000-square-ft advance factory is to be built at Ormlie, near Thurso.

The main growth area must necessarily be the Moray Firth, and the Moray Firth development (M.F.D.) policy is central to the Board's area development planning. The growth of population there in the past has been considerable (Table 14), and a recent survey has demonstrated that very extensive capacity exists for further expansion (Scotland, 1968a). A successful M.F.D. policy would reinforce Inverness as a major centre for the Highlands, with services and opportunities comparable with those available in other parts of the country, and would provide a wider market for local food

Table 14. GROWTH OF POPULATION IN THE MORAY FIRTH AREA, 1801–1961

	1801	Population ('000) in 1851	1901	1951	1961	Population change (1801 = 100) in the period from 1801 to 1851	1901	1951	1961
Inverness*	8·7	16·5	27·0	31·1	33·1	189	310	356	379
Dingwall, Invergordon and Tain†	5·8	9·6	9·1	9·7	10·0	167	157	168	173
Remainder of the Inverness area and Easter Ross	48·9	56·4	41·1	34·3	32·4	115	84	70	66
Total	63·4	82·5	77·2	75·1	75·5	130	122	118	119
Total population as a percentage of the population of the crofting counties as a whole	20·9	20·9	21·9	26·3	27·2				

* Figures for the parish of Inverness and Bona.
† Figures for the parishes of Dingwall, Rosskeen and Tain.

Source: *Census of Scotland*

producers and manufacturers. The Moray Firth has not only the physical capacity to hold upwards of 250,000 people and a good existing infrastructure, but also a major asset in the deep water of Cromarty Firth, capable of taking large tankers and ore carriers and with good sites immediately adjacent at Invergordon (Plate 24). This combination gives the area a distinct superiority over west-coast districts which contain fine anchorages but lack good sites which can be readily linked with existing services. Moreover, although the agricultural land around the Moray Firth includes much good arable, there is sufficient of it for the intrusion of industry to take place without great damage to farming interests.

In the past the main use of these resources has been for naval purposes, but as more centrally situated sites within Scotland become exhausted, a new importance is being attached to the area and to the port of Invergordon in particular. The aluminium smelter under construction and the petro-chemical complex projected thus represent the beginning of what may, over the very long term, be a major new industrial and city region with very high-quality building and amenity. A more immediate issue, however, is the danger that large industrial developments may be unsupported by further steady expansion, and thus a sudden increase in population may eventually be followed by the emigration of the incomer's children. A recent employment and population survey of Lochaber (Scotland, 1968*b*) emphasised that many more new jobs will have to be provided if present growth is not to be followed by renewed depopulation. Some future movement of population is inevitable, but it is clearly important to maintain an upward trend overall. Unless the pulp and aluminium plants can prove sufficiently propulsive to attract service industries or industries using their products, very careful planning will be needed.

Any industrial growth in the Highlands, however, has the positive effect of introducing a better balance to the overall employment structure, for only some 10 per cent of all jobs are in manufacturing. Fig. 30 demonstrates this imbalance in terms of labour exchange areas and also points to the concentration of such jobs in a limited number of places. It is particularly significant that increases in jobs in manufacturing during the early 1960s were largely restricted to Fort William, Inverness, Thurso and Wick exchanges, which endorses the three main areas considered to have major growth potential. While this is to some extent inevitable, it is important that the main growth areas should not suck in population from the west and the islands to the point of making these areas incapable of an economic recovery. Consequently, side by side with the policy of major growth areas runs a rural component which envisages the identification of village centres and the attraction of small industries in scale with the possibilities of the west and the islands.

RURAL DEVELOPMENT

Considerable interest is being shown in these local village centres, some of which are already quite large. Examples which come to mind are Mallaig and Lochaline in Lochaber, Scalloway in Shetland, Stromness in Orkney and Tarbert in the Outer Hebrides, but others are needed. Thus a counterweight to Stornoway in the south Hebrides has been suggested, and in the event of growth around Kyle–Kyleakin some attention to north Skye would be needed. Some small new industries have been introduced in these areas, notably precision engraving at Bernisdale in north Skye and perfume production in the island of Barra. Although small and insignificant when compared with the larger factories in Fort William and Inverness, these

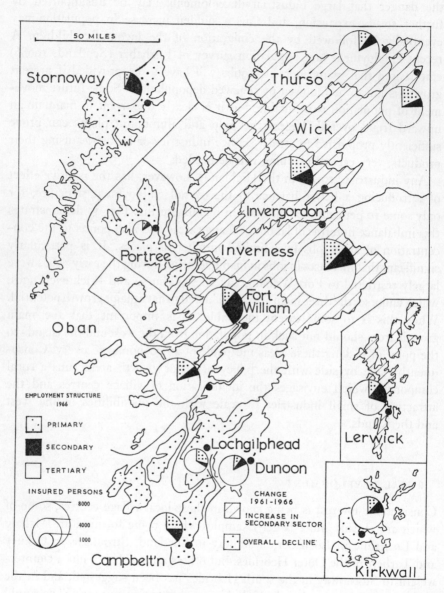

50 MILES

Stornoway

Thurso

Wick

Portree

Invergordon

Inverness

Fort
William

Oban

Lerwick

EMPLOYMENT STRUCTURE
1966

PRIMARY

SECONDARY

TERTIARY

INSURED PERSONS

8000

4000

1000

Lochgilphead

Dunoon

CHANGE
1961–1966

INCREASE
IN
SECONDARY SECTOR

OVERALL DECLINE

Campbelt'n

Kirkwall

Fig. 30 *Employment structure, 1961–6*

enterprises are equally important for Highland development and the stability of the landward areas, for they carry the 'growth point' idea down from district to local level. Combined with carefully planned local authority housing, much can be achieved in modifying and stabilising the rural settlement pattern.

So far the most remarkable example of village development has been at Strontian in north Argyll, where the first phase of the government project to revitalise small communities was opened in 1969. This building provides essential shopping services, a tea-room which can also be used for small functions, a tourist information desk and public conveniences. The second stage now being planned will include the erection of an old people's home, primary school, community hall building and public library. In addition general-purpose housing and a police station with associated cottages will be erected. Proposals for private housing development are being examined as well as a plan for a caravan park with access to the new facilities, while future possibilities include better car-servicing facilities, craft industries and adult evening classes. The choice of Strontian as the first centre for the application of these measures rests on several factors, including the lack of any coherent focus for the area hitherto and the growing agriculture– forestry and tourist economy, supporting a population which could not feasibly be based, on account of transport problems, in the nearest town, Fort William. But it is also significant that in Sunart the land is state-owned through the Department of Agriculture and the Forestry Commission, and hence the Government were determined to take a more comprehensive and imaginative view of their duties as landlords towards improving the quality and value of village life. Similar schemes will follow at Uig, Skye and elsewhere.

However, this new slant to rural development will still leave primary activities as a major element in the employment structure of areas with a predominantly scattered population, and hence the implications in terms of employment of any intensification of the agricultural or forestry effort can be decisive at this scale. The islands often show a particularly high level of dependence on such employment, and Mull has received a great deal of attention in terms of local comprehensive development because it is a large island yet lacks any basis for manufacturing and is so close to the mainland that its main service centre is across the sound at Oban. This makes it difficult for the island to establish tourism on any scale, and further hindrances lie in the unfortunate siting of the main settlement on the island, Tobermory, and the main tourist attractions, Iona and Staffa, on the distant, western side. The latter places, moreover, are reached only across poor roads and ferry crossings. Employment therefore depends heavily on primary industries, with some 140 jobs in agriculture and about sixty in forestry, maintaining the 7,000 acres of woodland planted by the Forestry Commission in Mull Forest. A further 500 acres per annum are being planted from the 6,000 acres which the Commission has acquired for planting. Agriculture occupies some 207,000 acres, made up of 6,000 acres of crops and grass and 201,000 acres of rough grazings and crofters' common grazings. Agricultural output has risen over the period 1938 to 1963, cattle from 2,869 to 4,267 and sheep from 51,318 to 79,063, but the labour force has dwindled to the present 140 from 240 in 1948.

In view of the numbers employed relative to area, the simple answer would appear to be one of expanding forestry in what is in fact one of the few islands where woodlands can be established with success. Some 29,000 acres are considered plantable, and further acquisitions by the Commission in north-west Mull may be made. But there are difficulties which arise from the unfavourable balance of arable land to rough grazings in the island; thus the sacrifice of even modest acreages of arable and sheltered grazings for forestry could have considerable repercussions for the remaining farmland. In addition the structure of farming is being upset by the changing balance. In the Ross of Mull there are typical crofting conditions and forestry has not made much impact, but in the north it is conspicuous on the margins of the rough deer-forest country, which is managed largely by a few big estates. Afforestation has therefore taken place on portions of large properties for the most part, but in addition there has been a growing attrition of the family farms, a number of which have been completely cleared for planting. The partial elimination of this small but important element of the local farming population is a cause for concern, for it runs parallel to a trend whereby more and more of the industry is falling into the hands of estate-owners without local connections, whose interests do not revolve solely around agriculture. They may employ two or three hired men on land which a working farmer would manage with seasonal help from his family. This situation in turn generates adverse publicity on agricultural conditions and probably deters practical farmers from establishing themselves there, and yet when knowledgeable people visit the island they are impressed with the possibility of the grazings. It would be unfair to blame forestry for creating a situation which stems from the large stalking grounds of the deer-forest era, but it would nevertheless seem to be contributing to this trend of depressing the vigour of the farming community by eliminating some of the remaining family farms.

A prejudice is therefore building up against forestry which is not altogether the fault of the Forestry Commission. It is complicated by the high costs of transport of feeding stuffs and materials to the island and of livestock back to the mainland sales, which makes agriculture correspondingly less remunerative than on an outlying mainland farm. This problem can be exaggerated, for lower farm valuations on the island must be taken into account, but it is certainly a barrier to large-scale land improvement by treatment with lime and slag and a barrier to heavier cattle stocks in view of the hay imports needed in the absence of land improvement. Thus the Land Use Report remarks that 'in its present state the agricultural prosperity of Mull depends largely on (*a*) ability to produce winter keep for hill cows and (*b*) management of hill sheep to produce lamb and wool crops at an economic level which is affected considerably by the variable market for store sheep' (Scotland, 1964, p. 82).

Forestry, however, is not subject to these constraints, since the activities of the Commission are financed ultimately by the taxpayer and the planting programme is planned on a national basis. It is difficult to know the precise costs of establishing a forest, but in view of the need to transport materials to the island the cost of doing this on Mull may be higher than normal. Again, while the long-term viability of the whole forestry programme is dependent on world timber prices and the effectiveness of substitutes, there are strong reasons for supposing the profitability of the Mull Forest to be less than normal owing to the lack of a local market for thinnings and to transport costs in bringing timber along island roads for shipment. It may well be that only very large forests of perhaps 20,000 acres in reasonably accessible locations can compete with the lower-cost produce of Scandinavia. Accurate figures of course cannot be given, but there are clearly reasons why local farmers should feel that in the specific case of Mull they cannot compete with the Forestry Commission over land acquisition and development as effectively as elsewhere. Yet there might well be equally profitable returns (or no heavier losses!) from farming if it were to receive the same measure of support from government funds. In 1965 a survey of the island by the School of Town and Country Planning in Edinburgh considered that the island could carry 22,000 cattle compared with the present figure of 4,000 and with this sort of intensification in mind the division of the larger estates had been advocated to establish state-owned family farms carrying a minimum of 500 ewes and 30–40 breeding cows, and with programmes of land improvement with treatment of rough grazings with lime and slag.

With this in mind the Highland Panel investigated the possibility of dividing a number of large properties as part of a programme of land settlement (Scotland, 1964, p. 84). On the Glen Forsa estate they considered that there was 'no doubt about the practicability of dividing the estate, though the resultant holdings would have the inconvenience of having to share the low ground arable which is wholly situated at the seaward end of the estate'. But the cost of creating these five or six family units, making maximum use of existing buildings which could be used for two holdings, would amount to £60,000 and would not support any more people than are now employed on the estate, which is at present operated as one unit. They concluded that 'the balance of advantage lay with the further development of the farm along present lines for some years', but added that in future the question of subdivision might be usefully reconsidered, perhaps with fewer holdings and greater integration with forestry, which would then increase the labour potential over and above the numbers employed at the moment.

This would seem to be the crux of the matter. Integration is certainly the policy in the Highlands as a whole, but it would appear that the present machinery is inadequate to deal effectively with Mull's conditions. With an imperfect economic and landholding structure the farming industry is additionally burdened by high transport costs. The island is one of few which can support forestry as an alternative form of land use, but, organised as a national body, the costs which embarrass agriculture can be more readily absorbed. Forestry may be justified on social grounds, following the 'social' argument for forestry discussed earlier, but farming should be given adequate support to enable a balanced partnership between the two interests to emerge. This is not happening under present conditions, where the situation is inflamed by the labour shortage and allegations of secrecy surrounding the Forestry Commission's future plans for the island, stockpiling of land and lack of objectivity in land surveying for future use. Significantly, therefore, some of the strongest calls for a Royal Commission on Land Use have come from Mull. The Highlands and Islands Development Board has suggested a programme of land improvement for agriculture on the basis of one acre of agricultural land improved for every five allocated to forestry. A greater interest in tourism by farming families is also suggested, and a new hotel at Craignure seems likely as a focus for this.

A useful contribution to Mull's problems is being made by dealing with products with a high value to weight ratio. Thus a large-scale market-gardening venture at Glengorm was started. Lettuce and celery are grown for sale to local stores between October and Christmas and the Glasgow market is also supplied. Greenhouse construction will enable tomatoes to be grown in future. Surprise has at times been expressed that the Highlands do not support greater numbers of such enterprises, but limited local consumption and the lack of a tradition in market gardening make progress difficult. Moreover the call of the hill often makes it difficult to specialise on the arable. However, as with the Hebridean bulb industry, progress in certain districts should be possible in future as the local home market builds up in the expanding towns. It is interesting to recall the plan outlined by the Scottish Vigilantes Association (1964, p. A3) to develop crofters' co-operatives along the lines of organisations already established in County Donegal in Ireland. Crofters would grow an appropriate range of vegetables and other crops on a contract basis to supply a chain of small canning factories in the Highlands. The problem of persuading pastoral farmers to grow food crops is recognised as an important factor, however.

SERVICES IN RURAL AREAS

An important factor in the search for stability in rural areas is the cost and reliability of services in these outlying areas compared with the situation in the main towns. There is a marked tendency for costs to escalate in the remoter places because of the difficulty of overcoming these terrific contrasts in accessibility. Although subsidies to help maintain essential services in the Highlands are often generous, there is still a considerable differential in costs within the Highlands. Certain services are provided at standard rates, notably postal services, many food items are sold at standard prices everywhere owing to the goods being sent 'carriage paid home' by manufacturers, and mobile banks, libraries and medical services are a great help. But even so the costs of isolation are still financially considerable, and it has been calculated that the community on Mull is consequently burdened to the extent of £70,000 per annum compared with a similar community on the mainland. The figure of 30s per week per family, which this is equivalent to, compares with 40s per family per week calculated after a separate study of the Orkney island of Westray.

There are many factors which account for this heavy imposition, the more obvious ones being increased transport costs on bulky goods like fuel and building materials along with animal feeding stuffs. Many food items are subject to a surcharge through small shopkeepers necessarily ordering in modest quantities from a wholesaler who cannot absorb the transport charge to destination. The cost of employing tradesmen away from their home town is of necessity high through accommodation charges in addition to the transport of men and materials. Shopping expeditions and access to professional services are correspondingly costly, involving high

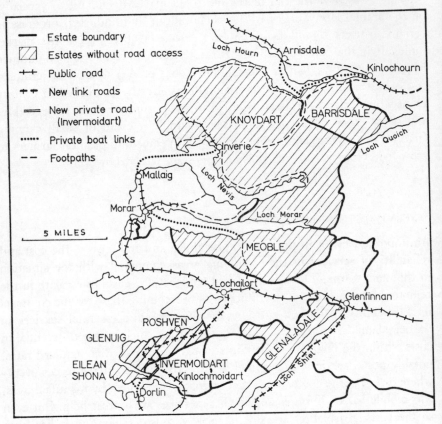

Fig. 31 *Estate communications in Arisaig, Glenelg and Moidart*

bus and steamer fares and the additional inconvenience of often having a short time for messages before beginning the return journey. The same problem affects farmers travelling to sales, and here the costs of overnight accommodation away from home are frequently unavoidable. More serious still are the costs of providing private transport links, as is necessary in the case of island estates and those without road access. In some coastal areas this is a common situation (Fig. 31).

But there are other difficulties and the costs are not always financial. Educational facilities can be provided at primary level in most communities of reasonable size, though even here considerable travelling is necessary for a minority of pupils, and often only a one-teacher school can be justified, a post which has increasing difficulty today in attracting teachers of high calibre. But at secondary level facilities must be concentrated at the main centres, a trend likely to increase with comprehensive education. At this stage, therefore, many more children are obliged to travel considerable distances daily or even stay in hostels. Fig. 20 shows how many primary schools in Lochaber are situated several hours' travelling time away from Fort William or Oban; for a number of pupils going on to secondary school even weekends at home are impossible owing to lack of Sunday transport and the impossibility of making the return journey early on Monday morning. With still higher grades of education such as college or university, living away from home becomes universally necessary, and though at this stage the situation is generally acceptable, separation at an earlier age can be a trial to parents and children alike.

Medical services have been decentralised to a considerable extent and the standard of service has been high since the Highlands and islands received a state medical service (the Highlands and Islands Medical Service) in 1915, several decades in advance of the country in general. Doctors are often maintained in small remote areas, such as the Small Isles, on social grounds but hospital facilities are concentrated in the main towns and travelling for attention is costly and time-consuming. In 1964, however, a scheme was launched whereby patients from the seven counties could claim part of their travelling expenses (those in excess of £1) when their journey exceeded thirty miles by land or five miles by sea. But more serious difficulties arise over emergency services, for night journeys to hospital can be hazardous from places normally dependent on steamer or ferry services to their main centre. Where air services are available the problem can be overcome, but certain districts like Mull and north Argyll are badly placed in an emergency since roads are poor and ferry services do not operate at night. Until a small hospital was built on Mull, 'mercy dashes' were made from time to time by small boats from Tobermory or Craignure to Oban (after a previous ferry crossing to Fionnphort in the case of Iona patients). For Ardnamurchan complications still arise from the poor state of the roads, even though the thirty-five-mile detour around Loch Eil to Fort William can be avoided now that the Corran ferry can operate at night.

Other services generally taken for granted are still not universally available in the Highlands and islands. Electricity supplies have not yet been taken to certain island and remote mainland districts, and postal services, though available everywhere at standard rates, are not of uniform efficiency, with necessary delays in delivery of mail to remoter places and only occasional deliveries when the postman needs to row his own boat or walk long distances to remote estates and shepherds' houses. Radio and television coverage is by no means complete, with the latter only having been available until recently through 'piped' television companies. In 1963 a series of V.H.F. sound and T.V. relay stations was built at Banavie, Ardgour, Mamore, Ballachulish and Oban to extend coverage from Rosemarkie (Black Isle), which relays signals direct from Kirk o' Shotts. But for T.V. only places within about fifteen miles of the relay stations (and with an electricity supply!) receive a good signal, and consequently many places are still without cover. Even when relay stations have been provided at Lochgilphead, Campbeltown and Kingussie there will still be 100,000 people in Scotland not receiving B.B.C. T.V. satisfactorily. Complete coverage of the Highlands will be an unattainable ideal for many years to come; a large high-power station for the whole area would not be practicable and the only solution is to build up a network of high-cost radio links, which can only be done slowly.

Telephones have a special importance in the Highlands, for a call to a tradesman or shopkeeper with orders is an effective alternative to making a long journey to town. Moreover at night the telephone is the lifeline of many small communities. It is therefore particularly desirable that the modernisation scheme for the telephone system in the west mainland and island districts should go through. Under the plans of the Scotland West area automatic service will be provided for all subscribers to meet the rising levels of trunk telephone traffic and to provide a more economical and reliable network, avoiding reliance on submarine cables, some of which have been prone to faults and are costly to maintain. A feature of the scheme is the introduction of multi-channel radio links, with radio stations in the remoter places working almost entirely automatically, without skilled attention, for long periods. Special equipment for trunk dialling will be located at automatic switching centres such as Stornoway, Benbecula, Mallaig, Oban, Fort William and Port Ellen (Islay). But this welcome overall improvement should not obscure local difficulties; certain communities find themselves at trunk-call distance from their nearest shopping centre, as is the case between the Small Isles and Mallaig, so that the telephoning of orders and inquiries becomes an expensive item. Moreover there are some isolated communities, like Barrisdale in Knoydart, where the high cost of providing telephone links is prohibitive and where the annual rental would amount to several hundred pounds. A commercial view by the G.P.O. is understandable, but the implications of this for the people concerned, when access to the outside world is restricted to their own boat, which cannot operate in bad weather, are an unsettling influence.

Services in the main centres and over much of the landward area are on the whole of a high standard. But this leaves a small minority of the population on the island and mainland where the comforts of the affluent society cannot be enjoyed except at great expense. These are the places with electricity, telephone and road access but a long way from shops, hospitals and professional services. They may also be communities where the Highlands and Islands Film Guild has been forced to discontinue shows through the 'self-imposed house arrest' which has followed the extended T.V. coverage, and where the Church of Scotland may not allow young ministers to accept charges. Or they may be even more isolated households almost entirely dependent on their own services and resources to maintain contact. To some extent one can advocate subsidising services to bring costs to the individual more in line with those in more central locations – this is the typical island argument – but there comes a time when the cost per head of doing this becomes excessive, and in these cases evacuation may be the only reasonable solution.

This is the typical pattern of events on the smallest islands, where glaring contrasts in opportunities between the island and the mainland induce depopulation to the point where even essential services cannot be maintained. Moisley (1966) has calculated that after rising to 120 by 1861 owing to pressure on land at the time of the clearances, the number of inhabited Hebridean islands has declined to seventy-three in 1961 (or eighty-two if lighthouses are included). With further refinements in servicing in future it is probable that the position of other islands will become critical, and in the same way a number of mainland habitations, which are effectively insular in their isolation, will be abandoned. But while such decline may be regretted, it represents in population terms a very small proportion of the total, as it has been estimated that the total population of the hundred or so Hebridean islands depopulated since the mid-sixteenth century cannot have been more than 2,500. Therefore desertion, 'though it may have some dramatic impact, is a small factor in the general depopulation of the Hebrides'.

Moreover desertion does not necessarily imply dereliction, for small islands are often profitable escape-proof grazings for cattle and sheep when organised as one unit by an absentee farmer. They may in fact be more profitable when used in this way than would be the case if the island was divided between a resident crofting population. But future repopulation may be effected as part of the growing trend of affluent southerners buying cottages for holidays or retirement. Of course proximity to roads is normally a necessity in the interests of costs and reliability, but the more affluent, resourceful and ambitious are moving to the small islands. Thus Castle Stalker in Appin and the small island on which it stands have been bought and the castle is to be made fit for habitation over the next few years for use when its owner retires. The island of Rona between north Uist and Benbecula will similarly support a regular population when the lodge currently being built for the island's new owner is finished!

CHAPTER ELEVEN

Conclusion

GATHERING together the many loose ends is no easy task, but some general conclusions must be attempted and possible future courses contemplated. An inescapable conclusion must surely be that the future of the Highlands can be a prosperous and secure one given adequate support from both within and without. For too long underdevelopment has been attributed to poor resources and an unfavourable peripheral position rather than to shortcomings in the use to which the admittedly modest endowment has been put. The lack of any coherent regional policy and doctrines of *laissez-faire* ensured that the richer resources of the coalfields would be emphasised in the eighteenth and nineteenth centuries, and it was precisely at this critical time that Highland separatism was finally destroyed as a military force. Small wonder that the economic convulsions which jolted the Highlands led to stagnation and depopulation, which turned the minds of people used to a changeless patriarchal society first to bewilderment and then to bitterness. Moreover change proved to be a continuous process, as witnessed by the several sudden waves of land-use change which ran through the nineteenth and early twentieth centuries. When these changes treated individual interests with only scant attention, can one be surprised when further change meets with resistance and suspicion?

The human side of the problem has been illustrated by Sir Robert Urquhart, who discusses the attitudes to the Highlands of Englishmen, Scotsmen and native Highlanders (1964, p. 188). The typical Englishman he regards as 'a mentally lazy man who makes a virtue of confessing to complete ignorance of Highland affairs and abandoning them to the care of Scotsmen. His mental attitude to the crofter is benignly romantic but unrealistic.' Scotsmen, however, are in the main Lowlanders who 'live too close to the Highlands and Islands to see them in perspective. Moreover they have a guilt complex which seeks solace in hostile prejudice'. The real Highlanders have for long suffered from lack of leadership and initiative, a condition which stems from the massive and selective redeployment of the Highland population which has taken place during the last two centuries. Against this background it is not to be wondered that Highlanders are seldom able to cope objectively with their problems. 'Their failure to communicate with their fellow citizens is in part due to a vehemence of expression which has become habitual in face of the prejudice of lowlanders and the bland incomprehension of the English. The crofter's mind is pervaded with a debilitating sense of ancient wrong and continuing injustice.'

Slowly, however, the situation has been improved. Steps were taken to stabilise the stake of the small farmer element by the crofting legislation of 1886, which gave security of tenure and rights to a fair rent and compensation for improvements made to the croft during the tenancy. This removed the causes of much unrest but failed to provide for future eventualities by introducing an element of rigidity into the smallest holdings which, by their very inability to provide a livelihood in themselves, were the ones most likely to require further regulation with changing economic and social circumstances. Subsequent legislation did bring more land into crofting, but mainly in order to provide further smallholdings rather than to enlarge the existing ones; in the course of time these new holdings inherited the problems of older ones, and security of tenure proved of limited worth when it was tantamount to enforced living at subsistence level; crofters showed their lack of confidence in the system by leaving the land in large numbers. The failure to develop the non-agricultural sectors of the Highland economy, coupled with the provision of a new skeleton network of steamer and rail services, ensured that problems of underemployment would be solved by movement to other regions of the country.

In the post-war period the Highlands have benefited from increased state interest in the security of both the individual and the regions. War-time subsidies to hill farming were continued and welcome development capital injected into agriculture through the MAP grants. At the same time the Taylor Commission, inquiring into crofting conditions, has been followed by legislation which goes some way to overcome the rigidity of the 1886 Act and set up the Crofters Commission once again to reorganise and develop this branch of the agricultural industry (though the 1955 Commission, like its predecessor of 1886, has not been allowed the finance and independence it would have liked). Legislation allowing subletting of croft land in 1961 was helpful in reducing the amount of croft land lying underused. Equally exciting, however, have been the recent attempts to integrate rural land use and remove some of the friction between farming, forestry and sporting interests. Most encouraging has been the trend to compensate for predictable losses from the land by establishing industry at selected growth points and by improving the infrastructure to produce environments more comparable in standard with those in other parts of the country. The existence of an Advisory Panel for the Highlands and Islands, succeeded in 1966 by the Highlands and Islands Development Board, charged with the task of reviewing all matters relating to the economic and social well-being and development of the Highlands and Islands, is indicative of this growing interest and determination. Regional development is thus gradually being conceived as a comprehensive operation and not simply as a sop to local unemployment problems, as was the case with the Special Areas and Development Areas legislation in 1934 and 1945 respectively. The later legislation of 1947 (the Town and Country Planning Act) and 1960 (the Local Employment Act) has paved the way for regional planning and development machinery for all parts of the country.

THE HIGHLANDS: A SPECIAL CASE?

This change is significant in that the Highlands cease to become a special case, with a trickle of aid to maintain the agricultural structure, and instead become one of a series of development areas where the first policy guideline is a 'concentration on objectives worth investing in' (Scotland, 1966, p. 55). It is tempting to insist that the Highlands be treated as a special case for development as well as given protection with fiscal incentives in excess of those granted to other peripheral regions. Given this approach, there are many schemes of an infrastructural nature which could be advocated in the Highlands: the Glen Feshie road from Aviemore to Braemar would provide a new link between the expanding urban areas of Fort William and Aberdeen and create an east–west road to detract from the more usual north–south orientation of major transport arteries. Completion of the coast road between Kyle of Lochalsh and Mallaig would be a boon to local amenity and wider tourist interests, while schemes such as a bridge to Skye would lay the foundation for a secure future for the island's economy. But such developments are likely to be resisted by a Treasury demanding proof of immediate economic necessity. Such proof could probably not be supplied, for the gain would come in the future, yet they are the sort of measures which a programme of radical rehabilitation would probably include, arguing that some of the glaring contrasts in local accessibility both within the Highlands and between the Highlands and adjacent regions must be reduced drastically if regional development policies are to make a significant impact.

It would be unreasonable to claim that the Highlands and islands do not receive any special aid for development. A scheme of loans and grants to be administered by the Development Board was approved in December 1965, including the unique inducement of special grants, and 'this was the first time that a regional agency of government had been given power of this kind . . . for the promotion and development of industrial and commercial concerns within its own area' (Report for 1967, para. 50). But rapid progress demands that exceptions from national policy be made consistently rather than occasionally, otherwise the advantages of one discriminatory measure will tend to be negated wholly or partially by subsequent moves which fail to make the same allowances for particular areas. Thus the confidence evoked by the appointment of the Highlands and Islands Development Board was partially dissipated by the uniform imposition of the Selective Employment Tax which, in its original conception, discriminated heavily against the Highlands because of the high proportion of the working population there employed in service industries. This is not to suggest that the Highlands should receive unlimited concessions, but rather to argue that the necessity of treating the Highlands with national as well as regional interests in mind must impose a ceiling on the amount of special aid which can be justified. For the Highlands and islands are a sub-region of Scotland, where the bulk of the population is concentrated in the Central Lowlands. Moreover the Scottish planning region probably has more autonomy and cohesion than its English counterparts, stemming from Scotland's legal and administrative independence.

What then constitutes a reasonable long-term objective? Maintenance, reduced attrition or growth of the Highland population as it stands at the moment? Although it seems that government is ready to justify increased sums in the interests of regional development, and although the local population is now probably more ready than ever before to accept a greater measure of industrialisation and urbanisation, investment will be directed only towards worth-while objectives. Moreover even with generous support to develop the periphery of the country, a zone of which the Highlands form a substantial part, the centre will continue to grow, probably at a faster rate, thus maintaining the differential in growth rates. The Highlands are peripheral but are not far enough away or sufficiently populated to permit an independent industrial economy to develop, as is the case with California, Siberia or Western Australia. In short the attraction of better jobs and amenities in the south cannot be easily countered and must be expected to remain indefinitely as one of the characteristics of British geography; to arrest or reverse the trend would seem impracticable even if it were considered desirable.

One line of argument is that the periphery will in future be aided in its rehabilitation by the labour shortage in the south and by congestion in the older industrial areas, thus making for a desire to decentralise in the Development Areas, a possibility which government financial incentives will then develop. This may be interpreted generously for the Highlands to suggest that great value will in future be placed on anchorages such as Loch Eriboll in north-west Sutherland and industrial sites along the east coast, while pockets of local unemployment will be seen from afar as potential labour forces for new industry. But such a rosy view would be an overestimation; certainly the existence of a labour force in the Development Areas constitutes a powerful attraction, but the reservoir is not always large nor do numbers of unemployed persons necessarily indicate a labour force for light industry. Often the quality of labour in the Development Areas in terms of its skills may be very inferior to that in the centre, and hence many of the unemployed may be virtually unemployable as far as any particular industrialist is concerned. Nevertheless if a labour force is available then this will certainly act as a powerful attraction. In the past the availability of labour in the Highlands has been surprisingly low owing to the tendency to migrate south in the event of unemployment, but a novel attempt is being made to overcome this by compiling a register which now contains the names and skills of thousands of people who would return to the Highlands if and when suitable jobs became available. The scheme is known as 'Operation Counterdrift', and the Highland Board hope that it will increase the attractions of the Highlands for industrial growth. But such a scheme is unlikely to upset the balance of advantage currently in favour of concentration on a limited number of growth points.

STRATEGY WITHIN THE HIGHLANDS

Regional as well as national politics are an important factor, and any development programme needs to show evidence of a balance between the centre and the periphery. Aware of the need to have a strong focal point in the Highlands, plans are to develop Inverness by expanding along the Beauly Firth. Coupled with expected industrial growth in the Cromarty Firth area, this would create a 'linear city' for the 'Golden Triangle' stretching from Nairn to Inverness and round to Dingwall and Invergordon, and would contain service industries on a par with those enjoyed nationally. Included in particular would be a technical college, and possibly a university, which would improve the resources of the Highlands for skilled labour. Yet from the analysis of population material it is evident there are two worlds within the Highlands, with the prosperous factory worker in Inverness feeling few of the misgivings of the Hebridean crofter conscious of his limited stake in the peat moss on the edge of Europe. The Highland problem in some areas at least is one of how to cope with embarrassingly rapid growth rather than a search for new palliatives to arrest decay. There are consequently many people on the fringes of the Highlands who view with suspicion the plans to develop Inverness, arguing that the 'Golden Triangle' is already the most favourable location in the Highlands and that further development there will have the unwelcome effect of drawing population from the periphery towards this central point. This move to the centre has received considerable attention in recent years when considered at national level, and no doubt regional policies are the result of investigations into this problem. But the examination of similar forces within each region has not received the same attention and commentators frequently make the error of generalising too much about the Highland economy, thus giving an exaggerated impression of extreme optimism or despair as the case may be.

In the regional interest, then, should the Board continue to encourage development selectively along the axis of growth, with subsidies to the flagging economies of outlying islands, or should it attempt to stimulate growth more evenly? Applying the national argument at regional level there is the same contrast between the centre (the 'Golden Triangle') and the periphery (the Hebrides, Orkney and Shetland), with growth easiest to accomplish in the centre and more difficult on the periphery, where stability is needed yet where local inaccessibility and poverty of resources make this difficult to accomplish. Interest is being shown in the localities marginal to the 'Golden Triangle', namely Caithness, Lochaber and Argyll, which produces a long narrow growth axis running down the east coast, the Great Glen and its continuation into Argyll. On the west mainland and islands small industrial projects are appropriate, and fishing and tourism are receiving close attention since the agricultural and forestry potential is, of course, very limited. Services must be improved in these areas, particularly housing and transport, and even though rapid improvement cannot be reasonably anticipated it is imperative that the present pattern of services should not be eroded away by inopportune closures of rail, steamer or bus services. It is also important that each peripheral locality should have a dynamic central place, and it is with this in mind that one local authority is being suggested for the whole of the Outer Hebrides, with the concentration of services, including secondary education, in Stornoway rather than on the mainland. Such ideas have been condemned on the mainland as tantamount to the setting up of a 'Hebridean Curtain', but it is merely the logical projection of the regional argument down to a more local level; just as the Highlands as a whole must have a thriving focal point in Inverness, so the peripheral locality of the Outer Hebrides needs, at this lower-tier level, a prosperous central place.

A healthier balance is all the more necessary since the co-operation and determination of all sections of the Highland population is required, for it is most important to create a more coherent regional identity in the Highlands. Intense and narrow loyalties should not be allowed to obscure the vision of the wider good. But can the Kintyre farmer and the Unst crofter both be brought to feel that they have common problems and that Inverness is the logical centre in which to seek solutions? Functionally Argyll's links with Glasgow and the orientation or Orkney and Shetland to Aberdeen and Edinburgh would seem to compromise the emergence of a regional feeling for the seven counties. With Scotland such a clear entity, is there scope for regional feeling to intervene between local loyalties on the one hand and patriotism on the other? The unit of the crofting counties has proved to be one of the most resilient features of the Highland scene, for this administrative unit, demarcated arbitrarily in 1886 with the effective crofting area in mind, has been consistently endorsed by later legislation and is the sphere of influence of the Highland Board. The only flexibility allowed is that adjacent areas may be included to secure better co-ordination of development; this applies to schemes such as tourism in the Cairngorms with the consideration of the Banffshire and Aberdeenshire sections of this growing holiday area. Where to draw the line is bound to be an inconclusive argument, but nevertheless the crofting counties unit would seem to have little justification now for permanence. Certainly the effective crofting area has receded, and on that basis a smaller unit, taking either the area north of the Caledonian Canal, as recommended by the Vigilantes Association, or the more restricted areas of the north-west mainland and islands, might be more appropriate. Alternatively, if it is argued that crofting is no longer an appropriate common denominator in view of the decreasing proportion of the Highland population which this form of agriculture represents, then there would seem to be no logical reason for omitting adjacent counties like Bute, which is in a more difficult economic position than many parts of Argyll, and Moray and Nairn, which are for the most part functionally linked with Inverness. Fig. 32 compares the extent of the crofting counties with the smaller area administered by the Congested Districts Board at the

9

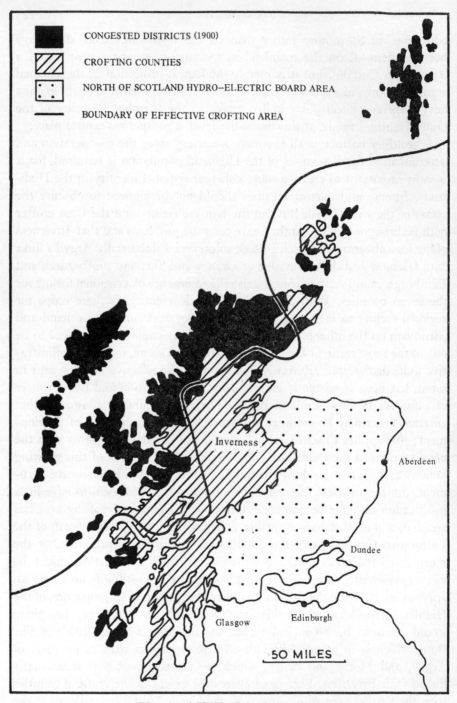

Fig. 32 *A Highland development area*

Legend:

- CONGESTED DISTRICTS (1900)
- CROFTING COUNTIES
- NORTH OF SCOTLAND HYDRO—ELECTRIC BOARD AREA
- BOUNDARY OF EFFECTIVE CROFTING AREA

Inverness

Aberdeen

Dundee

Glasgow   Edinburgh

50 MILES

turn of the century and the larger Highland unit over which the North of Scotland Hydro-Electric Board has responsibilities today.[1]

THE REGIONAL PROBLEM IN EUROPE

The Highlands and islands are one facet of the regional problem in Britain, though on grounds of position, resources and history the area has a unique character. But most countries have problems of this nature, and it is reassuring therefore to notice that they have similar difficulties in ameliorating conditions in their peripheral areas. Interest was expressed in Norway by the Advisory Panel (1961), for the Norwegians have been following the policy of setting up 'cornerstone' industries in the most promising locations in the backward regions, some government-run and others private. This was part of the north Norway Development Programme, which was launched in 1952 with an emphasis on the speeding-up of hydro-electric power exploitation and an extension of vocational education. The north Norway Development Fund was also established, to provide guarantees for private enterprises unable to obtain sufficient finance through normal sources, the incentives discriminating in favour of north Norway relative to the rest of the country. In 1962, however, the scheme was incorporated in a more general programme for all the backward regions of Norway, and the General Development Fund appeared. There are clearly many parallels with the Highland position, though the hydro-power resources of the Highlands are not so substantial and are no longer so highly valued nationally (as witnessed by the brake recently applied to further construction schemes), while it is doubtful if the financial aid is as generous. The Highland Panel also stressed the strength and freedom of financial aid to the development of north Norway, coupled with the absence of a burdensome rating system. However, it is significant that in Norway, as in Britain, financial aid is necessarily directed to the periphery in general rather than to one segment of it in particular. The 'special case' is difficult to justify on a permanent basis, necessary though this is for sustained action, and just as north Norway cannot maintain its special status indefinitely, it is easy to see how the crofting counties, a much smaller unit relative to the national economy, cannot command unlimited attention.

Another well-known 'problem area' is the Italian south, which has tended

[1] The Royal Commission on local government in Scotland has recommended that the Highlands and islands should comprise one of the eight regions which will form the basis of the new scheme. This has brought objections from those who advocate fuller autonomy for the main island groups and from others who argue that the whole area should either be divided into two or partially absorbed by the Glasgow region.

to fall further behind the more prosperous north with its industrial growth packed into the Milan–Genoa–Turin triangle. Since the war the south has received the attention of a special agency, the 'Cassa per il Mezzogiorno', which has sought to inject development capital in liberal doses. However, even with the investment of funds and expertise the south accounted for a smaller proportion of the total Italian Gross National Product (G.N.P.) in 1961 than it did in 1951. Moreover, to prevent dissipation of funds by attempting a proliferation of small schemes in a large number of localities, the most promising regions of Campania (Naples) and Puglia (Bari, Brindisi and Taranto) have received a disproportionate share of the funds in order to develop 'growth poles'. This now familiar policy has also been adopted by French planning in their concept of 'metropoles' and 'regional centres', and must inevitably foreshadow some redistribution of population within each region, as is happening in the Scottish Highlands.

Regional policy everywhere has a number of built-in restraints. Decentralisation from national level to regional and local government and planning can only be partial and can only go as far as is permitted by the national interest, where the bulk of power and vested interest is concentrated. In the same way the trends towards the setting-up of supranational organisations such as the various economic groups within Europe can only proceed as far as the individual member states desire. With this hierarchy of scale components appearing in planning, decentralisation immediately demands the formulation of policy guidelines by the national government to avoid major conflicts and weakening of the national fabric. But the impossibility of real independence for a Highland development authority need not be interpreted pessimistically; the wider areal context in which Highland affairs are discussed may not change, but there is certainly greater sympathy and understanding now than at any time since 1886, if not since 1745, and an increasing number of ways in which Highland resources can be developed.

Bibliography

THE most valuable general work on Highland geography is the volume by
A. C. O'Dell and K. Walton (1962), entitled *The Highlands and Islands of
Scotland*. But there is no shortage of other reading matter in the form of
articles, books and reports, and the list that follows is intended as a selection
of those items which have relevance to the themes taken up in this book. A
number of categories may be identified. For eighteenth-century affairs there
are a number of travel accounts (Pennant, 1769; Knox, 1787; Newte, 1791)
which give a valuable insight into conditions, as well as the work of historians
(Brown, 1908; Dickie, 1920; Grant, 1918). But a much greater weight of
material relates to the nineteenth century, when the improving movement
stimulated much literary effort. There were several agricultural accounts on a
county basis (Robertson, 1813), while the Old and New Statistical Accounts
deal with the situation in each parish in the 1790s and 1840s, giving a useful
indication of conditions before and after improvement in many areas. Other
commentaries are to be found in the pages of the *Transactions of the Highland
and Agricultural Society of Scotland*, and local material is often available in
the form of estate documents and maps, many of which are still in the hands
of proprietors or available in Edinburgh at the National Library or Register
House. The maps produced by General Roy in his survey of the Highlands
in the mid-eighteenth century are valuable guides to the settlement pattern
on the eve of improvement.

The impact of economic changes on the population of the Highlands and
the resultant emigration prompted considerable writing on the social
question, and works cited by Alison (1847), (1826), Brown (1806), Mac-
Culloch (1824) and Selkirk (1806) represent a cross-section of the opinions
expressed. These themes were afforded greater attention later in the nineteenth century with the appearance of local newspapers and the appointment
of Royal Commissions (Scotland, 1884, 1895) to examine local conditions.
The evidence and maps presented with these official reports form a valuable
source of evidence for the reconstruction of the Highland scene several
decades after the improving movement, when the golden age of farming had
given way to policies of deer afforestation and land settlement. Detailed
analysis of census material is a valuable support here and is facilitated by the
availability of the actual enumeration books for consultation in Edinburgh
for the censuses conducted between 1841 and 1891 (Storrie, 1962c).

The twentieth century has so far produced an even greater wealth of material in the form of reports by government agencies and committees, not to mention the growing output from interested persons in learned journals. Land use has always been a popular theme; contributions on farming, with emphasis on the problems of small farms and land improvement, come from Beilby, Braid, Fenton, Fraser, Gorrie, Scola, Symon and others, while the work on forestry by Hutcheson, Steven and Walker is very important. Among the historical work the contributions of Adam, Grimble, Kermack, MacLeod and Prebble are prominent, with work in the field of economic history by Grant, Gray, Haldane and Hamilton and in archaeology by Fairhurst and Small. Economists have made a number of assessments, notably those by MacKay, Noble, Munby and Simpson. But of particular prominence in recent years has been the contribution from geographers, for the earlier work by Geddes and O'Dell has been followed up by a large number of workers including Caird, Coull, Gailey, Kirk, Miller, Moisley, Skewis, Spaven, Storrie and Wheeler. References on natural history can be found in Darling and Boyd (1964) and on the physical landscape in O'Dell and Walton (1962).

M. I. ADAM (1918–19), 'The Causes of the Highland Emigrations of 1783 to 1803', *Scottish Historical Review*, XVI 280 and XVII 73.

—— (1921), 'Eighteenth-century Highland Landlords and the Poverty Problem', *Scottish Historical Review*, XIX 1.

ADVISORY PANEL ON THE HIGHLANDS AND ISLANDS (1961), *Report on a Visit to Norway, September 1961*.

W. P. ALISON (1847), *Observations on the Famine of 1846 and 1847 in the Highlands of Scotland and Ireland*.

J. ANDERSON (1785), *An Account of the Present State of the Hebrides and West Coast of Scotland*.

ANON. (1826), *A Critical Examination of Dr MacCulloch's Work on the Highlands and Western Isles of Scotland*.

—— (1918), 'The Lochaber Deer Forests', *Scottish Journal of Agriculture*, I 465.

—— (1957), 'Forestry, Agriculture and Marginal Land', *Journal of the Forestry Commission*, XXVI 1.

G. D. BANKS (1950), 'Hydro-electric Development in the Highlands', *Scottish Geographical Magazine*, LXVI 65.

O. J. BEILBY (1948), 'The Problem of Marginal Farms', *Journal of the Agricultural Economics Society*, VII 306.

J. S. BLACKIE (1885), *Scottish Highlanders and the Land Laws*.

J. L. BLAKE (1962), 'Pasture Improvement Schemes in the Island of Lewis', *Scottish Studies*, VI 108.

D. C. BOWSER (1951), 'Private Forestry in Scotland', *Scottish Forestry*, V 10.

K. W. BRAID (1934), 'Bracken as a Colonist', *Scottish Journal of Agriculture*, XVII 59.
—— (1957), 'Bracken Eradication', *Transactions of the Royal Highland and Agricultural Society of Scotland*, n.s., II 16.
P. H. BROWN (1891), *Early Travellers in Scotland up to the End of the Nineteenth Century*.
—— (1908), 'Scotland in the Eighteenth Century', *Scottish Historical Review*, VI 343.
R. BROWN (1806), *Strictures and Remarks on the Earl of Selkirk's Observations*.
W. M. BROWNLIE (1949), 'Observations on the Performance of Sheep Breeds Other than Blackface on an Argyllshire Hill Farm', *Transactions of the Royal Highland and Agricultural Society of Scotland*, LXI 32.

H. M. CADELL (1923), 'Scottish Canals and Waterways', *Scottish Geographical Magazine*, XXXIX 73.
A. A. L. CAESAR (1961), 'Problems of Regional Planning in Great Britain', in *Problems of Applied Geography* (Proceedings of the Anglo-Polish seminar, 1959) 39.
—— and D. E. KEEBLE (eds) (1965), 'Regional Planning Problems in Great Britain', *Advancement of Science*, XXII 177.
J. B. CAIRD (1951), 'The Isle of Harris', *Scottish Geographical Magazine*, LXVII 85.
—— (1956), 'Survey of South Uist', *Glasgow Herald*, 18 Oct.
—— *et al.* (1958), *Park: A Geographical Study of a Lewis Crofting District* (Geographical Field Group, Nottingham).
—— (1962), 'The North-West Highlands and Hebrides', in J. B. Mitchell (ed.), *Great Britain: Essays in Regional Geography*, 543.
—— (1964), 'The Making of the Scottish Rural Landscape', *Scottish Geographical Magazine*, LXXX 72.
—— and H. A. MOISLEY (1961), 'Leadership and Innovation in the Crofting Communities of the Outer Hebrides', *Sociological Review*, IX 85.
—— and —— (1964), 'The Outer Hebrides', in J. A. Steers (ed.), *Field Studies in the British Isles*, 374.
J. A. CAMERON LEES (1897), *History of Inverness*.
R. H. CAMPBELL (1959), 'The Highland Economy, 1750–1850', *Scottish Journal of Political Economy*, VI 59.
—— (1960), 'The Industrial Revolution and the Scottish Countryside', *Transactions of the Gaelic Society, Inverness*, XV 15.
L. V. CHILTON (1950), 'The Aluminium Industry in Scotland', *Scottish Geographical Magazine*, LXVI 153.
A. COLLIER (1955), *The Crofting Problem*.
H. M. CONACHER (1936), 'The Relations of Land Tenure and Agriculture', *Journal of the Agricultural Economics Society*, IV 167.
CONGESTED DISTRICTS BOARD (SCOTLAND) (1898–1910), *Annual Reports*.
A. COOPER (1966), 'Inwintering of Sheep', *Outlook on Agriculture* (I.C.I.), V (2) 80.
J. T. COPPOCK (1968), 'The Countryside (Scotland) Act and the Geographer', *Scottish Geographical Magazine*, LXXXIV 201.
J. R. COULL (1962a), 'The Geography of Crofting in Scotland' (unpublished Ph.D. thesis, Aberdeen University).
—— (1962b), 'The Island of Tiree', *Scottish Geographical Magazine*, LXXVIII 17.
—— (1963), 'Melness: A Crofting Community on the North Coast of Scotland', *Scottish Studies*, VII 180.
—— (1964), 'Walla: A Shetland Crofting Parish', *Scottish Geographical Magazine*, LXXX 135.
—— (1966a), 'Population Trends and Structures on the Island of Westray, Orkney', *Scottish Studies*, X 69.

J. R. COULL (1966*b*), Economic Development of the Island of Westray, Orkney', *Scottish Geographical Magazine*, LXXXII 154.

—— (1967), 'A Comparison of Demographic Trends in the Faroe and Shetland Islands', *Transactions of the Institute of British Geographers*, XLI 159.

I. A. CRAWFORD (1962), 'Kelp Burning', *Scottish Studies*, VI 105.

E. CREGEEN (1959), 'Recollections of an Argyllshire Drover', *Scottish Studies*, III 143.

CROFTERS COMMISSION (1886–1910; 1955–), *Annual Reports*.

J. CRUICKSHANK (1961), 'The Black Isle, Ross-shire: A Land Use Study', *Scottish Geographical Magazine*, LXXVII 3.

A. CUNNINGHAM (1918), 'The Revolution Government in the Highlands', *Scottish Historical Review*, XVI 29.

F. F. DARLING (1937), *A Herd of Red Deer*.

—— (1945), *Crofting Agriculture*.

—— (1947), *Natural History in the Highlands and Islands*.

—— (ed.) (1955*a*), *West Highland Survey*.

—— (1955*b*), 'Review of A. Collier on the Crofting Problem', *Scottish Historical Review*, XXXIV 64.

—— and J. M. BOYD (1964), *The Highlands and Islands*.

G. L. DAVIES (1958), 'The Parish of North Uist', *Scottish Geographical Magazine*, LXXII 65.

J. R. DAY (1918), *Public Administration in the Highlands and Islands of Scotland*.

D. R. DIAMOND (1965), 'Regional Planning: The Scottish Approach', in A. A. L. Caesar and D. E. Keeble (eds), 'Regional Planning Problems in Great Britain', *Advancement of Science*, XXII 183.

J. M. DICKIE (1920), 'The Economic Position in Scotland in 1760', *Scottish Historical Review*, XVIII 14.

M. A. M. DICKIE (1959), 'Rural Development Surveys in Scotland', *Forestry*, 32.

—— (1960), 'The Crofting Counties: Problems and Prospects', *Transactions of the Royal Highland and Agricultural Society of Scotland*, V 1.

M. E. M. DONALDSON (1926), *Further Wanderings, Mainly in Argyll*.

—— (1935), *Scotland's Suppressed History*.

R. L. DREW (1966), 'Regional Development with or without Science', *University of Strathclyde Regional Studies Group Bulletin*, II.

W. DRUMMOND-NORIE (1898), *Loyal Lochaber*.

C. L. D. DUCKWORTH and G. E. LANGMUIR (1967), *West Highland Steamers*.

H. FAIRHURST (1954), 'The Natural Vegetation of Scotland', *Scottish Geographical Magazine*, LXX 193.

—— (1960–4), 'Scottish Clachans', *Scottish Geographical Magazine*, LXXVI 67 and LXXX 150.

—— (1967), 'The Rural Settlement Pattern in Scotland, with Special Reference to the West and North', in R. W. Steel and R. Lawton (eds), *Liverpool Essays in Geography: A Jubilee Edition*, 193.

E. W. FENTON (1936), 'The Spread of Bracken in Scotland', *Agricultural Progress*, XIII 66.

—— (1937*a*), Some Aspects of Man's Influence on the Vegetation of Scotland', *Scottish Geographical Magazine*, LV 16.

—— (1937*b*), 'The Influence of Sheep on the Vegetation of Hill Grazings in Scotland', *Journal of Ecology*, XXVIII 438.

J. B. FLEMING and F. H. W. GREEN (1952), 'Some Relations between Town and Country in Scotland', *Scottish Geographical Magazine*, LXVIII 2.

R. G. FLETCHER (1953), 'Cattle Rearing at Ardlussa, Jura, 1946–1951', *Scottish Agriculture*, XXXII 68.
FORESTRY COMMISSION (1919–), *Annual Reports*.
T. B. FRANKLIN (1952), *A History of Scottish Farming*.
A. FRASER (1954), 'The Scottish Sheep Industry of Today', *Transactions of the Royal Highland and Agricultural Society of Scotland*, LXVI 23.

V. GAFFNEY (1959), 'Summer Shielings', *Scottish Historical Review*, XXXVIII 20.
R. A. GAILEY (1960*a*), 'Settlement Changes in the South-West Highlands of Scotland' (unpublished Ph.D. thesis, Glasgow University).
—— (1960*b*), 'Settlement and Population in Kintyre, 1750–1800', *Scottish Geographical Magazine*, LXXVI 99.
—— (1961*a*), 'Tenant Mobility on a West Highland Estate', *Scottish Historical Review*, XL 136.
—— (1961*b*), 'The Role of Subletting in the Crofting Community', *Scottish Studies*, V 57.
—— (1962), 'The Evolution of Highland Rural Settlement', *Scottish Studies*, VI 155.
A. GARNETT (1939), 'Diffused Light and Sunlight in Relation to Relief and Settlement in High Latitudes', *Scottish Geographical Magazine*, LV 271.
P. GASKELL (1967), *Morvern Transformed*.
A. GEDDES (1936), 'Lewis', *Scottish Geographical Magazine*, LII 217, 300.
—— (1944), 'Landscape and Ecology in Relation to Afforestation', *Scottish Forestry Journal*, LVIII 53.
—— (1945), 'Ecology and Landscape and the Forester', *Scottish Forestry Journal*, LIX 29.
—— (1947), 'The Development of Stornoway', *Scottish Geographical Magazine*, LXIII 57.
—— (1948), 'Conjoint Tenants and Tacksmen in the Isle of Lewis, 1715–1726', *Economic History Review*, I 54.
—— and F. D. N. SPAVEN (1947), '*The Highlands and Islands: Their Regional Planning*' (Outlook Tower, Edinburgh).
J. GIBB (1938), 'Problems of the Highlands', *Geographical Magazine*, VII 1.
R. M. GORRIE (1947), 'Shelterbelts and Cottage Industries in Scottish Planning', *Scottish Geographical Magazine*, LXIII 11.
A. GRANT (1809), *Letters from the Mountains, being the Real Correspondence of a Lady between the Years 1773 and 1807*.
I. F. GRANT (1924), *Everyday Life on an Old Highland Farm, 1769–1782*.
—— (1930), *The Social and Economic Development of Scotland before 1603*.
—— (1934), *The Economic History of Scotland*.
—— (1935), *The Lordship of the Isles*.
—— (1961), *Highland Folkways*.
J. S. GRANT (1959), 'Reflections on Past and Present Developments in Lewis', *Scottish Agriculture*, XXXIX 113.
K. W. GRANT (1918), 'Peasant Life in Argyllshire at the End of the Eighteenth Century', *Scottish Historical Review*, XVI 144.
M. GRAY (1951), 'The Kelp Industry in the Highlands and Islands', *Economic History Review*, IV 197
—— (1954), 'The Highland Potato Famine of the 1840s', *Economic History Review*, VII 357.
—— (1955), 'Economic Welfare and Money Income in the Highlands, 1750–1850', *Scottish Journal of Political Economy*, II 47.
—— (1957*a*), *The Highland Economy, 1750–1850*.
—— (1957*b*), 'The Consolidation of the Crofting System', *Agricultural History Review*, V 31.

M. GRAY (1964), 'The Place of Fishing in the Economy of the North-West, 1886–1914', in L. D. Stamp (ed.), 'Land Use in the Scottish Highlands', *Advancement of Science*, XXI 90.

M. J. F. GREGOR and R. M. CRICHTON (1946), *From Farm to Factory: The Evolution of an Industrial Community in the Highlands.*

I. GRIMBLE (1962), *The Trial of Patrick Sellar: The Tragedy of the Highland Evictions.*
—— (1965), *Chief of Mackay.*

A. R. B. HALDANE (1952), *The Drove Roads of Scotland.*
—— (1962), *New Ways through the Glens.*

H. HAMILTON (1932), *The Industrial Revolution in Scotland.*
—— (1959), 'Economic Growth in Scotland, 1720–1770', *Scottish Journal of Political Economy*, VI 85.

W. A. HANCE (1952), 'Crofting in the Outer Hebrides', *Economic Geography*, XXVIII 1.
—— (1953), 'The Fishing Industry of the Outer Hebrides', *Economic Geography*, XXIX 168.

P. D. HANCOCK (1960), *Bibliography of Works Relating to Scotland, 1916–1950.*

G. C. HAYES (1952), 'A Survey of West Highland Agriculture', *Proceedings of the Agricultural Economics Society*, X 35.

J. HEADRICK (1859–61), 'On the Practicability and Advantages of Opening Navigation between the Moray Firth at Inverness and Loch Eil at Fort William', *Transactions of the Highland and Agricultural Society*, 355.

G. F. HENDRY (1958), 'Grass Silage in Scotland', *Scottish Agricultural Economics*, IX 45.
—— (1962), 'Scotland's Part-time Farms', *Scottish Agricultural Economics*, XII 112.
—— and O. J. BEILBY (1957), 'The Small Farm in Scotland', *Scottish Agricultural Economics*, VIII 28.

R. HERON (1794), *General View of the Agriculture of the County of the Hebrides.*

HERRING INDUSTRY BOARD (1935–), *Annual Reports.*

S. HIBBERT (1822), *Description of the Shetland Islands.*

HIGHLANDS AND ISLANDS DEVELOPMENT BOARD (1967), *Annual Reports.*

HIGHLAND TRANSPORT BOARD (1967), *Highland Transport Services.*

H.M.S.O. (1918), *Report of the Reconstruction Committee (Forestry Sub-Committee)* (Acland Report), Cd 8881.
—— (1922), *Report of the Committee on National Expenditure* (Geddes Committee), Cd 1582.
—— (1931), *Report of the Select Committee on National Expenditure* (May Committee), Cmd 3920.
—— (1957), *Forestry, Agriculture and Marginal Land*, Report of the Natural Resources (Technical) Committee (Zuckerman Committee).
—— (1958), *Report of the Enquiry into Inland Waterways*, Cmnd 746.
—— (1961), *Report of the Committee of Enquiry into the Fishing Industry* (Fleck Committee), Cmnd 1266.

J. W. Hobbs (1951), 'The Great Glen Cattle Ranch', *Scottish Agriculture*, XXX 183.

P. HOBSON (1949), 'The Parish of Barra', *Scottish Geographical Magazine*, LXV 71.

J. H. M. HOME (1954), 'Private Forestry in Scotland, 1854–1953', *Scottish Forestry*, VIII 26.
—— (1957), 'Land for Forestry', *Scottish Forestry*, XI 11.

J. W. HOUSE (1966), 'Margins in Regional Geography', in J. W. House (ed.), *Northern Geographical Essays*, 139.

K. M. HUGGINS (1938), 'The Scottish Highlands: A Regional Study', *Scottish Geographical Magazine*, LI 296.

A. M. A. HUTCHESON (1963), 'A Study of Hydro-electric and Forestry Developments in the Highlands' (unpublished Ph.D. thesis, Edinburgh University).

A. IRVINE (1804), *An Enquiry into the Causes and Effects of Emigration from the Highlands and Western Isles of Scotland.*

S. JAATINEN (1957), *The Human Geography of the Outer Hebrides.*
P. JACKSON (1948), 'Scottish Seaweed Resources', *Scottish Geographical Magazine*, LXIV 136.

T. KEITH (1912), 'The Influence of the Convention of the Royal Burghs of Scotland on the Economic Development of Scotland before 1707', *Scottish Historical Review*, X 250.
J. G. KELLAS (1962), 'The Crofters' War, 1882–1888', *History Today*, XII 281.
W. R. KERMACK (1947), *The Scottish Highlands: A Short History.*
W. T. KILGOUR (1908), *Lochaber in War and Peace.*
W. KIRK (1957), 'The Primary Agricultural Colonisation of Scotland', *Scottish Geographical Magazine*, LXXIII 65.
—— (1962), 'North-East Scotland', in J. B. Mitchell (ed.), *Great Britain: Geographical Essays*, 509.
J. KNOX (1787), *A Tour through the Highlands of Scotland.*
J. G. KYD (1952), *Scottish Population Statistics, including Webster's Analysis of Population, 1755* (Scottish History Society).

K. J. LEA (1962), 'Hydro-electricity and Industry in the Highlands of Scotland', *Drumlin*, IX 26.
—— (1968), 'Hydro-electric Power Developments and the Landscape in the Highlands of Scotland', *Scottish Geographical Magazine*, LXXXIV 239.
A. T. A. LEARMONTH (1950), 'The Population of Skye', *Scottish Geographical Magazine*, LXVI 77.
M. M. LEIGH (1928–9), 'The Crofting Problem, 1790–1883', *Scottish Journal of Agriculture*, XI 4, 131, 261, 426 and XII 26.
LORD LOVAT (1911), *Forestry Survey of Glen Mor and a Consideration of Certain Problems Arising Therefrom* (Royal Scottish Arboricultural Society).

DAVID MACBRAYNE LTD (1951), *A Hundred Years of Progress, 1851–1951.*
J. MACCULLOCH (1824), *The Highlands and Western Isles of Scotland.*
A. MACDONALD and J. M. KAY (1957), 'Electricity in the North of Scotland', *Scottish Journal of Political Economy*, IV 18.
C. MACDONALD (1948), 'New Light on the Croft', *Transactions of the Highland and Agricultural Society of Scotland*, XXVII 181.
C. M. MACDONALD (ed.) (1961), *The County of Argyll: Third Statistical Account.*
D. J. MACDONALD (1965), *Slaughter under Trust.*
J. MACDONALD (1811), *General View of the Agriculture of the Hebrides and Western Isles of Scotland.*
R. H. MACDONALD (1885), '*The Emigration of the Highland Crofters.*
W. MACDONALD (1872), 'On the Agriculture of Inverness-shire', *Transactions of the Highland and Agricultural Society of Scotland*, IV 1.
D. R. MACGREGOR (1968), *The Island of Tanera Mor* (unpublished MS.).
M. MACINTOSH (1939), *A History of Inverness.*
A. MACKENZIE (1881), *History of the MacDonalds and Lords of the Isles.*
—— (1914), *The Story of the Highland Clearances.*

A. M. MacKenzie (1951), 'Post-war Trends in Hill Sheep Farming in Scotland', *Scottish Agricultural Economics*, II 43.

W. C. MacKenzie (1903), *History of the Outer Isles.*

D. I. MacKay (1965), 'Regional Planning in the North of Scotland', *Aberdeen University Review*, XLI 75.

—— and N. K. Buxton (1965), 'The North of Scotland Economy: A Case for Redevelopment', *Scottish Journal of Political Economy*, IV 23.

A. McKerral (1947), 'The Tacksman and his Holding in the South-West Highlands', *Scottish Historical Review*, XXVI 9.

D. S. MacLagan (1957), 'Stock Rearing in the Highlands, 1720–1820', *Transactions of the Highland and Agricultural Society of Scotland*, II 63.

J. P. MacLean (1923), *History of the Island of Mull.*

R. C. MacLeod (1921), 'The Western Highlands in the Eighteenth Century', *Scottish Historical Review*, XIX 33.

—— (1925a), 'The Norsemen in the Hebrides', *Scottish Historical Review*, XXII 42.

—— (1925b), 'A West Highland Estate during Three Centuries', *Scottish Historical Review*, XXII 161.

—— (1926), 'The West Highlanders in Peace and War', *Scottish Historical Review*, XXIV 122.

A. MacPherson (1959), 'Land Use Problems in the Hill Areas of Scotland', in R. Miller and J. W. Watson (eds), *Geographical Essays in Memory of A. G. Ogilvie*, 68.

—— (1964), 'Scotch Whisky', *Scottish Geographical Magazine*, LXXX 99.

M. D. MacSween (1959a), 'Settlement in Trotternish, Isle of Skye, 1700–1958' (unpublished B.Litt. thesis, Glasgow University).

—— (1959b), 'Transhumance in North Skye', *Scottish Geographical Magazine*, LXXV 75.

—— and A. Gailey (1961), 'Some Shielings in North Skye', *Scottish Studies*, V 77.

N. MacVicar (1799), 'On the Means of Introducing Linen Manufacture into the Highlands of Scotland', *Transactions of the Highland and Agricultural Society of Scotland*, 150.

M. S. Martin (1703), *Description of the Western Isles of Scotland.*

J. Mason (1947), 'Conditions in the Highlands after the '45', *Scottish Historical Review*, XXVI 134.

J. Mathieson (1924), 'General Wade and his Military Roads in the Highlands of Scotland', *Scottish Geographical Magazine*, XL 193.

—— (1938), The Tragedy of the Scottish Highlands', *Scottish Geographical Magazine*, LIV 257.

J. S. Maxwell (1954), 'Scotland's Forests, 1854–1953', *Scottish Forestry*, VIII 191.

S. Mechie (1960), *The Church and Scottish Social Development, 1780–1870.*

G. Meiklejohn (1927), *Settlements and Roads of Scotland.*

R. Miller (1959), 'Orkney: A Land of Increment', in R. Miller and J. W. Watson (eds), *Geographical Essays in Memory of A. G. Ogilvie*, 7.

—— (1964), 'The Geography of the Scottish Highlands', in J. A. Steers (ed.), *Field Studies in the British Isles*, 360.

H. A. Moisley (1961a), 'North Uist in 1799', *Scottish Geographical Magazine*, LXXVII 89.

—— (1961b), 'Harris Tweed: A Growing Highland Industry', *Economic Geography*, XXXVII 353.

—— et al. (1961), *Uig: A Hebridean Parish* (Geographical Field Group, Nottingham).

—— (1962a), 'Population Changes and the Highland Problem', *Scottish Studies*, VI 94.

—— (1962b), 'The Highlands and Islands: A Crofting Region', *Transactions of the Institute of British Geographers*, XXXI 83.

—— (1964), 'The Geographical Background', in L. D. Stamp (ed.), 'Land Use in the Scottish Highlands', *Advancement of Science*, XXI 141.

H. A. MOISLEY (1966), 'The Deserted Hebrides', *Scottish Studies*, X 44.

D. L. MUNBY (1954), 'Transport Costs in the North of Scotland', *Scottish Journal of Political Economy*, I 75.

—— (1956–7), 'Electricity in the North of Scotland', *Scottish Journal of Political Economy*, III 67 and IV 27.

NEW STATISTICAL ACCOUNT OF SCOTLAND (1834–45).

T. NEWTE (1791), *Prospects and Observations on a Tour of England and Scotland.*

A. NICOLSEN (1930), *A History of Skye.*

T. A. F. NOBLE (1954), 'The Future of Crofting', *Scottish Journal of Political Economy*, I 174.

NORTH OF SCOTLAND COLLEGE OF AGRICULTURE (1966), *Survey of Crofting Practice in North and South Uist, 1963.*

NORTH OF SCOTLAND HYDRO-ELECTRIC BOARD (1945–), *Annual Reports.*

A. C. O'DELL (1933), 'The Urbanisation of the Shetland Islands', *Geographical Journal*, LXXXI 501.

—— (1934), 'Lerwick: A Port Study', *Scottish Geographical Magazine*, L 27.

—— (1939a), *The Historical Geography of the Shetland Islands.*

—— (1939b), 'Development of Scottish Railways', *Scottish Geographical Magazine*, LV 129.

—— (1953), 'A View of Scotland in the Middle of the Eighteenth Century', *Scottish Geographical Magazine*, LXIX 58.

—— (1959), 'Excavations on St Ninian's Isle', *Scottish Geographical Magazine*, LXXV 41.

—— and K. WALTON (1962), *The Highlands and Islands of Scotland.*

W. G. OGG (1930–7), 'Reclamation and Cultivation of Peat Lands in Lewis', *Scottish Journal of Agriculture*, XIII 121, XIV 131, XV 174, XVI 218, XVIII 153 and XX 179.

A. G. OGILVIE (1945), 'Land Reclamation in Scotland', *Scottish Geographical Magazine*, LXI 77.

OLD STATISTICAL ACCOUNT OF SCOTLAND (1780–8).

OSBORNE (1958), 'The Movements of People in Scotland 1851–1951', *Scottish Studies*, II 1.

E. PAGET (1960), 'Comments on the Adjustment of Settlements in Marginal Areas', *Geografiska Annaler*, XLII(B) 324.

H. B. PEIRSE (1954), 'Forest Policy and Legislation Affecting Scotland, 1854–1953', *Scottish Forestry*, VIII 15.

T. PENNANT (1769), *A Tour of Scotland.*

J. PREBBLE (1961), *Culloden.*

—— (1963), *The Highland Clearances.*

—— (1966), *Glencoe.*

G. S. PRYDE (1962), *Scotland from 1603 to the Present Day.*

RED DEER COMMISSION (1959–), *Annual Reports.*

H. A. RENDEL-GOVAN (1941), 'Crofting on Bogs', *Scottish Geographical Magazine*, LVII 9.

J. RITCHIE (1919), 'Some Effects of Sheep Rearing on the Natural Conditions of Scotland', *Scottish Journal of Agriculture*, IX 190.

—— (1950), 'Some Observations on Problems of Hill and Marginal Land', *Economic Journal*, LX 740.

I. M. L. ROBERTSON (1949), 'The Head Dyke: A Fundamental Line in Scottish Geography', *Scottish Geographical Magazine*, LXV 6.

J. ROBERTSON (1813), *General View of the Agriculture of the County of Inverness.*

W. C. A. ROSS (1934), 'Highland Emigration', *Scottish Geographical Magazine*, L 155.

R. N. SALAMAN (1949), *The History and Social Influence of the Potato*.

J. B. SALMOND (1938), *Wade in Scotland*.

P. M. SCOLA (1961), 'Scotland's Farms and Farmers', *Scottish Agricultural Economics*, XI 59.

SCOTLAND (1884), *Report of the Royal Commission on the Condition of Crofters and Cottars in the Highlands and Islands of Scotland* (Napier Commission), Cd 3980.

—— (1895), *Report of the Royal Commission on the Highlands and Islands* (Deer Forest Commission), Cd 7681.

—— (1910), *Report of the Departmental Committee on the Work of the Congested Districts (Scotland) Commissioners for the Improvement of Agriculture*, Cd 5457.

—— (1912), *Report of the Departmental Committee on Forestry in Scotland*, Cd 6085.

—— (1914), *Scottish Land* (Report of the Scottish Land Enquiry Committee).

—— (1922), *Report of the Departmental Committee on Lands in Scotland Used as Deer Forests*, Cd 1626.

—— (1943), *Report of the Committee on Hydro-electric Development in Scotland* (Cooper Committee), Cd 6406.

—— (1944), *Report of the Commission into Hill Sheep Farming in Scotland* (Balfour Commission), Cd 6494.

—— (1950), *A Programme of Highland Development*, Cd 7976.

—— (1954), *Report of the Commission of Inquiry into Crofting Conditions* (Taylor Commission), Cd 9091.

—— (1956), *Report of the Hill Lands (North of Scotland) Committee*, Cd 9759.

—— (1959), *Review of Highland Policy*, Cd 785.

—— (1961), *Natural Resources in Scotland* (Scottish Council (Development and Industry)).

—— (1962), *Report of the Committee on the Generation and Distribution of Electricity in Scotland* (MacKenzie Committee), Cd 1859.

—— (1964), *Land Use in the Highlands and Islands* (Department of Agriculture and Fisheries for Scotland).

—— (1966), *The Scottish Economy, 1965–1970*, Cd 2864.

—— (1967), *Population and Places in Scotland* (H.M. Registrar-General for Scotland).

—— (1968a), *The Moray Firth: A Plan for Growth in a Sub-region of the Scottish Highlands* (Holmes Report; Highlands and Islands Development Board).

—— (1968b), *Lochaber Study: Employment Survey, 1966–1981* (Scottish Council (Development and Industry)).

—— (1969), *By Bridge to Skye* (Scottish Council (Development and Industry)).

J. F. SCOTT (1954), 'The Parish of Morvern', *Scottish Geographical Magazine*, LXX 79.

SCOTTISH TOURIST BOARD (1959–), *Annual Reports*.

SCOTTISH VIGILANTES ASSOCIATION (1964), *Highland Opportunity*.

W. SCROPE (1884), *Days of Deer Stalking*.

EARL OF SELKIRK (1806), *Observations on the Present State of the Highlands of Scotland*.

D. R. F. SIMPSON (1962), 'An Economic Analysis of Crofting Agriculture' (unpublished Ph.D. thesis, Harvard University).

W. D. SIMPSON (1969), *Portrait of the Highlands*.

J. SINCLAIR (1795), *General View of the Agriculture of the Northern Counties and Islands of Scotland*.

—— (1831), *Analysis of the Statistical Account of Scotland*.

W. I. SKEWIS (1962), *Transport in the Highlands and Islands*.

A. SMALL (1966), 'Excavation of Underhoull, Unst, Shetland', *Proceedings of the Society of Antiquaries of Scotland*, XCVIII 225.

—— (1968), 'The Historical Geography of the Norse Viking Colonisation of the Scottish Highlands', *Norsk Geografisk Tidsskrift*, XXII 1.

J. SMITH (1805), *General View of the Agriculture of the County of Argyll.*

J. H. SMITH (1957), 'Post-war Trends in Scottish Agriculture', *Scottish Journal of Political Economy*, IV 249.

W. A. SMITH (1888), 'West Coast Fisheries', *Transactions of the Royal Highland and Agricultural Society of Scotland*, XX 132.

T. C. SMOUT (1964), 'Scottish Landowners and Economic Growth, 1650–1850', *Scottish Journal of Political Economy*, XVIII 218.

F. D. N. SPAVEN (1954), 'Decline and Stability in Highland Areas', *Planning Outlook* III(2) 5.

L. D. STAMP (1964), 'Land Use in the Scottish Highlands', *Advancement of Science*, XXI 141.

R. G. STAPLEDON (1945), 'The Improvement of Hill and Marginal Land in Scotland', *Scottish Journal of Agriculture*, XXV 8.

H. G. STEERS (1962), 'The Grampians', in J. B. Mitchell (ed.), *Great Britain: Geographical Essays*, 527.

H. M. STEVEN (1951), 'The Forests and Forestry of Scotland', *Scottish Geographical Magazine*, LXVII 110.

—— and A. CARLISLE (1959), *The Native Pinewoods of Scotland.*

A. STEVENS (1928), 'The Highlands and Hebrides', in A. G. Ogilvie (ed.), *Great Britain: Essays in Regional Geography*, 357.

D. STEWART (1822), *Sketches of the Character, Manners and Present State of the Highlands of Scotland.*

J. I. STEWART (1931), 'The Scottish Herring Fishing Industry', *Scottish Geographical Magazine*, XLVII 217.

M. C. STORRIE (1961a), 'Islay: A Hebridean Exception', *Geographical Review*, LI 87.

—— (1961b), 'A Note on William Bald's Plan of Ardnamurchan and Sunart', *Scottish Studies*, V 112.

—— (1962a), 'Landholdings, Land Utilisation and Settlement in Certain Isolated Areas of West Scotland' (unpublished Ph.D. thesis, Glasgow University).

—— (1962b), 'The Scotch Whisky Industry', *Transactions of the Institute of British Geographers*, XXXI 97.

—— (1962c), 'The Census of Scotland as a Source in the Historical Geography of Islay', *Scottish Geographical Magazine*, LXXVIII 152.

—— (1962d), 'Two Early Resettlement Schemes in Barra', *Scottish Studies*, VI 71.

—— (1965), 'Landholdings and Settlement Evolution in West Highland Scotland', *Geografiska Annaler*, LXVII(B) 138.

J. A. SYMON (1949), 'The Agricultural Revolution, 1750–1850', *Scottish Agriculture*, LXXVIII 80.

—— (1954), 'The Falkirk Trysts', *Scottish Agriculture*, XXXIII 117.

L. SYMONDS (1959), 'The Economic Conquest of the Hills', *Scottish Geographical Magazine*, LXXV 18.

B. M. W. THIRD (1957), 'The Significance of Scottish Estate Plans and Associated Documents', *Scottish Studies*, I 39.

J. THOMAS (1965), *The West Highland Railway.*

J. THOMSON (1791), *The Value and Importance of the Scottish Fisheries.*

D. T. TIMINS (1901), 'The Mallaig Extension of the West Highland Railway', *Railway Magazine*, VIII 400.

J. TIVY (1965), 'Easter Ross: A Residual Crofting Area', *Scottish Studies*, IX 64.

D. Turnock (1965), 'Hebridean Car Ferries', *Geography*, L 375.
—— (1966), 'Lochaber: West Highland Growth Point', *Scottish Geographical Magazine*, LXXXII 17.
—— (1967a), 'Evolution of Farming Patterns in Lochaber', *Transactions of the Institute of British Geographers*, XLI 145.
—— (1967b), 'Population Studies and Regional Development in West Highland Scotland', *Geografiska Annaler*, XLIX(B) 55.
—— (1967c), 'Glenelg, Glengarry and Lochiel: An Evolutionary Study in Land Use', *Scottish Geographical Magazine*, LXXXIII 89.
—— (1968), 'Fort William: Problems of Urban Expansion in a Highland Area', *Tijdschrift voor Economische en Sociale Geografie*, LIX 260.
—— (1969a), 'Crofting in Lochaber', *Scottish Studies*, XIII 33.
—— (1969b), 'North Morar: The Improving Movement on a West Highland Estate', *Scottish Geographical Magazine*, LXXXV 17.

R. Urquhart (1964), 'Highland Crofting', in L. D. Stamp (ed.), 'Land Use in the Scottish Highlands', *Advancement of Science*, XXI 188.

H. A. Vallance (1938), *History of the Highland Railway*.

F. T. Wainwright (ed.) (1962), *The Northern Isles*.
J. Walker (1808), *Economic History of the Hebrides and Highlands of Scotland*.
K. R. Walker (1958), 'The Competition for Land between the Forestry Commission and the Agricultural Industry in Great Britain' (unpublished Ph.D. thesis, Oxford University).
J. W. Watson (1939), 'Forest or Bog: Man the Deciding Factor', *Scottish Geographical Magazine*, LV 148.
A. Watt (1952), 'The Forests of Scotland', *Scottish Forestry*, VI 23.
P. T. Wheeler (1960), 'Travelling Shops and Mobile Shops in Sutherland', *Scottish Geographical Magazine*, LXXVI 147.
—— (1964), 'The Sutherland Crofting System', *Scottish Studies*, VIII 172.
—— et al. (1964), *The Island of Unst, Shetland* (Geographical Field Group, Nottingham).
—— (1966), 'Landownership and the Crofting System in Sutherland Since 1800', *Agricultural History Review*, XIV 45.
G. K. Whitehead (1960), *The Deerstalking Grounds of Great Britain and Ireland*.
G. P. Wibberley (1954), 'Some Aspects of Problem Rural Areas in Britain', *Geographical Journal*, CXX 43.
—— (1959), *Agriculture and Urban Growth: A Study of the Competition for Rural Land*.
J. D. Wood (1964), 'Scottish Migration Overseas', *Scottish Geographical Magazine*, LXXX 164.
W. Wood (1950), *Morar and Moidart*.
M. Wright (1965), 'Regional Development: Problems and Lines of Advance in Europe', *Town Planning Review*, XXXVI 147.

Index